"Joyce Brooks has a flair for travel that is easily understood by people who love to go with her. Read this book and think of the possibilities."

—GEORGE E. AKER, President, Heritage Clubs International LLC (for Group Travel Directors), Reno, Nevada

"Superb! Yet again, Joyce Brooks has captured both the mind and spirit in this marvelous creation chronicling her world conquests. Insightful, in-depth, inspiring and fun ... *Seven Before Seventy* is sure to entertain as well as educate both the experienced world traveler and those who like to live vicariously through the magnificent storytelling of a true master ... a MUST READ for anyone who has yearned to travel the globe!"

—JAMES "JIM BOB" REINCKE, The Tourism Guru of Motivation Nation, President/CEO, The JPR Group, Inc., Salem, Illinois

"Joyce Brooks has spent the better part of her life doing a different kind of T.V—Travel Vacations! In *Seven Before Seventy* she takes readers along on her myriad adventures abroad and at home. Whether it's a sea voyage to Antarctica, climbing Ayers Rock in Australia, seeing Heyerdahl's Easter Island monuments or interacting with her guide who is the grandson of a Sultan in Kalimantan in Borneo, you're along for each exciting ride with her. She writes with a lively, honest, and keenly observant pen. This book is like a Pedi Cab dash through the streets of Hanoi ... very enjoyable reading!"

—MIKE DALY, Vice President, Collette Vacations, Pawtucket, Rhode Island

"*Seven Before Seventy* is an engaging travelogue that will be of interest to anyone who dreams of world travel ... The book should be particularly useful for people planning to travel to any of the places mentioned. I particularly enjoyed her description of her journey to Antarctica. But even for people who don't travel, Joyce offers insightful commentary on numerous places that will give anyone a better understanding of the world—its vast diversity of culture and landscapes, plus the universal hospitality of its people. Joyce's writing style is conversational and makes for a quick and entertaining read."

—TOM BENGTSON, President and CEO, NFR Communications (producer of several magazines including one devoted to bank club travel), Minneapolis, Minnesota

# Seven Before Seventy

*One Woman's Quest for the Seven Continents*

## JOYCE BROOKS

EAKIN PRESS  Austin, Texas

*To*
*seven very special people in my life—*
*Keith, my husband and beloved travel companion,*
*and*
*my six grandchildren*
*Lauren, Rachel, Zachary, Katie, Nathan and Jenni—*
*May peace reign so they can enjoy the world in their*
*grandmother's footsteps.*

*All photographs from the Joyce Brooks collection.*

FIRST EDITION
Copyright © 2003
By Joyce Brooks
Published in the United States of America
By Eakin Press
A Division of Sunbelt Media, Inc.
P.O. Drawer 90159 ☏ Austin, Texas 78709-0159
email: sales@eakinpress.com
💻 website: www.eakinpress.com 💻
ALL RIGHTS RESERVED.
1  2  3  4  5  6  7  8  9
**1-57168-803-X**

Library of Congress Control Number: 2003108048

# Contents

# Acknowledgments

Special thanks to:

My son, Corky Cootes, for without his unwavering patience and constant assistance regarding the computer, this book could not have been a reality. He also is responsible for my web page and teaching me how to use my new laptop and projector for speaking engagements. Corky—without you, Mom would have never made it in the computer world.

My family editors—Karon Wheeless, my stepdaughter, and Heidi Frock, my daughter—for taking time from your busy schedules to proofread my manuscript and offer words of encouragement.

Virginia Messer of Eakin Press, for giving me one more chance by publishing my second book.

# Prologue

I hope you took the exciting journey with me via my first book, *Around the World in the Middle Seat: How I Saw the World (and Survived!) as a Group Travel Leader*. In *Seven Before Seventy* I continue my exploits as a group travel leader and my personal travel adventures, but this sequel concentrates on the more exotic and less traveled areas of the seven continents and surrounding areas of this wonderful world of ours.

At the age of nine, lying on my half-filled cotton sack between the tall rows of cotton on a farm in Central Texas, I vowed to travel around the world and write a book about it. I declared that my life would be complete if I could see Paris, France, the Taj Mahal in India, and the wild animals in Africa. I managed to do that in my travels to six continents. Finally, at the age of sixty-nine, I stepped on my seventh continent—Antarctica. Thus the title, *Seven Before Seventy*. My childhood aspiration has become reality, as I have now been to all seven continents and written two books. In the process, I have visited 116 countries and escorted over 200 group tours. As the saying goes, I've been there, done that—but I'm not ready to call it quits! I want to share the memories that are stored in the chapters of my private book of life.

My childhood declarations did not materialize quickly. I was forty-two years old before I saw my first dream destination—Paris. And I was sixty-eight before my first book was published. Through the years, however, I never lost sight of my goal. Born of middle-class farming parents, I worked my way through college and obtained a degree in journalism. My first taste of wanderlust came at the age of sixteen, when I entered a farm magazine essay contest and won an all-expenses paid trip to New York City and Washington, DC. They say that it's hard to keep them down on the farm after they have seen "Paree," and that was true for me when I saw New York! I was hooked on travel. Yet my fantasies were put on hold as I married, had two children, and continued to work at various newspaper jobs and as program director for a YMCA, public relations director for a junior college, and fundraiser for a public television station. Travel was not an option; at that time of my life I was simply trying to pay the bills and be a mother and a career woman. Then to add to the problem, I found myself divorced at age forty with two kids to support.

Good fortune came my way in the form of Keith Brooks. We were married, and he became a wonderful stepfather to my seven- and ten-year-old children. He had another quality that appealed to me: He liked to travel. We saved and took one big trip a year, which did not sufficiently scratch my traveling itch. So I tried being a travel agent, and soon discovered that travel agents *send* people on trips but rarely go themselves.

Timing is everything. When I called on a local bank, seeking their bank travel club's business for the travel agency, the president had just fired the person in the position, and he offered me the job. Discontent as a travel agent, I jumped at the chance.

This opened the door to my commitment to see the world! I started out small, with one-day trips, and later branched out to further destinations. I became a "Pied Piper" and soon had a group that would follow me nearly anywhere in the world.

None of this came easy. I worked very hard taking care of the customers' needs and comforts, plus providing interesting and stimulating destinations for them. When things would go wrong (as they frequently do when you are traveling, especially with forty or more people), I would wonder if the stress was worth it. Then I would re-member my love of travel and the satisfaction I received in helping senior citizens enjoy their later years. Some of my "faithful followers" have said they would never have ventured out of the United States if they hadn't gone with Keith and me, for they knew that we would take care of them if anything happened. So from 1981 to 1999, we were group travel leaders, and when we wanted to go to a place that was "too far out" for my followers, I was able to arrange special discounts as a member of the travel industry to journey to more remote sites of the globe by ourselves.

*Seven Before Seventy* explores our expeditions in places that are not the "run of the mill" destination. I selected my favorite locations and included some tips to share with you. Time causes changes in countries, as we personally found out in the United States on September 11, 2001. My stories reveal conditions at the time of our visit and my facts concerning locales are from our native guides, which I believed to be accurate. I am relating the adventures just as we experienced them. Everything is true. I received no compensation from any of the places or companies mentioned here; in fact, they did not even know I was going to write a book when I was there. The only exception was the Orient Lines, who were advised I was an author researching Antarctica for my second book.

So come along with me as we peek inside my special places on the seven conti-nents and many areas of the oceans and seas. I think you will enjoy the trip.

# Antarctica

They say that seven is a lucky number. It certainly was true in my case, for when I stepped on my seventh continent of Antarctica on January 14, 2003, my childhood dream became a reality.

I wanted to write my second book about the special places on all seven continents. I had been to the other six several times, but had never made it to the bottom of the world—to the land of ice and snow. My husband, Keith, said he definitely did not want to go. One reason was his tendency to get seasick, and it is a known fact that the Drake Passage, which is necessary to cross from the tip of South America to Antarctica, boasts the roughest seas on the planet. But this certainly did not deter me. Confronted with the possibility of high seas, I wanted to go on a ship that was the largest and most stable in the area, and therefore I selected the *Marco Polo* cruise ship of the Orient Lines. They graciously assisted me in making my venture to my last continent.

It was with mixed emotions that I prepared for this adventure alone, having never been outside the United States without Keith, but I was determined not to pass up this opportunity. To get ready for the cold climates, I purchased silk thermal underwear and insulated rubber boots. I already had rain pants from our fishing trips in Alaska, warm gloves and fur hat from skiing, and the cruise line was to furnish a parka aboard ship.

At 2:00 P.M. January 9 Keith said goodbye to me at the Austin airport. I could hardly keep from crying. But I thought: *Joyce Brooks, if you can lead forty or more people all over the world, you can certainly manage just yourself!* I had never been on an escapade like this before—to be gone from Keith for twelve days and to go so far away. As my daughter, Heidi, had cautioned me, I would not know anyone on this trip, my "faithful followers" would not surround me, nor would I have Keith.

I checked in at the American Airlines desk and was then directed over to the new monster machine to x-ray my checked luggage. Immediately I missed Keith when I had to lift that heavy bag up on the conveyer belt.

"Is the bag unlocked, and do you have any film in it?" the security guard asked.

I responded no to everything and was instructed to wait on the other side.

"We need to look inside your bag," the officer stated, and then proceeded to take it to the back, where I could not see what was going on. I had packed everything so carefully and had even sat on the bag to get it closed. We had put a luggage strap around it for fear the bag would come open since I had to leave it unlocked. The new security rule had just gone into effect that all checked luggage must be left unlocked for inspection. Maybe they wanted to look inside the bag because of those big old rubber boots. Anyway, it was returned closed and the strap back in place. I explained that I was going to Buenos Aires, Argentina, and would like to have my bag locked. To my surprise, they took my keys and locked it.

As I went through the next security check, I had no problems at all. They did not go through my roller bag or take off my shoes.

The plane departed on schedule at 3:00 P.M. Just as we were coming in to the Dallas/Fort Worth airport, I remarked to the woman next to me: "I land in airports all over the world, and everything is fine until we arrive at DFW ... then it goes to pot!"

Just as I said that, the plane stopped on the runway. The captain announced: "With DFW's new security system, somehow a person slipped through the checkpoint into the boarding areas and they were unable to stop him, so they have now evacuated all three terminals. You need not worry about missing your connecting flights, for the whole airport is shut down."

There we sat, on the runway, for nearly two hours. Nothing was served to us. Fortunately, I have learned to travel with my water bottle. When we were finally allowed to arrive at the gate and deplane, I was told that my flight to Miami would depart in twenty minutes. And true to DFW fashion, I came in at Gate 2 in Terminal A and my departure plane was at Gate C29! With no passenger cart in sight, I moved as fast as possible and made it with five minutes to spare. It was then around 6:00 P.M.

As I was getting into my seat, the woman across the aisle said to me: "Did you have to wait a long time out on the runway? I'm a smoker and I've not had a cigarette since I left Los Angeles at 8:00 A.M. I'm about to die!"

She asked the flight attendant if there would be any food served on the flight to Miami.

"There is no food served on any flights under four hours since 9/11, plus all the airlines are losing money every day," she said haughtily. Later, a more congenial flight attendant told us there was room in business class if we wanted to move up there, but there would be no food or free drinks. Since I was used to sitting in the middle seat coach class, I jumped at the opportunity to move up to a nicer seat to starve in.

We arrived in Miami at 9:30 P.M. and were scheduled to leave at 10:10 P.M. By this time, I was getting very hungry, with only a package of stale pretzels to eat since I began my journey. The woman at the American desk assured me they would serve dinner, plus breakfast, on the eight-and-a-half-hour flight to Buenos Aires. With that assurance of food in the near future, I went back to the gate area.

A young man, who had noticed the Orient Lines luggage tag on my roller bag, approached me. "Going to Antarctica?" He was meeting a friend from New York City in Buenos Aires. From there they were flying commercial, not on the cruise charter flight, to Ushuaia, where we would board the ship. We had a nice talk and promised to visit during the cruise.

The call was made to board the plane and every seat was full, but fortunately I had an aisle seat. The captain then announced that we had an equipment problem, which was not too comforting, since this was the same plane that I had just flown in from DFW. Finally everything was fixed, and we took off at 11:10 P.M. Around midnight, I was delighted to receive some food. I don't know if it was because of my extreme hunger, but it was a fairly good meal, especially for airline food today. In the past, alcoholic drinks were free on international flights due to the foreign competition. But that isn't the case anymore. So I went all out and spent $4 on a small bottle of Merlot, and was able to sleep in snippets until 6:00 A.M., when wakened for a breakfast sandwich of grilled ham and cheese.

On one trip to the restroom at the back of the plane I overheard the airline personnel say they had been informed that the man at DFW was trying to go through security with plastic explosives. What if he had planned to get on my plane? It was a frightening thought!

We arrived at Buenos Aires at 10:00 A.M. Friday. While standing in the immigration line, I met a man from Boston who was going fly-fishing for brown trout in the Tierra del Fuego area. We had a short and friendly conversation.

The custom officials x-rayed my bags again, and I proceeded through the gates. I was thrilled to see a smiling woman holding an Orient Cruise Lines sign. She collected four men cruise passengers besides myself, and we headed for a van for the forty-five-minute ride to the city and the Sheraton Hotel. There must have been 100 or more armed policemen standing in front of the hotel. Out in the street facing them were hundreds of demonstrators with signs and drums. Our guide said they were protesting Argentina's dire economic crisis. Their money used to be tied to the U.S. dollar; at this time it had been devaluated to three pesos to one U.S. dollar. The guide had the policemen open the barrier to the hotel so our van could enter.

I was very glad to settle into my lovely room after being up for over thirty hours. I quickly undressed and crawled into the king-size bed, but terrible chanting and drumbeats intruded from outside. My window on the seventeenth floor faced the front of the hotel, and even more protesters had gathered to vent their frustrations. I don't know why they thought the Sheraton Hotel was the best site for this event. Periodically, the police would fire shots (I certainly hope into the air). Regardless, there would be no sleeping for me with all that commotion going on outside. I lay there and tried to at least rest the old body before getting ready for the city tour offered by the cruise line.

I had been to Buenos Aires three times before and had enjoyed three city tours, but I thought I might as well take in another one. The three-hour excursion around this European-influenced city was very interesting and we did go to some residential areas I had not seen before. I enjoyed revisiting the picturesque La Boca, with its colorful buildings and art displays. The area was settled and developed by Italian immigrants, and today it is an artists' colony. The tango originated here, and I had to have my picture taken dancing the tango with a handsome male Argentinean. We drove down Avenue 9 de Julio (July 9), the widest street in the world, which was lined with jacaranda trees, unfortunately not in bloom at this time as they put on their show in November.

Death is usually an equalizer, but not in Buenos Aires. When the wealthy die, their bodies are brought to the Recoleta Cemetery, where generations of the elite repose in

*Dancing the tango with a handsome Argentinean.*

magnificent mausoleums. Evita Peron rests there in a modest tomb of the "Familia Duarte" (her maiden name). I noticed that the Evita admiration must be fading with the passage of time, for there were less flowers adorning her grave than when I had visited some years back. As my group strolled through the cemetery, I heard someone call my name. I turned, and to my surprise, there was the fisherman from Boston whom I had met at the airport. He introduced me to his two fishing buddies, and we commented that it was ironic that we would meet again in a cemetery.

Back at the hotel, exhausted from lack of sleep, I ordered room service and fell into bed at 8:00 P.M. for a wonderful night's rest.

Saturday morning the Orient Lines offered a buffet breakfast for us at the hotel, and then we were transferred to the domestic airport for our appointed Chilean Airlines charter flight (there were three planes to accommodate all the passengers). As I approached the departure gate, the attendant wanted to take my roller bag, stating that it was too large to go in the overhead bins. I assured them that it would fit under the seat, where I promptly put it when I entered the plane. Before takeoff, a stewardess came and removed my bag, saying that it could not stay there. They would check it and I could pick it up when we arrived in Ushuaia. That bag held everything necessary to my well being, plus my cameras and all my film. However, I had no choice but to let her take it.

Sitting next to me (I had an aisle seat) was a charming couple from Michigan, Laurie and Bill. They had a very delightful story. They met at school in Munich, Germany, as they were "army brats." (They showed me a picture taken on their date to the senior prom.) Then their soldier-fathers were transferred, and they lost contact. Laurie married and moved to California and some years later was widowed. Bill returned to Michigan but never married. About eight years ago, Bill noticed Laurie's name and address in a military newspaper. Not knowing her marital status, he sent her a Christmas card. Not knowing his marital status, she answered him. One thing led to another, and now they are happily married and living in Michigan. Bill said the reason he never married was that he was waiting for Laurie.

Across the aisle was a woman whose nametag said "Tour Manager." I introduced myself and told her I had been a group leader for many years. Bea was leading a group from Great Britain, and we promised to talk sometime while at sea.

It is over 1,000 miles from Buenos Aires to Ushuaia, the southernmost city in the world at the very tip of the South American continent, or as the locals say, the bottom of the world. When we landed, I expected to pick up my bag outside the plane. The security guard said that it would be delivered inside the terminal. Everyone was going to the transfer buses and I still didn't have my carry-on. Finally, a ship representative said that it would be delivered to my cabin on the *Marco Polo* ship. I felt very uneasy about this situation, as the bag was not locked. It contained my cameras, plus $300 in cash. When traveling alone I like to separate my cash between my carry-on and my purse, so I wouldn't be completely without funds in case one was stolen. Also, all my medications and cosmetics were in that bag!

A short drive brought us to the *Marco Polo*, docked next to the city of Ushuaia. The ship is not large in terms of cruise ships today, but for me it was just the right size. With a maximum speed of 20.5 knots, it is 578 feet in length and has eight passenger decks. There are 425 cabins for a cruise capacity of 850, but on this Antarctica cruise there were only 500 passengers. Amenities included four lounges, two restaurants (one designated seating for dinner), library, card room, casino, Internet center, beauty shop and spa, and a fitness center.

As we entered the ship, we had to produce the cruise card that had been mailed to us. It looked just like a credit card, and when swiped at the entrance computer the screen acknowledged that I was indeed Joyce Brooks, Cabin #634. The women in the group were presented a red carnation, and a cabin steward led me to my room. What a pleasant surprise when I opened the door to find a beautiful flower arrangement sent

*The luxurious* Marco Polo *glides supremely along in the Antarctic waters.*

by my daughter and son-in-law, Heidi and Gary. There also was a letter from the social hostess welcoming me on board and stating that she would arrange for me to meet with the captain.

Neither my big bag nor the roller bag were there, so I strolled over to the city to locate a place to send an e-mail home. I passed the Hotel Ushuaia, where we had stayed with our group on a Collette Vacation tour of South America in 1993. I quickly located a place where I was able to send e-mails and check my messages—all for fifty cents! On the way back to the ship, a six-foot penguin wanted me to pose for a photo. For $1, who could refuse? It isn't every day that you can have your picture taken with a big penguin!

*Strolling along the streets of Ushuaia, I met a handsome six-foot penguin.*

When I returned to the ship, I became more upset, as the bags still had not arrived. It was now 4:30 P.M. and time for the safety drill. I put on the life vest from the cabin and went up to my muster station. The explanation of the way you should jump into the water if necessary seemed a little useless, for in the Antarctic waters you would die of the cold in a few minutes anyway.

Returning to my room, I noticed a bunch of bags stacked in the gangway. My little green roller bag was there! I grabbed it and ran to my room. Everything was intact. At least now I could survive, even if I had to wear the same clothes for the entire cruise. As my big bag was still not there at dinnertime, I marched off to the dining room dressed in the same clothes I had been wearing since I left home.

As I was traveling alone, I had requested a large table at the early seating. What a pleasant surprise to find I was at a table for nine—and nine of the most interesting and delightful people you would ever meet. There were three men and six women. We laughingly noted that we had three countries represented: three were from Texas, one from Great Britain, and five from the United States.

After a delicious dinner (especially appreciated after the airline food), I returned to my room to joyously find my big bag. As I unpacked, I realized that without Keith I had all kinds of room for my clothes and personal items. But I still missed him.

At 8:00 P.M. I could feel the ship moving as it began to make its way through Beagle Channel out to the Drake Passage on our route to the Antarctica Peninsula, more than

*Every evening I looked forward to dining with my interesting table companions. Front row, left to right: Ruth—Encino, CA; Kip—Dallas, TX; Joyce—Evant, TX; Judy—Tallahassee, FL. Back row: Willard—Houston, TX; Sandra—Eugene, OR; John—United Kingdom; Marcia—Las Vegas, NV; Jackie—Cherry Hill, NJ.*

600 miles away. I went out on the back deck and there met Bea, the English tour conductor. She and I had a grand time exchanging group tour war stories. We looked up in the sky and saw the most astounding rainbow I have ever seen. It rose from one side of the ocean and formed an arc that concluded in the water on the other side. Each color was brilliant, shading from reds to yellows to blues to purple. I could really believe that there was a pot of gold at the end of this magnificent display. As Bea and I continued talking, I told her that my husband did not come because he did not want to take a chance of seasickness on the crossing of the Drake Passage. She said that she had that concern as well, and had purchased the sea wristbands to avoid seasickness. I told her I was not wearing them yet because I wasn't sure where to put them to get the maximum value. As she was showing me that you take your three middle fingers and place them where your hand joins the wrist, a woman came around the corner.

"You must be discussing how to apply the sea wristbands," she said.

We told her that was the case, and that she was very astute to recognize this.

"I was the ship nurse for two years before I realized that the zodiac drivers were having more fun, so now I drive a zodiac boat. So I have lots of experience in applying these bands," she explained, and introduced herself as Barbara.

"Wait just a minute and let me go get mine," I said as I quickly ran to my cabin.

When I returned, she expertly applied them, and I was set for any rough waters in the Drake Passage. Barbara told us that she was from Inverness, Scotland, the home of the Loch Ness Monster. She said she spent two months a year on the *Marco Polo*, and was a nurse in Scotland the rest of the year. She told us the crew looked forward to reuniting each year, and that they had become a regular family. She had been with the crew for eight years and was the token woman zodiac driver.

The entertainment that evening was Showtime by the onboard musicians and singers, all very talented. They presented a very lavish and enjoyable program of song, dance, and magic.

That night when I took a shower I did not want to get my wristbands wet, so I marked with a pen the pressure point and removed them. It was 11:30, and when I looked out my window it was still twilight outside.

As I climbed into bed, I checked the television monitor in my room that had a map of our cruise route and indicated where the ship was at that precise moment. I saw that we were well into the Drake Passage, and the ship was just barely swaying; in fact, it felt nice to be rocked to sleep.

After a good night's rest, I awoke at 7:30. We were deep into the Drake Passage, and it wasn't rough at all. I opted not to put on the wristbands.

I went up to breakfast at Raffles, the buffet café that has windows all around and seating outdoors. I could see nothing but slight waves and occasionally some birds following the ship in hopes for a meal from whatever the ship's movement would bring to the surface.

I quickly ate breakfast to attend the lecture on "Exploration of the Antarctic Peninsula" by David Wilson. David and his brother, Christopher, were part of the *Marco Polo* Expedition Team and were great nephews of Dr. Edward Wilson, who died with Captain Scott and his party on their return from the South Pole in 1912. David had written a book about his uncle, entitled *Cheltenham in Antarctica,* which I purchased and had him personally autograph to me. David devotes his time to promoting Britain's historic Antarctic heritage and recently helped produce a CD of Antarctic expedition songs.

David explained that Antarctica, unlike any other continent, is believed to have existed long before it was actually discovered. The ancient Greeks around 530 B.C. thought that the Earth was round, and that an ice area at the bottom should equally balance the northern icy region. As early as 700 B.C. a Phoenician fleet sailed from the Red Sea south along the African coast to the Straits of Gibraltar. In 650 A.D., according to Polynesian legends, one of their boats sailed so far south it reached a place where the sea was frozen. The Portuguese made attempts in 1487 by sailing around the southern tip of Africa, as far as present-day Mozambique. In 1497 Vasco de Gama found the way around Africa to India. Portuguese Ferdinand Magellan led the first circumnavigation of the globe in 1519-22. He discovered and named the Tierra del Fuego area at the southern tip of South America. In 1577-80 Englishman Francis Drake made the second circumnavigation of the globe and titled the wild seas below the end of South America as Drake's Passage. People believed that a land existed farther south, but the Southern Ocean's terrifying storms, high waves, and impenetrable pack of ice kept the continent's white face hidden from inquiring adventurers for centuries more.

A Yorkshire man, James Cook, who went around the world three times and discovered more territory than anyone else in history, penetrated farther south than anyone else before. He crossed the Antarctic Circle on January 17, 1773, but with three tries southward he never found the southern continent. In 1819 British mariner William Smith discovered the South Shetland Islands, which led to an influx of British and American sealers. This "seal rush" nearly led to the extinction of seals in that area. During the sealing period, up to 1892, more than 1,100 ships visited the Antarctic regions in their quest for seals, but there were no reports of landing on the continent itself.

The Antarctic continent was first seen by human eyes in 1820, although historians disagree whose eyes were really first. Credit for being the first man to see the continent has been divided between the three who made separate voyages that year: Fabian von Bellingshausen, a captain in the Russian Imperial Navy; Edward Bransfield, a captain in the British Navy; and Nathaniel Brown Palmer, an American sealer.

Frenchman Dumont d'Urville was the first person to actually set foot on Antarctica in 1840. Some historians say that it could have been John Davis, an American sealer in 1821, but he was unsure if he landed on the continent or a nearby island.

Joseph DeGerlache of Belgium was the first to photograph Antarctica. He was heading a ship that was stuck in the Antarctic ice and was forced to stay the entire winter in 1897. In 1899, Carsten Borchgrevink led a British-funded expedition and was the first to set up base and winter on Antarctica. Their two huts still stand today. The Briton Captain Robert Scott led an expedition often referred to as the "Discovery Expedition," for many important scientific and geographical discoveries were made on this journey. Ernest Henry Shackleton, an Irishman, led a group bound for the South Pole. He brought with him Siberian ponies that proved to be unsuited to the task. Shackleton, along with three companions, pioneered the route to the polar plateau, but unfortunately on January 9, 1909, they were forced to turn back when they were within 180 kilometers from their goal of the South Pole. On December 11, 1911, Norwegian Amundsen and his party of five reached the South Pole with the aid of dog teams and sleds.

Following close behind was Captain Scott, with his party of five, using man-pulled sledges. They arrived at the Pole on January 17, 1912, only to find that Amundsen had beaten them by thirty-five days! Sadly, Scott and his men perished in a blizzard on their return to the camp. Found with their frozen bodies were many geological samples that have greatly aided scientific studies of Antarctica. American Robert Byrd made the first flights over the South Pole.

Today Antarctica has the unique distinction of being the only place in the world where there has never been war, where the environment is fully protected and pure, and where research has priority. This is because of the Antarctic Treaty, which originated with twelve nations in 1961 and today has grown to forty-five nations. The treaty stipulates that no nation has sovereignty, and Antarctica should forever be used exclusively for peaceful purposes and never be the object of international discord. Special rules were put into place to protect the native flora and fauna. Wouldn't it be nice if the rest of the world were governed like this?

Following this presentation, Chris Wilson told us about the various species of penguins we would encounter on our cruise around the Antarctic Peninsula.

I noticed in the daily ship bulletin that it was now time for an art auction at Sea Preview. Not sure what it was, I decided to go have a look, especially since complimentary champagne would be offered. Was I surprised! In the *Marco Polo* lounge they displayed 200 or more pieces of art, all nicely framed, and definitely not your garage-sale variety. These were signed lithographs by Dali, Picasso, Chagal and Rockwell. A suggested price tag was displayed on each. When the auctioning started, I was amazed at the bargains; they were selling for less than half of the appraised value. The purchased art would be shipped to your home, anywhere in the world. As I don't have an inch of wall space available in our home, due to the worldwide trinkets I have accumulated through years of globetrotting, I was not an interested buyer. But if you are looking for art, this is an excellent place to pick up some good buys. I found out that the art program is part of fundraising for non-profit organizations around the country and is operated by the Heart of Giving, a subsidiary of Fine Art Wholesalers, Inc.

Now it was time for my meeting with the cruise director, the lovely Shani Reay. I presented her with my book, *Around the World in the Middle Seat,* for the ship's library. She invited me to be a guest at the captain's table for dinner that evening. Needless to say, I was thrilled! As I had the first seating for dining, she requested that I come to the second seating of Captain Roland Andersson's Welcome Cocktail Reception, and afterwards we would go down to the dining room together.

After lunch, Russell Thompson, retired senior lecturer as meteorologist/glaciologist in the Department of Geography at the university in Reading, Britain, spoke on "Antarctic Rocks and Ice." We were still out at sea in the Drake Passage, and I was ready to see some of that ice.

I found out that Antarctica is about the same size as the continent of Australia. The terrain is about 90 percent thick continental ice sheet and 2 percent barren rock, with average elevations between 2,000 and 4,000 meters. There are mountain ranges up to about 5,000 meters. Glaciers form ice shelves along about half of the coastline, and floating ice shelves constitute 11 percent of the area of the continent. When the glaciers break off, they become floating icebergs, some as big as large buildings. What amazed me is that the portion you see above the water constitutes just about one-tenth of the ice formation. It has been estimated that there are about 300,000 icebergs in the Southern Ocean at any one time. Ultimately, they melt completely as they drift to the northern warmer waters. Antarctica is the coldest, driest, and windiest place in the world. The

record low temperature recorded to date was minus 128.5 Fahrenheit—a little too cold for this Texas gal.

After the talk I went out on the deck, and there, floating past the ship, was my first iceberg! Wow! As I looked around, I could see them everywhere—pristine white with shades of blue in the crevasses ranging from pale turquoise to deep blue.

But I had to go back inside for the information lecture on riding in the zodiacs and landing on Antarctica—what I had been waiting sixty years to do! The ship's expedition leader, Nigel Sitwell, informed us of the rules. Nigel, an internationally recognized naturalist who has led more than fifty cruising expeditions to Antarctica, has been with the Orient Lines since 1993. This native of Great Britain helped draft the original guidelines of conduct currently followed by all principal ships visiting Antarctica. First he explained what to wear. Logically, he suggested to go out on deck and see what the weather was, and dress accordingly. He suggested thermal underwear, warm shirt, jeans, thick socks, cap, gloves, rain pants and rubber boots, and of course, the lovely bright red parka that was delivered to our room compliments of the Orient Lines. Everyone would be issued a colored tag with a letter (I was blue B), and these would be clipped on the parka pocket flap. Groups of about twelve would go at scheduled times to board the zodiacs for excursions. When your group was called, you would proceed down to the

loading dock, where crewmen would outfit you with a life preserver, then down the outside stairwell to the waiting zodiac. You boarded by clasping the crewman's wrist, and he would clasp yours, enabling you to enter the inflatable rubber boat safely.

The naturalists would carefully monitor the passenger's conduct on shore. The rule was to never get closer than fifteen feet to the penguins; however, if a bird decided to come up to see you, that was fine. You should remain still and let him have the right of way. The viewing area would be blocked off with markers, and we were never to stray from the designated area. There would be no smoking, gum chewing, or eating of any kind on land. We were cautioned to go to the toilet before departing the ship, for there certainly were no facilities on land, and it is a "no-no" to go behind a rock. We were also told to be sure not to drop any film, papers, or camera batteries on the ground.

We were still sailing along in the Drake Passage, and the seas were relatively calm. My next option was to go to Tea Time, but I decided to skip the extra calories and donated $10 to the ship's casino.

The evening meal was formal, so I dressed in the best I had brought with me for my evening with the captain. For the welcome aboard cocktail party, the captain and Shani greeted everyone at the door to the Ambassador Lounge, and the photographer snapped a picture of each passenger and the captain—a sure sell.

Following the reception, Shani and the captain met their ten dinner guests to go down to the dining room. I was honored to sit next to Captain Andersson and across the table from Peter Hillary, who had just completed his second climb to the summit of Mt. Everest, a feat first accomplished by his father, Sir Edmund Hillary, in 1953. National Geographic filmed Peter's latest achievement. Peter, one of the ship's guest lecturers, is a native of New Zealand. He has climbed Mt. Vinson, the highest mountain in Antarctica, and made news in 1999 when he and two companions forged a new overland route to the South Pole, dragging 440-pound sleds for 900 miles, battling blizzards, frostbite, and illness. Peter Hillary was one of the most interesting individuals I have ever had the privilege of meeting. He had fascinating tales of exploits with his father on the highest mountain ranges in the world, on both the North and South Pole, as well as stories about their jet boat ride up the sacred Ganges River from the Bay of Bengal in India. He was the first to cross the "roof of the world," a 3,000-mile route from Sikkim through Nepal and India to Pakistan at an average altitude of over 13,000 feet. Today he assists his father in the building and maintaining of schools and hospitals in Nepal.

Traveling with Peter Hillary was his close friend and attorney, Alexander Witten-Hannah, who was sitting next to Peter and across from me at the Captain's Dinner. Alex lives in Auckland, New Zealand, and has quite a list of adventures in his life—such as secretly climbing to the top of the Great Pyramid in Egypt to watch the sun set on the desert, assisting Sir Edmund Hillary on school and hospital building projects for the sherpa people, and in 1982 he joined Peter on the expedition to climb Lhotse, the South Peak of Everest. He has traveled to more than forty countries. (He also volunteered to be photographer with my camera to take the pictures of me with the Captain and Peter.)

My dinner host on the Marco Polo was Capt. Roland Andersson. A native of Sweden, he has been a member of the Royal Swedish Navy, the Merchant Marine, and was in charge of many vessels before becoming the head man for the Orient Lines on the Marco Polo. This was his eighth season to command the ship to the Antarctic region.

When the wine was served, Captain Andersson sampled it, but then refused to be served. He said that recent rules from the Orient Lines prohibited him from having even a glass of wine with dinner while he was in charge of the vessel.

This was a most stimulating evening, complete with interesting and charismatic people, outstanding food and wine. A treasured souvenir photo of the dinner guests was delivered to my room the next day.

After dinner, I was rushing

to the night's entertainment, and my strap sandal shoe broke. I was grateful that hadn't happened when we were going down to dinner with the group. Quickly, I ran to my room to change shoes before going to the show.

I was so keyed up after the delightful night's activities, I could hardly go to sleep. At midnight I looked out my cabin window, and it was still twilight. According to the daily program, the sun would rise at 3:35 A.M. The seas were still very calm. When we had remarked to the captain at dinner about the smooth passage, he quickly replied: "We are not back to Ushuaia yet."

I woke at 6:00 A.M., rushed to the window, and there floating past were numerous icebergs—all sizes and shapes. The many shades of blue create different illusions. The variance of light causes the various shades of blue to appear in the icebergs. Glacial ice ranges in color from white to milky blue because the air bubbles trapped in the ice scatter white light efficiently. The shades of blue change with the color of the sky, ranging from deep indigo to light turquoise.

I quickly donned my parka and fur hat and headed out on the front deck. The wind was blowing and it was very chilly, but I wanted to see everything. We were in what is referred to as Neptune's Bellows, so named as it is a narrow channel and very strong winds blow through the strait of sloping snow-covered walls rising to 1,914 feet. This is the entrance to Deception Island, a ring around a collapsed volcanic cone, providing one of the safest natural harbors in the world. As we cruised around the harbor surrounded by the land-ring of Deception Island, it was like I would picture the moon surface, covered with snow and ice. All was white with the exception of some black spots created by wind on small mountainsides. As we sailed along, I noticed little black things darting all around in the water. I was told that these were penguins out feeding. Black and white petrels were flying all around. We cruised past some uninhabited buildings that were said to belong to Argentina and Spain.

As I was standing at the ship rail, a Japanese man came up to me and motioned that he would like to take my picture. Not accustomed to being a model, I smiled in agreement (he did not speak English, and my Japanese is certainly lacking). He set up

*It was so exciting to walk along the ship's deck and see the many icebergs floating past.*

his camera on a tripod, and got everything set and then came over beside me to get in the picture. I guess he wanted to tell his friends in Japan he had met a tall American (I was about a foot taller than he was). He bowed and handed me a gift of Japanese trinkets, which looked like hair ornaments. I smiled and bowed also.

The passengers on the ship were about 40% American, 40% British, and 20% Japanese. The Japanese passengers had earphones, and every lecture and announcement on board ship was interpreted for them by Ruriko Hosaka Lindblad, a Japanese native and wife of the late Lars-Eric Lindblad, who pioneered Antarctic cruise expeditions.

*From the rubber zodiac boats we could get up close and personal to the icebergs.*

In the afternoon we finally got to go out in the zodiacs to cruise around Cuverville Island. We would not step on land on this excursion, but I was excited to get out and see some penguins and icebergs up close from the vantage point of the small inflatable boat. I got outfitted in my arctic gear, and at 3:30 P.M. my group was called to march down to the exit. Everything was orchestrated beautifully. Once down there, one crew member puts a life vest on you, and then you go down the ladder to the loading platform, where two crewmen assist you into the zodiac. We sat around the sides of the rubber boat. I was pleased to see that the driver was Barbara, the woman who had assisted me with the sea bands.

Cuverville is a small, rocky island just off the west coast of the Antarctic Peninsula. The zodiac boat brought us close enough to see our first penguins—the Gentoo species.

*My first sighting of penguins on land—they were everywhere!*

The island is known to be home to about 5,000 pairs of Gentoos. For an hour we glided along the island's rock-strewn beaches that rise to dramatic cliffs, some topped with abundant green moss. Overhead storm petrels, southern black gulls and Antarctic terns swirled about. But the most interesting aspect of this outing was the icebergs. They were all around us, and the zodiac could get up very close for us to view the many shades of blue on some hunks of ice

*The penguins come out to greet the* Marco Polo.

that would be fifty or more feet high (I remembered that only one-tenth was showing above the water). The sea was calm and the air was cold. It was reported to be about 30 degrees, with all the clothing I had on it didn't seem that cold. I had now been in the zodiac, seen penguins and icebergs, but I wanted to step on my seventh continent. I was advised that I would get that honor the next day. Nearly everyone on this cruise had come here to experience their seventh continent, making this a very extraordinary and well-traveled collection of individuals.

The entertainment that evening was by Shani, who not only does a magnificent job as social hostess but can sing a great tune and presents a fabulous show. Sunset was at 11:20 P.M.

I rose at 6:00 A.M. to see the entrance to Lemaire Channel, a steep-sided narrow pass, just about 1,450 yards wide that continues for about seven miles. There were icebergs all about, and the ship maneuvered very slowly to avoid them. It was snowing lightly, but the seas were calm, even though there was a gusty wind through the passage. The scene was incredibly beautiful, with walls of ice and snow all around us. I could not believe that I was really there, seeing this surreal landscape. Even in all my winter gear I was cold, so I went inside to the *Marco Polo* lounge. There I could comfortably sit and view the monstrous icebergs, the black and white landscape tinged with shades of blue, forming a tapestry with many patterns. Low clouds hovered overhead. The *Marco Polo* has numerous areas to watch the passing scenery.

*Icebergs surrounded the ship, but through technology on the bridge, the captain was able to make his way safely around them.*

An announcement was made of whale sightings. I rushed over to see two water-spouts and the back of the whales, but they were too distant for a picture.

We docked just off Port Lockroy, a small harbor on the west side of Wiencke Island. This British station is a popular tourist stop, as it is one of the few protected anchorages in the area for ships and is surrounded by spectacular mountainous scenery. Until 1931, Port Lockroy was a major harbor for whalers, and evidence of this is the numerous whale bones along the shore. The British have reconstructed a whale skeleton on shore.

We were notified that two officials would come on board and sell stamps that we could affix to our postcards and they would mail them for us with an Antarctica postmark. Of course, we were all eager to do this, but were informed that the cards would remain at Port Lockroy until the mail boat came the next week. Then they would go to the Falkland Islands, where they would await a mail plane headed for London, and in London they would be sorted for the various destinations around the world. My card was postmarked January 14, and I received it March 15. The officials, a man and a woman, were happy to see cruise ships to take advantage of a shower and excellent meals. There are no shower facilities in the small hut they occupy on shore.

*At last—my lifelong dream come true—I had been to all seven continents! The ship's photographer had all the nation's flags ready to take your picture when you landed.*

January 14, 2003 was the big day—the long-awaited time had come! My group loaded in the zodiacs at 2:55 P.M. headed for Port Lockroy. As I departed the boat and walked up the rocky incline, I could not believe it. I really had set foot on my seventh continent, Antarctica. My childhood fantasy was finally realized, sixty years from the time in a Texas cotton patch that I vowed to see the world. I thought to myself: *I finally accomplished my goal at age sixty-nine.* Then it hit me: that I had visited seven continents before turning seventy. Thus the title of my book was born. This was an emotional experience, impossible to describe. The ship's photographers were there to take our pictures with our respective country's flag and a sign commemorating the date (another sure sell).

Waiting for us on the barren rocks with patches of snow were (according to the naturalists) about 2,000 Gentoo penguins, with about the same numbers of

*Here I am—standing on Antarctica!*

the rookery out fishing. The birds were sitting on or standing in nests of small rocks accompanied by one or two chicks, about two to three weeks old. The birds return to this area each year in the Antarctic summer (October-February) to hatch and raise their young. Penguins as a rule mate for life and share the responsibility of sitting on the nest, about thirty-one to thirty-nine days of incubation period, and fishing for food. Their average lifespan is fifteen to twenty years. They usually lay two eggs, but rarely does more than one make it to maturity. The chicks are little fat puffballs, sitting right between the parent's feet. The bright orange beak and a prominent brush-type tail distinguish this species. The adults are about twenty-four to thirty inches in height and weigh around twelve pounds.

*"Why don't you want my pebble?" The romantic bachelor tries to woo an uninterested female.*

We were careful to stay at our allotted distance of fifteen feet, but the penguins were very friendly. When we stood still, they frequently would come right up to us. They showed no fear of humans; in fact, they totally ignored us. Several came within two or three feet of me as I stood perfectly still.

One young male bird came up to a female standing by a nest and dropped a pebble he carried in his mouth at her feet. She refused to pick it up. The naturalists said this was part of a courtship ritual. Males would bring rocks to the female to make a nest. He pointed out that this was a young bachelor looking for a mate, but obviously this lady was not interested. The birds do not mate until they are around four years of age. Rebuked, the young suitor just waddled off. When the penguins walk, their flippers are extended, and the entire body swings side to side on two feet. They can jump from one rock to another, and it is funny to see them sliding down an incline.

The penguins were constantly squawking to each other, or maybe just to themselves. They emit a sound similar to *"graanntee"* over and over.

The terrain was rocky with patches of ice, making it very difficult to walk, especially in those big rubber boots. I was very careful strolling through the penguin poop (which, after a while, did not smell as bad as when we first arrived), and I had more fun taking photos of the scenery and birds.

After about an hour or more, we lined up to have our boots washed. Several unlucky ship crewmen had drawn the short straw to have the duty of washing the passengers' filthy boots. At the edge of the water, they had a chair for you to balance yourself as you lifted each boot to be cleaned with a brush and water. When we

reached the ship, we were directed to an area with chairs, where more crewmen pulled off our boots, put them in a plastic bag for us to carry up to our room, and then handed us a cup of hot lemonade. One class act!

I quickly showered and changed clothes because I wanted to hear Amanda and Peter, current residents of Port Lockroy, talk about living in that remote place. They said there had been another man with them, but he had departed the day before.

*After tromping through the penguin poop, the ship's crewmen give our boots a good washing (not a popular job).*

Peter was about forty and Amanda looked to be in her early thirties, both very attractive. I wondered what kind of relationship they had in the small hut on a remote continent. They get their fresh water for use on land from the nearby floating icebergs. The outpost is occupied just during the four summer months. Amanda is a penguin specialist and was studying the migration by attaching a satellite device to the penguin's tail. The small satellite sends signals to Cambridge University in England where the data is analyzed. Peter was conducting a study to implement the control of fishing in the area. I can't imagine living in these conditions for four months, with only 4,000 penguins as neighbors.

*A Filipino chef creates a swan from a chunk of glacial ice at the "red parka party."*

After dinner, we had a "parka party." Everyone showed up in his or her red parkas on the open back deck. It was snowing lightly, but not really cold as there was no wind. One of the ship's chefs was carving on a block of glacial ice about three feet square. He was going at it furiously with all kinds of small hatchets and knives and in a very short time produced a stunning swan. Drinks were served over glacial ice. I couldn't tell the difference except that these were hunks of ice instead of cubes. A good time was had by all.

The next morning I slept until 8:00. Looking out my window, I could see we were sailing into Paradise Harbour. People often think of paradise as a place on a tropical island, but there is an undeniable beauty in the bay, from the sublime icebergs to the backdrop of mountains and glaciers reflected in the water. This is now the site of the Chilean station where scientists from Chile reside during the summer months.

I went out to the front deck. It was a great morning—temperature in the thirties and lightly snowing. I watched the crew unload the eight zodiac boats that are stored at the front of the ship. A crane lifts the large rubber boat up from its storage and swings it over the side and then lowers it many feet below to the water. Amazingly, the zodiac driver was standing in the boat during the whole process. That looked very frightening to me.

*The zodiac driver must ride the boat from the deck many feet to the icy waters below.*

I was scheduled to go ashore at 12:30 and decided to have a large breakfast and skip lunch. Before long, it was time to get dressed to go out. This was a little like preparing for skiing, but I had learned that it was not cold enough for the heavy sweater plus the parka.

On the short ride to land, our driver commented how lucky we were to have today's weather, clear and calm. He said he had seen it so foggy that they had to use a compass just to find the *Marco Polo* less than a mile away. The water was incredibly clear. The driver said there was visibility up to 200 feet deep, and he had scuba dived in these waters.

As we approached the landing, a Chilean flag hung lifeless in the still air. The flag is similar to the Texas flag: a white star in a field of blue and two stripes, one red and one white. The Texas flag has the red stripe on the bottom and the Chilean is red on top. As far as we could see in this protected cove were Gentoo penguins, grouped in their

*This Gentoo penguin proudly protects two baby chicks.*

individual communities. Occasionally there would be one nesting over by itself, but as a rule the nests were very close together. These chicks were younger than the ones we had seen the day before, and many parents were still sitting on eggs. The surrounding water was full of penguins, swimming and diving under the surface seeking krill (a shrimplike crustacean), squid, and small fishes. The adult catches the prey with its bill and swallows it whole while swimming. They then return to feed their own offspring, which are recognizable by the chicks' distinctive call. The chick sticks his head deep into the parent's throat to receive the regurgitated food.

The number-one enemy of the Gentoo is the snowy white sheathbill birds that swoop in and grab eggs or chicks. I heard a terrible ruckus, and saw that nearby a sheathbill was walking among the nesting penguins. The parent would make a loud noise, wave its

*Mama regurgitates her catch from the sea into the baby's mouth.*

flippers wildly, and attempt to bite the bird, but they never left the nest where the chick or egg was safely lodged.

We had lots of time to roam among the rookeries, and the penguins didn't seem to mind the "tall birds in red parkas" that were milling about taking pictures of them.

On the return ride we spotted a leopard seal resting on an iceberg. His coat was dark gray on top with "leopard" spots on the throat, shoulders, and sides. This fellow was about eight feet long. The zodiac driver said he was probably a young male, as the adults get to be eleven feet long weighing about 700 pounds. The seal was alone on this chunk of ice, waiting for a penguin dinner to swim by.

When I awoke Thursday morning, we were at Half Moon Bay. The sun was shining brightly, and I could see tall, snow-covered mountains, a few icebergs, and three small red huts near the water. Half Moon Island is a one-and-a-quarter-mile-long, crescent-shaped island in the South Shetland Islands. In 1956 the Argentine government established a station here, but it was unoccupied during our visit.

This was to be our last shore excursion, and I was very sad to think that the excitement and sights were coming to an end. The day was climaxed with perfect weather—clear, calm, and about 50 degrees. I didn't even wear my fur hat, just my earmuffs on my head. One naturalist said that this was the best weather he had ever experienced in the nine years he had been visiting there. He said that on previous occasions he had seen waves so high in the harbor that they could not even land.

This was our only wet landing, where we had to disembark in about twelve inches of water. No problem with my knee-high rubber boots. A short walk up an incline over water-worn rocks brought me to the Chinstrap Penguin Village. These darling creatures are smaller and more slender than the Gentoos, weighing in at about nine pounds. They have blue-black backs with white cheeks and white underparts and a black bill. Their name derives from a thin black line, like a chin-

*This smiling feller is a Chinstrap.*

*Mother Chinstrap talks to her baby chick.*

*"I'm King of the Rock!" At least that seems to be what he is saying, and everyone is agreeing with him.*

strap, that crosses the chin and runs back under the eye to join the nape. I think this makes them look like they have a permanent grin. Most of them had one or two chicks about three to four weeks old.

I guess the ship personnel knew that we would be reluctant to leave, as this was our last stop, so they did not pressure us to leave after one hour. We had plenty of time to bond with the Chinstraps, and it was a treasured experience. I sat down on a rock and watched them as they shuffled down to the water and dived in. When they returned, they would come out on shore and shake themselves, and then make their way up to the family to share dinner.

The Chinstraps make a much higher pitched sound than the Gentoos. The area around the penguin colonies was very rocky and icy. On the return ride, we circled a large iceberg where two seals were sunning themselves. One was a Weddell seal, one of the largest of all seals, which has a smiling small face on a big body. The other one was a small elephant seal, the largest seal in the world. Our driver said this elephant seal was probably a young teenager.

Back on the *Marco Polo* I reflected on my extraordinary adventures in Antarctica. I had a mixed feeling of sadness and joy as I realized that I would never return this way again; however, I was so thankful that I was able to see it. One Irish passenger expressed my feelings exactly when she said: "I so hated to leave the wee pets."

We were now setting sail northward back to Ushuaia. The resident helicopter (the ship's eye in the sky) took off from the top deck to check our pathway to make sure that there were no icebergs blocking our route. We watched icebergs carrying seals float by, and many birds followed our wake. Several whales were spotted in the distance.

Friday—our last day at sea. We thoroughly enjoyed lectures by Peter Hillary. He entertained us with his many extraordinary adventures, combining humor with fascinating information.

The final night was the Captain's Farewell Dinner, so I had a beauty appointment. The hairdresser did a good job (my local stylist would die if she knew that I paid $38.50 for the same treatment she does for $12). While I was in the beauty shop, the announcement came that we were going around Cape Horn, an island that is the final upward burst of the Andes mountain range at the tip of South America. When the ship rounds the Horn in the Drake Passage, the ocean is pinched to little more than 300 miles wide by the Antarctic Peninsula. The Horn is about as far south of the equator as Juneau, Alaska, is north of it. Weather conditions at the Horn are known to be very nasty, causing numerous shipwrecks. But on that day there were just a few white-caps on the water's surface. Upon our return to Ushuaia, Captain Andersson said it had been the smoothest crossing of the Drake Passage he had ever had in his eight years in the area. I can say that I was truly lucky to be on this voyage. Would anyone like to purchase practically new sea wristbands, worn only a few hours?

That last afternoon I sat in the *Marco Polo* lounge reflecting on my trip alone, an experience I had not had before. It was surprising how many people on this cruise were single travelers, and how many had spouses at home who just didn't want to go to Antarctica (I was one of those). One man said his wife would not come because she said she had seen the movie *Titanic*. I met some very interesting people and acquired some new lifetime friends, but I hope I don't have to travel without Keith in the future.

The Farewell Dinner was quite a production. After we had feasted on lobster and all the trimmings, followed with Baked Alaska, the Filipino waiters, wine stewards and kitchen staff presented an outstanding choir presentation. I have been on many, many cruises, but this was the first time I have been entertained by dining personnel in a musical show.

When I awoke Saturday morning we were in Ushuaia. Having been to Antarctica through the Drake Passage with perfect weather all the way, here it was raining and yucky. We had the day to kill, and I signed up for the Escondido Lake BBQ and presidio tour. As we left the town in the motor coach, the guide pointed out that we were on the Pan American Highway. That same highway runs from the Canadian border through the United States, and comes right through Evant, Texas, where I live. You can continue south on it until you reach the Panama Canal. On the other side of the canal it continues all the way through Central America to the bottom of the world at Ushuaia.

We traveled through lush countryside with snow-capped mountains in the distance. The guide said that they could cross-country ski here almost year-round. There were peat bogs just like the ones I had seen in Ireland that they use for fuel. As we came along a lovely stream, I noticed that on either side of the water for about fifty feet the trees were dead. The guide said that a few years ago they had brought in thirty-five pairs of beavers from Canada to start a fur trade. The fur business had declined, and the beavers increased to over 50,000 and were destroying the trees.

We had a delicious Patagonian lamb barbecue lunch at a ski lodge, followed by an authentic Argentinean gaucho dance show. Back in Ushuaia, we stopped at the old Prison Museum. The town started as an Argentinean penal colony, and the museum is in the original penitentiary. The building, built in 1902, once held as many as 600 inmates. It closed in 1947 and was incorporated into the local naval base.

I decided to leave the tour and walk downtown to do a little shopping. I found a couple of T-shirts before returning to the ship. Antarctica is the first place I have ever been that does not have gift shops! Very refreshing.

Bags had to be packed and outside the door by 10:00 P.M. It took some doing, but I did get everything in the suitcase and locked, including those big rubber boots.

Sunday morning we took a tour of Tierra del Fuego National Park prior to going to the airport to catch our chartered flight at noon. This park was created in 1960 to protect the vegetation and animals unique to this area at the end of the world. The first inhabitants of this region were Indians who wore no clothes. In the sub-arctic climate they coated their bodies with seal fat to stay warm. When they hunted seals, in canoes, the women rowed, the men speared the sea lions, and the children tended the fire in the center of the boat. They never let the fire go out. When the first explorers came to this area, they saw the fires, and named the area Tierra del Fuego—"Land of Fire." The Indians died out when white men brought diseases from which they had no immunity.

We sat at the airport until 4:30, because planes could not come in due to the dense fog. Orient Lines provided lunch and drinks for us. I could not believe that such a small airport restaurant staff could make sandwiches for 500 people, but they did. Although it wasn't the greatest sandwich I'd ever eaten, at least it was something. After all the food on the ship, we were having withdrawal symptoms after stuffing our stomachs for eight days.

As I walked around the waiting area to pass the time, I saw my friend Laurie sitting in a wheelchair with a cast on one leg from her toes to her knee. I was shocked to hear that she had stepped off a curb while walking around in Ushuaia, and had a spiral fracture from her ankle up her shin. She would have to have surgery when she returned to Michigan. What a terrible way to end such a wonderful trip.

When the charter flight reached Buenos Aires, I was left still standing at the baggage carousel as my shipmates picked up their luggage and took off for customs. My charter flight was the first one to arrive of the three, but my bag was the *last* bag to come in. I grabbed it, and had to walk what seemed like miles to the international terminal. On my regular schedule I was to have about a four-hour layover in Buenos Aires, but with the delay of the charter flight and my baggage arrival, I barely made it to the departure gate in time and boarded the American Airlines plane bound for Miami—4,427 miles and eight hours away. We arrived at Miami at 5:00 A.M., and the temperature in Miami was 46 degrees, not much warmer than it was in Antarctica! We would leave for DFW from the same gate we arrived, so I thought this was going to be a piece of cake.

Never assume. It was a long walk to immigration, and the escalators were not working so I had to carry the bags up (another time I really missed Keith). I cleared immigration smoothly, and all was going great until I arrived at customs. They asked if I had been to Antarctica. This was difficult to disclaim when I was wearing an Antarctica jacket and T-shirt with penguins on it. They put my luggage through x-ray and then directed me to the Agriculture Department. There I had to take off my tennis shoes to be disinfected (even though I had never worn them in any penguin area).

Then I had to open the big bag, unpack the rubber boots, and they disinfected them. I couldn't imagine what we might bring back from a pure and pristine land, plus the boots had been washed after each excursion. I really think the penguins should have had *us* disinfect our boots before we stepped on their land, coming from the rest of the world loaded with germs!

Surprisingly, we arrived at DFW on time and departed for Austin on time. When we landed, I ran to meet Keith, who was waiting for me at the Austin airport luggage area. I had been up over forty-eight hours and was flying over twenty of those hours. I was totally exhausted, but so thankful to be home and have so many wonderful memories of my seventh continent, Antarctica.

One gentleman from Canada on the ship offered me this saying, and I think it represents what I was feeling as I traveled home:

"Yesterday is history,
Tomorrow is a mystery,
Today is a gift; that is why it is a present."

*Sadly I had to leave this wonderful continent of ice, snow, and lovable penguins. But I was happy that I had the opportunity to see Antarctica, and I did it before I was seventy.*

# Australia and Pacific Area

For friendly people and beautiful scenery, plus no language barrier (most of the time), a wonderful destination is Australia and New Zealand. Australia is about the same size as the United States in landmass, but most of the population is centered on the eastern part of the continent. I think of Australia as "the U.S. East Coast and West Coast—with Arizona in between." In our four excursions there we visited most of the eastern cities, plus the barrier reef. We also made it to the outback but, regrettably, never ventured over to the western town of Perth.

## Australia

Our first trip "down under" was just Keith and me. In my other book I related the difficulty we had in obtaining visas. (I stupidly thought that a visa was just a credit card, so we did not have the visa document necessary to enter Australia, thus costing us many extra dollars and missed time on our tour.)

We had a very short time in Melbourne, but we did get to take the tour down to Phillip Island, located ninety miles south of Melbourne, to see the darling fairy penguins. These lovable creatures look just like regular penguins but are toy size, just about eight inches high. Hundreds of them make their home at Summerland Beach on Phillip Island, living in a hole in the sand about twenty to fifty yards up the beach. Each day they swim out into the ocean to feed and at dusk return home. At first you see the water stirring, and then, one by one, the little birds come ashore, shaking themselves. Fairy penguins mate for life. One bird will come out of the water, walk up and down the beach until it locates its spouse, and then the two of them waddle together up the beach to their home in the sand. You can see two little black heads sticking up out of the hole—so romantic.

The first time Keith and I saw the Penguin Parade was in 1977. At that time the area was roped off, with one light pole for illumination. We stood behind the rope, and the penguins walked right beside us up to their nests in the sand. The last time we were there, with a group in 1993, the experience had been ruined, in my opinion. There were large concrete viewing stadiums, with lights everywhere, and the birds had to walk underneath the seating area to get to their homes. Also, even though there was a sign stating "No Photos" and the announcement was made on a loudspeaker before the penguins arrived, people were still flashing pictures right in the poor little birds' faces. The special allure of the place had been replaced with too many people and concrete bleachers—too commercialized. But I guess that is the norm now in many tourist spots.

Leaving Melbourne, we flew to the Australian famous "outback" town of Alice Springs, located in the center of the continent. This small town is an oasis surrounded by the stark and desolate beauty of miles and miles of desert and rock mountains. From here we took a small propeller plane 275 miles over red-colored earth without any vegetation to Ayers Rock, the purpose for coming all this way. Ayers Rock is the largest single rock in the world, rising over 1,100 feet above the desert and extending nearly two miles. I was determined to climb it.

We stayed at Inland Motel, near the rock, and were the only non-Australians there. That evening after dinner, hot tea was served. We were never served any liquid during the meal, unless it was wine. I could barely get through the meal without some type of beverage. I remarked to the woman next to me that in Texas we drank a lot of iced tea.

"Oh," she exclaimed, "how do you make it?"

I couldn't believe people had not heard of iced tea, which probably ranks as the number-one beverage in Texas. I explained that you just make the hot tea, let it cool, and add ice. Since the average temperature was around 100 or more in the outback, I thought iced tea certainly would be appropriate.

"That sounds very interesting," she said. "I will have to try it sometime."

At sunset and sunrise Ayers Rock takes on different colors, from bright orange to deep rust with shades of purple. The rock also displays various shades and colors at different times of the year. We were there in the winter (June), and the colors at sunset changed from pink to dusky burnt orange.

The next morning, we were "up and at 'em" before sunrise to see what the morning view of Ayers Rock had to offer. Regrettably, it was cloudy that morning, and we failed to see much color transformation. But we did get to climb the monolith. I fool-

*The stark beauty of Ayers Rock.*

ishly had on leather-soled boots, inappropriate for climbing solid rock surfaces. A pathway had been marked to follow at an angle up the rock, and life-saving chain handrails were installed for ill-prepared and clumsy people like me. But determination won out, and we did reach the top of Ayers Rock for the heart-throbbing view of harsh and barren land with the naked Olga Mountains on the horizon. There was not a tree in sight. We had made it to the top, but then came the hard part: getting down. This I accomplished mostly on my rear end. My shoe soles were so slippery that I could not get any traction, and the safest way was to sit and slide down the steepest part. This wasn't good for the seat of my pants or my bottom, but it was better than falling.

When we reached the ground, our motel staff had left a box with breakfasts. Never has cold cereal tasted so good. An Ayers Rock Climber's Certificate certifying that we actually climbed to the top on June 15, 1977, is one of our prized possessions.

After breakfast, we took a walk around the base of the formation to see Aboriginal rock paintings in many of the caves. The sketches were primitive, but very artistic. (Later I would find in Gladstone a colorful Aborigine painting on a kangaroo skin, which now graces the wall of my office.)

In the shadow of the rock, an Aborigine man sat cross-legged playing a didgeridoo, a long, hollow wooden pipe about four feet long. When blown into, this instrument produces a strange wailing sound. Several tourists tried but failed to make a sound. We would have explored more, but the flies were driving us wild. Our backs and caps were covered with the horrible little pests. I now know why the Australian Bushmen are shown with corks hanging down from the brims of their hats—to shoo the flies away.

The strikingly lovely city of Sydney reminds me of San Francisco because of the similar bay and the up-and-down terrain of the streets. If you closed your ears and did

*The koala bear is cuddly, but his sharp claws can dig into your skin.*

not hear the Aussies talk, you would think you were in San Francisco, for the people look and dress the same. There is one outstanding difference: the impressive Opera House building jutting out into the bay. I was overwhelmed that they had raised the money for the building and maintained it with lottery funds. (I have never seen anything built with Texas Lottery State funds.) A tour of the building is a must. The various performance halls are not only attractive, but the acoustics are impeccable. Do not miss a performance when you are there.

In Sydney we went to the zoo to see the animals found only in Australia: kangaroos, wallabies, emus, koalas, and the duckbill platypus (a very strange half-duck, half-otter looking creature that paddles around in the water). The most frightening sight was the wild dingo dog. Looking ferocious with large sharp teeth, these canine beasts paced back and forth next to the barrier fence.

We have been to Australia four times, two personal trips and two on group tours. On the last trip, Bill of our group mastered the art of playing the didgeridoo.

If it were not for the terribly long flight to and from there, I would go more often. You will love the people, the scenery and the unique wildlife. Australia is like no other country in the world.

## New Zealand

I am frequently asked what is my favorite country, and I have very many, but I consider New Zealand one of my favorites as it has so much to offer in such a small space. The country showcases snow-capped mountains, glaciers, fjords equal to Norway, trout streams, hot geysers, native Maori culture, and the exclusive kiwi bird and kiwi fruit. Made up of two islands called, logically, North and South Island, they cover about 1,000 miles total in length. This is home to more than four million people and seventy million sheep.

On our first trip to New Zealand, Keith and I landed in Auckland, rented a car, and toured the North Island. The first thing we noticed when we drove into Rotorua was the strong odor of hydrogen sulphide. This natural gas rises from the underground thermal springs. Nearby is the Maori village, which is somewhat touristy. Here we walked through the thermal area similar to Yellowstone National Park, with its bubbling mud pools and spouting geysers.

In the evening the local Maoris presented a concert of their cultural music and dance. They were dressed in authentic native costumes of straw skirts with feather adornment. We were amused by the men's dance, where they stick out their large tongues. This was sup-

*The native Maori people on the North Island of New Zealand present a colorful musical show for the tourists.*

posed to frighten the enemy, but it seemed to me the only way this would be a deterrent was that the opponent might die laughing.

On a different visit with our group, we attended a hangi (Maori feast). As we entered the banquet hall, a Maori man and woman in native dress greeted us. There a photographer snapped a souvenir photo of each tourist with the natives. Everyone bought a picture except one woman in my group. When asked why she didn't want it, she remarked: "Why would I want a picture of me with people I do not even know?"

On the North Island, another attraction is Waitomo's famous Glo Worm Grotto. When Keith and I were there, the caves were flooded and closed. We did get to see them on the next trip with the group. We went down a staircase quietly (you don't want to wake the glowworms and have them fall on your head), boarded a flat-bottomed boat, and glided into the darkness of the cave. When our eyes became adjusted, we looked up and saw thousands of tiny lights shining from the roof. It was an unbelievable experience, and hard to explain—one of those things you just have to see for yourself. We were told that the tiny insects are not glowworms but are the larvae stage of a fungal gnat, with luminous excretory tubes. The long, sticky lengths resemble beads, and at the extreme end is a miniscule light intended to trap tiny insects. Whatever they were, it was something to see—and certainly spooky!

To get from the North Island to the South Island, you can either fly or take the ferry across the very rough Cook Strait. We have done both, and I definitely recommend flying, especially if you have a tendency to become seasick. Over half the people, Keith included, became very seasick on our crossing.

On the south island of New Zealand, Mt. Cook is the centerpiece, rising 12,349 feet to the sky. We stayed at the Franz Josef Hotel, a picture-book lodge with a view of the nearby glacier. From there Keith and I took a ski plane ride to the top of Franz Joseph glacier, which is about eighteen miles long and two miles wide. As we prepared for takeoff, the pilot said that the weather wasn't favorable for landing, but he could give us a good view regardless. Since this was the only time we had for the venture, we decided to go ahead. The five-passenger plane had skis on the base next to the wheels that could be lowered to land on the ice and snow. After we had been aloft for about fifteen minutes, he said that he had clearance to land if we wished. Of course we did!

I looked down and all I could see was ice with deep cracks that looked blue. All of sudden, we were skidding to a stop right on top of the sparkling glacier that was

*A special thrill was landing on 2,000 feet of ice and snow of Franz Joseph Glacier, South Island of New Zealand.*

over 2,000 feet deep. What an electrifying feeling to be on top of this magnificent glacier! As we deplaned, we sank in fresh snow up to our knees. We had a great time throwing snowballs at each other and taking in the eye-popping view from this vantage point. In the distance, Mt. Cook stood in all its shining glory.

I began to wonder: It was easy skiing to a stop in the landing, but how would we take off from an icy runway? No problem. The pilot just brought the plane around on the skis, revved up the engine, and took off as if he had wheels and had been on an asphalt or concrete runway. I will always remember this as one of the many highlights of our travels.

On another excursion, Keith and I were driving around New Zealand on the South Island en route to Milford Sound. It was around dusk when we approached a tunnel. As we proceeded through this approximately two-mile tunnel, I commented how narrow it was and that I surely would not want to meet a bus in there. We made it through without seeing any vehicle, and continued on to the Milford Hotel with its stunning view of the mountains that tumble right down into the sea.

As we were checking in, the clerk said: "Did you have a long wait at the tunnel, or did you arrive on the right half hour?"

This proved God takes care of those who do not have enough sense to take care of themselves. What we did not see in the low light of the evening was a sign stating that northbound traffic goes through on the first half hour and southbound traffic on the last half hour. We had no idea on what portion of the clock we passed through the tunnel.

The Milford Hotel is attractively decorated and located with marvelous views of the fjord-like canyon in front of it. From there you can take a boat trip along the sound to closely view numerous cascading waterfalls and sheer rock walls that rise thousands of feet out of the water.

On the return trip we were careful to pass through the tunnel at the correct time. We drove north and enjoyed the scenery of mountains and streams, accented with fields of lupine (just like our Texas bluebonnets, but much larger and in colors of purple and pink). As we came around a curve, we saw a car that had just crashed headfirst into a tree at the side of the road. We stopped to see if we could be of assistance. Out of the car jumped a young man, around thirty, and he ran over to the driver's side and extracted a woman in her sixties.

"Are you OK?" we inquired.

"Yes," the man replied, "but Mum's quite shook up."

"We just passed a work crew not too far back. We'll take you there and see if they can contact help. Come get in our car," Keith invited.

Leaving the car with the front smashed in next to the tree, they climbed into the back seat.

The woman started crying.

"There, there, Mums. Don't cry. I think all you will need is a new bonnet," the son said reassuringly.

I thought I was going to die trying not to laugh. I knew the New Zealanders and Aussies called the car hood a bonnet, but the idea of her needing a new bonnet struck me as very funny.

Do not miss New Zealand when you plan a trip to Australia. Once you are in the area and you have already paid for the airfare, take in its outstanding scenery and gentle people.

# Papua New Guinea

When I told my daughter that Keith and I were going to Papau New Guinea, she said, "Isn't that where they put people in a pot and eat them?"

Maybe they did many years ago, but not any longer. However, they still dress strangely (according to our standards), and certainly this is one of the most interesting cultures in the world and one of the most intriguing places we have visited.

In 1996 we flew from Austin, Texas, to Los Angeles and then fourteen hours and twenty minutes to Hong Kong. (Yes, I was in the middle seat!) After overnight in the airport hotel, we flew to Singapore, one of my favorite cities. Everything is so clean and orderly.

In Singapore it is against the law to litter, chew or possess chewing gum, spit or feed birds in public areas. If caught littering, the offender is arrested and has to pay a fine of 300 Singapore dollars. On the last Sunday of each month, the guilty parties have to report to a city park, where they are outfitted in a bright orange vest imprinted "LITTERBUG" on the front and back and must work all day cleaning the park. The local paper publishes their picture on the front page Monday morning. Reports are that the first time this was enforced, they had more than 100 litterbugs in the picture. Now rarely does anyone disobey the law. Very effective.

After several days in Singapore, with day trips over to neighboring Malaysia, we flew to Port Moresby, the largest city and capital of Papua New Guinea, often referred to as PNG. We made tour arrangements through *Melanesian Discoverer,* a luxury catamaran that sails around the islands and rivers of Papau New Guinea.

As we wanted to see some of the interior of the country, we first visited the highlands region. This area is so remote and covered with dense foliage that even the tribes are isolated from each other. This has resulted in 740 different languages. Today natives communicate in pidgin, a sort of midway meeting point for verbal communication. The PNG pidgin has taken words from many languages, but mostly from German and, English, as the country was ruled by Britain and Germany and, lastly, Australia. In 1964, Papua New Guinea obtained its independence. The outside world did not learn about the mountain tribes until 1933, when the first white man ventured deep into the highlands. And in 1996, Keith and Joyce Brooks arrived.

A flight of almost two hours in a two-engine prop plane with an Australian pilot took us from Port Moresby to Tari, the main city of the highlands, close to the center of the country. Looking down, we could see lush green mountains and valleys with an occasional village of five or six grass-roofed huts dotting the hillsides. Small gardens could be spotted nearby.

As our plane landed, I noticed standing by the airport fence an assortment of people. All had very black skin. Some were dressed in western attire, but the majority were in native dress. For the men the ensemble consisted of a waistband with one banana leaf hanging down in front and one banana leaf hanging down in back, and a huge headdress of hair that stood out up to two feet high around and on top of their head, decorated with feathers and flowers. The wig might be black, red, yellow, or a combination of all three. That is all: banana leaf, wig, flowers, and feathers. To add to this, many men's faces were painted with red and yellow designs.

*We look very dull pictured with the Wig Men of Papua New Guinea—especially our headwear.*

The women wore cloth skirts that wrapped around their waists. Some had on blouses, some had bare tops. A "bilum bag," a woven net bag of various sizes, up to three or four feet across, completed her attire. Inside the bag would be vegetables, firewood, children, or small pigs. These bags are transported on the woman's back, with the carrying strap across her forehead for leverage. I never saw a man with a bilum bag. All we ever witnessed the male carrying was a spear or "killing stick," a two-foot stick with a sharp cassowary bone attached. The large cassowary birds, related to the Australian emu, but stockier in build, at one time were numerous in the wilds of PNG. But the use of the bones for weapons and tools, meat for food, and feathers for adornment has greatly depleted the species, and today they are rare.

Entering the airport building, we immediately spotted our driver, who would transfer us to our lodge. As we waited in the van for him to collect our luggage, there appeared at the open door quite a sight. An old man was standing there, staring at us. He had the traditional banana leaf loincloth and a typical hair wig. His neck was adorned with a large, half-moon shell necklace about six inches across that I instantly coveted. I later found out that this was called a "kina shell," made from the gold lip pearl shell and in the past was used as money.

I smiled and said hello. He just looked at me. I'm sure I looked as strange to him as he did to me. He never said a word—just stood there and stared. I kept smiling (a method I have used successfully around the world to make friends), but his expression never changed. After several minutes, I felt rather uneasy. When our driver returned, he clarified that the man was the self-appointed welcoming committee for Tari—a most unusual form of "welcome wagon." Anyway, I started looking for a kina shell necklace and later found one at a village market. When I tried to bargain with the owner, he said, "This is our money. We don't devalue it." So I forked over the number-one asking price.

We stopped at the Tari market. Our driver explained we were to pick up Ray and Julie, Peace Corps workers at the Catholic High School located on the way to our lodge. They were a young couple in their mid-twenties from Washington, DC. He taught math and she English. Julie had just started a class on sex education for the students, which she thought very important as their parents still practiced all the old tribal rules and are uninformed about birth control and AIDS. Ray and Julie were glad to visit with Americans. They were rather homesick.

Along the drive to our lodge, about twenty miles over a very rough and unpaved road, the scenery was out of the ordinary, with high mountains and little native villages displaying small gardens growing mostly sweet potatoes, the main staple of their diet. Their sweet potatoes are white and long, and have a sweeter taste than our white potatoes.

The landscape scenes were amazing, but the real attraction was the people. Everyone walks. We didn't see any personal motorized means of transportation except in the cities. Only the lodge or government officials operate vehicles out in the countryside. Sitting along the road was the local form of entertainment. Large groups would be gathered there—some playing games, some selling vegetables, and, in most cases, just sitting there doing nothing. Those walking were a sight to behold. There was no set fashion. Some men wore nothing but the banana leaf; others would have the leaf loin wrap and a western shirt. I saw one man with a yellow construction hard hat on top of his large hair wig. But the most unusual sight was a woman walking down the road carrying a pig wrapped up just like a baby—the real "pig in a blanket." Others would have a pig on a string, leading it like a dog.

In the highlands, the measure of wealth is pigs, land, and women, in that order. The number of pigs he possesses, the land he owns, and the number of wives are the mea-

*Now here's a real pig in a blanket!*

surements of a man's standing in the community. This has led to many tribal and inter-tribal wars in the past, and skirmishes frequently occur to this day. We were scheduled to visit a certain village but could not as they were at war with their neighbors.

One day as we were driving along the road, we had to stop and wait while a battle was waged by one group on one side of the road and another on the opposite side. The weapons were bows and arrows and spears. As we waited some distance away, the conflict consisted of considerable yelling back and forth. Then, for some unknown reason, they just parted and went their separate ways. I don't know if it was coffee break time or if talk had settled their differences.

Our hotel, the Ambua Lodge, was located at an altitude of 7,000 feet in the mountains. Forty individual traditional looking *casitas* were built using local materials. Inside were many amenities: a sweeping view of the valley, a private bathroom, and even electric blankets on the beds to keep us warm during the cool nights. Delicious meals were served in the large dining room in the main building.

From the lodge we drove up to 9,000 feet in search of the elusive Bird of Paradise. Here our guide located the "King of Saxony" bird, with two long black feathers on each side of his head that swept down about three feet. What a thrill to see this magnificent bird in the wild! PNG is home to thirty-eight of the world's forty-three spectacular and gaudy species of Bird of Paradise. Because of the Bird of Paradise's significance to tribal ceremonies and dress decoration, they have become endangered and are now protected by the government.

At the "Wigmen's Village" the next day, we were informed that a few selected men go to wig school for eighteen months. There they eat a special diet to make their hair grow fast. When it is about eight inches long, they attach a cone-shaped bamboo frame underneath the hair on their skull and then let the hair grow over it to form a mushroom shape. The hair is then cut and made into a wig, and adorned with Bird of Paradise feathers and flowers. The wigs can be removed for sleeping and are kept on racks by their beds. Those who cannot grow enough hair can use tree moss. The men also paint their faces with red and yellow dye.

Most villages are protected with high bamboo fences, and some even have a tunnel to

*Musical instruments are formed from bamboo.*

pass through for admission as a safeguard from their enemies. Inside the village, the men sleep in one building called a long house. The husband owns the separate hut where his wives, children, and pigs sleep. He will visit his hut during the night but always returns to the men's building later to sleep. The highlands man can have as many

*My* National Geographic *shot. This old woman was sitting in the doorway of a hut on one of the PNG islands.*

wives as he can afford. A wife usually costs thirty pigs, plus sometimes several bilum bags or kina shells. The women do all the work of growing the food and caring for the pigs. The men hunt and fight wars. Fighting tribal wars is a national pastime, but today the warriors are rarely wounded or killed.

Villages usually consist of one family, clan, or tribe. The village people have a strong alliance with each other, and if someone from another village wrongs one of their members, the entire village combines for the "payback." They also help each other with food and money. Through the "Wantok" system, virtually everybody is fed and clothed, even if they are unemployed. "Wantok" literally means "one talk," and those with a common language look after one another and share the clan's wealth. The first mate on our cruise ship around the PNG islands and rivers explained that because he had a good job and income, he sent most of his paycheck to his village on the Sepik River. This was a Wantok responsibility he accepted without question.

But the Wantok system, regrettably, encourages unemployed youths to venture to the cities in hope of making money for their clan. There they are unable to find work, as they are uneducated and unskilled. This leads to crime, which is prevalent in Port Moresby.

After two extremely interesting days around Tari, we took the small plane back to Port Moresby to overnight. The name of the airline was "Southwest Air," which reminded me of the popular airline in Texas. But I knew I was not in Texas when the man sitting beside me on the plane did not have on a Stetson hat and boots but was dressed in the PNG traditional banana leaf and hair wig. Unfortunately, we did not belong to the same "Wantok," so I missed an opportunity to discuss the local politics.

Next morning we flew to the southeast coast of the island to board our floating hotel for twelve days, the *Melanesian Discoverer*. The small catamaran ship has twenty-one cabins, and there were thirty passengers on board for this cruise, including a group of Germans who spoke very little English, a couple from Poland (he was a doctor and had an excellent English vocabulary), a Travcoa tour group of twelve from the

United States, three Australians, and Keith and me. Quite a mixed bag. We had become good friends with the Australians—a couple, both doctors, and a single woman, a world traveler. (Naturally we gravitated to each other because we all spoke English—although sometimes we had difficulty between the Australian and Texan accents.) We still communicate with Christmas cards and e-mail.

With the capable leadership of the cruise director, Jan, who, incidentally owned the ship, everyone blended together and the cruise was totally delightful and most informative. Jan and her husband, Peter, are both native Australians. Peter was in the PNG government cabinet. Jan graciously gave us her personal cabin, the only one on the top deck. It was a large room with a king-size bed (almost unheard of on a small cruise ship). Each evening she would join Keith and me for cocktails on the back deck. Jan would have a margarita, and we would have our vodka gimlets. She enjoyed eating my snack mixture of nuts and dried fruit. (I sent her a large package of the nut mixture the following December as a Christmas present. She received them the next September. Don't know what they tasted like by then.)

Each day we would stop at one or more of the Trobriand Islands that dot the waters off the southeastern area of the mainland. The islanders have strong Polynesian characteristics and look very different from the highlanders. A chief dominates each island, and inheritances are passed through the female side of the family. This means the chief's sons belong to his wife's clan and they can be superseded by one of her oldest sister's sons.

Where the sign of prestige in the highlands is land and pigs, yams (potatoes) reign in the islands. Not only are yams the primary staple food, they are elements of a ritual between villages and clans. The quantity and size of the yams grown are very important. At harvest time, usually July or August, the potatoes are dug up and brought to the village for display and then placed in the yam houses, which are small storage huts built upon stilts with openings between storage shelves for ventilation. The chief's yam house, always the largest and most decorative, was filled first from the harvest. One chief's yam house displayed a four-foot potato.

The island villages are all laid out in circular fashion. Yam

*This fancy building is where the chief of the island stores his yams, the staple food of the tribe.*

houses form the inner ring, surrounded by sleeping houses (in this area the husband sleeps in the same house with his possessions—wives, children, and animals). In this small area lived all the clan, plus the pigs, dogs, and chickens. The houses were made of poles with palm leaf roofs and dirt floors. The area in the middle plaza was usually swept very clean.

Sexual customs in the islands are rather unusual. From puberty, teenagers are encouraged to have up to seven partners (I don't know how they keep count). When a young man reaches puberty, he moves into a bachelor hut that is closed in for privacy. A girl can visit a bachelor hut and experiment to see which man she wishes to marry.

Upon marriage, the couple settles down and are monogamous, with the exception of an occasional fling during the wild yam harvest, which is acceptable. With all this premarital activity, surprisingly very few children are born out of wedlock. This is attributed to an herbal contraceptive that is given the morning after.

Each island we visited had a little different culture, and all had to perform an exotic dance for us upon arrival, complete with native dress, or in this case, undress. The young men always had the banana leaf costume, and the ladies and girls had just the grass skirts with bare breasts. At one location, an older woman was dancing

*(Above) A real fashion statement—the head matriarch gets to wear a bra! (Below) Beautiful young ladies decked out in local costumes perform a dance for us.*

in her grass skirt, but instead of bare on the top, she wore a white cotton brassiere, similar to the old popular "Maidenform" ads. When I inquired about this fashion statement, it was explained that she was the head matriarch and was entitled to wear a bra as a symbol of her position. (And to think I've been wearing one for all these years and did not realize its significance …)

We arrived on Thursday at an island that designates this day at school as "Native Day." The children dress in traditional costume and sing and dance traditional programs. We were privileged to witness 380 students perform six dances. These were the most beautiful children I have ever seen. They had exceptional well-developed bodies, and their chocolate-colored skin glistened. They apply coconut oil and then sprinkle on golden pollen from flowers that shine like flecks of gold on their skin. We noticed one child with totally white skin and hair. He was an albino, and his sister was the same way. Jan said that the children accepted them, but sadly they would probably not live very long as with such thin skin they would develop skin cancer from the intense sun.

The island school was furnished with crude tables and stools for desks. The teacher proudly showed us the students' artwork, which was very expressive. In PNG about 70 percent of the children begin elementary school and about 30 percent make it through to the sixth grade and on to high school. Attendance on the islands is bet-

ter than in the highlands because the villages are closer together and island life is more peaceful than in the mountains. The island people's diet is also more nutritious due to the plentiful seafood.

Wares for sale were always displayed immediately when we stepped from the shore launch, and I am always a sucker for native crafts. We bought ebony woodcarvings and seashells.

Practically all adults in PNG chew betel nut, the nut of the Areca palm. It is generally mixed with lime from sea coral and seed stalks from a pepper plant. The reaction between the lime and the nut produces a mild narcotic effect. Smiles were repulsive to me, since their teeth and gums were bright red. They would spit wherever they were, leaving along the footpaths bright red spots that looked like blood. Prolonged use leads to black teeth and, in some cases, mouth cancer. Betel nut was sold at all the markets and frequently along the sides of the road. Men and women both have brightly woven straw bags in which they carry their betel nut supply. These were not sold as souvenirs, but I wanted one.

*These straw bags are used to carry their beetle nut, and I was able to trade a pack of Marlboros for one. I also traded for the boar's tooth necklace around her neck.*

One woman was enticed to empty out her betel nuts and trade her bag to me for one pack of Marlboros.

Smoking is widespread among both men and women in PNG. Traditionally they smoked grass roots or rolled up paper. Now cigarettes are available, but to obtain an American brand that they all desire is very expensive. I have never smoked, and personally do not endorse the practice. But in many third world countries, smoking is very prevalent. Since I could not be a one-woman force to change the habit, I found that American cigarettes had great trading value. At one time I exchanged a package of Marlboros for an extremely large and colorful helmet seashell. Various other souvenirs were obtained for one or two cigarettes.

We completed our magical island cruise at Madang on the north shore of PNG and then continued for a five-day cruise inland on the Sepik River. The Sepik has the same relevance to PNG as the Congo in Africa or the Amazon in South America. It is one of the largest rivers in the world in terms of water flow. The Sepik is over 180 miles long and most of it is navigable, so it serves as a main transportation route where roads are impossible. At places the river was so wide it was impossible to see across. Within this region dwells another unique PNG culture.

Villages appear all along the river. As we cruised the muddy waterway that resembled a chocolate milkshake, we stopped and toured the villages and markets. Here the people's skin was darker than that of the islanders. They wore primarily western dress for the tropics: shorts and T-shirts for the men, wrap-around skirts and shirts for the ladies. Most of the children were naked.

The architectural difference here was the Haus Tambarana, or spirit house. Tall, carved poles twenty to thirty feet long support the buildings. The roof spire at each end stretches up to ten feet high. Only men can enter the spirit houses, unless you are a foreign tourist, and then you can enter because that is where they have their carvings

*Life is simple along the Sepik River, with a dugout canoe the only means of transportation.*

*Haus Tambarana, or Spirit House, symbolizes the different architecture along the Sepik River.*

for sale, and they know women are the best shoppers. The long house was filled with exquisite woodcarvings for sale. The Sepik men are known for their excellent carvings, and of course we had to have several. We eyed an artfully carved set of two spears, about six feet in length. We remarked we liked them, but there was no way we could get them back on the plane. The merchants were prepared. The vendor quickly showed how the spears could be taken apart into easy-to-carry, two-foot lengths that would fit in our checked luggage. They now hang above a door in our home.

Another tradition found only in the Sepik region is the "crocodile" initiation of young men. Today it is not as widely practiced as in the past, although our guide said that it seemed to be getting re-established. Any time after puberty, a young man enters a long period of confinement, training, and education of the initiation rite. This culminates with the skin-cutting ceremony, where incisions are made on the person's upper body. The cuts

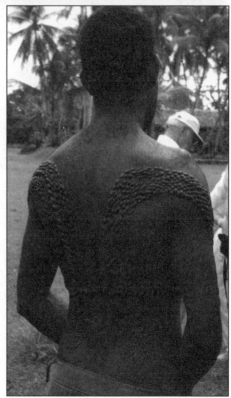

*A young man of the Sepik River displays his "crocodile" initiation scars.*

today are made with a razor blade, instead of bamboo knives. Deep slashes are made in circular patterns, and the process takes about an hour. The young man is given only beetle nut to chew to help deaden the pain. Clay and ashes are then rubbed into the cuts to insure they heal as raised scars—like crocodile scales. At one village we were allowed to photograph a young man, age nineteen, who had undergone the scarification. His whole back was a pattern of bumps. It was difficult for me to look at him.

*A typical PNG market offering beetle nut and vegetables.*

The gardens along the river produce a greater variety of vegetables than those found in the highlands or islands. Jan would purchase fresh vegetables from the women each day for the ship. One vegetable I had never seen was called "snake beans." It was a green bean about two feet long and one-half inch in diameter. We had them that night for dinner on the ship. They tasted a little like celery.

Our river cruise ended back at Madang, where we caught Southwest Air. We flew to Mt. Hagen, just southeast of Tari. This city is quite bustling, with about 50,000 people. Our guide took us to a market that offered all types of vegetables, but what caught my interest was a cassowary bird, all trussed up in a basket holder. It was a real treat to see one of these uncommon creatures up close. It looked a lot like an emu. Our guide explained that this ostrich-type bird is now almost extinct, and we were fortunate to be able to see one. I had purchased a chief's headdress in the Sepik and was advised that the plumes were cassowary. I hoped that the bird did not have to die to decorate this headdress.

There was very little out of the ordinary at Mt. Hagen—just a large city. We toured a tea plantation where they export the finished product to Europe. Then we went riding out in the countryside. Our driver stopped and spoke to two men in regular western attire at the side of the road. A short time later, we came back to this area and were directed to a village hut. The man who came out to greet us in native dress was one of the men we had seen on the side of the road, this time ready to put on a show for the tourists. He entertained us with their method of building a fire, and demonstrated their primitive weapons.

*This quick-change artist quickly became the "native" to entertain the tourists.*

Keith and I have reflected that among all our many trips, we have to rate Papua New Guinea as one of our all-time favorites. This is credited to the extraordinary culture, wild and varied scenery, and the excellent handling of our arrangements by Jan and the *Melanesian Discoverer* staff. If you are looking for a different and unusual destination, select Papua New Guinea.

# Guam

On our trip around the world (during my brief stint as a travel agent, when Keith and I traveled with the owners of the agency), one of our destinations was Guam, about halfway out in the Pacific Ocean between Japan and Australia. Guam is the westernmost possession of the United States; thus this is where the day starts for the U.S. This is also where the deepest place known in the ocean, the Marianas Trench, lies at 39,198 feet. This information makes you think before going swimming around there.

We contacted the Guam Visitors Bureau, and they sent the current Miss Guam, Vivian, to be our lovely guide. Not only was she beautiful, she was very knowledgeable about her island.

Guam belongs to the United States, and the people are American citizens, but they have no vote and have one non-voting member in the House of Representatives in Washington. The island was settled by the ancient Chamorro civilization, and remnants of the culture are latte stones. These mushroom-shaped rocks are found all over the island, and it is a mystery as to the precise purpose or significance of the stones.

As we passed a Catholic church, we noticed eight couples lined up, all obviously waiting to be married. The girls were all in long white wedding gowns and veils, and the young men decked out in tuxedos. Vivian explained that 75 percent of Guam

*Lucky Keith poses with the lovely Miss Guam.*

tourists are from Japan, and of these, about half are honeymooners. It is very expensive to have a wedding in Japan, so wedding packages are very popular in Guam. The couple purchases a package that includes airfare, wedding gown and tuxedo, church ceremony with an interpreter (the Catholic priest speaks only Spanish), and a honeymoon stay at a Guam hotel with meals and transportation. The wedding business has become Guam's biggest source of income.

When Vivian came to pick us up at the hotel the next day, she asked if we would mind having some other people on our tour of the southern part of the island. We told her that would be fine. Forty nuns in full-dress habit greeted us when we boarded the bus. We felt a little underdressed in our shorts. The nuns were off for a day of relaxation from their duties at the convent and school. They had guitars and tambourines that accompanied their singing all the way to the southern coast. They also had baskets of food and insisted we join them for lunch.

The southern area of the island is where U.S. troops landed in World War II and took twenty-one days to win the island from the Japanese, who had held it for thirty-three months. This was also the area where Magellan arrived when he discovered Guam. The island is lush with tropical plants and flowers, but the most enjoyable part of Guam was spending the day with forty singing nuns.

## Tahiti Islands

The South Pacific Islands are known to be paradise "escape islands," where the scenery is lush and tranquil, the way of life slow and easy, and the natives very friendly. There are 118 islands in this French colony known as the "Tahiti Islands." There are five groups, called The Society, Tuamotu, Gambier, Australs and Marquesas, each with its own particular character. The most familiar is the Society group, and that is where we have visited twice. I escorted a group on a cruise of five of the Society Islands on the American Hawaiian Cruise Line (mentioned in my first book).

Keith and I stopped there on our way to Australia on our first visit to the South Pacific in 1977. We flew from Los Angeles to Papeete, the capital of Tahiti. From there we went to Bora Bora, a tiny tropical fantasyland just about an hour flight from Papeete. The airport is on a tiny offshore island because Bora Bora is too mountainous for a landing strip. From there you collect your luggage and go by transfer boats for about twenty minutes to the Bora Bora island proper, where the hotels are located. We were met by "le truck," a truck with benches in the back, which serves as the island taxi service.

The ride to Hotel Bora Bora is about four miles on the island's only road around the beach. When we arrived, we were transformed to an idyllic South Pacific hideaway. Guest quarters were individual Polynesian-style bungalows with thatched roofs, some located on the private sugar white beach, while others were built right over the water accessible by bridge walkways. From these cozy cottages you could view the underwater creatures by gazing through the "window" in your floor. To get up close and personal, all you had to do was step right off your private verandah and instantly have a refreshing swim or snorkel among the colorful fishes and coral in the crystal clear waters. Our accommodation was on the beach with a hammock for lazing on the front porch. The water was an incredible lovely shade of blue (said to be seven different shades) that seems to change at different times of the day. The lagoon was totally calm, as it is protected with an outer reef in the near distance. Meals were served in the main house built out over the water, and the food, with a Polynesian flavor, was excellent.

This is the place for the ultimate in beauty and serenity. The hotel provided bicycles for us to tour the twenty-five-mile unpaved road the entire distance around the island. We saw land crabs scurrying into their mud holes on the beach, native huts with pigs tied up in the yard, and unwrapped long loaves of French bread obviously recently delivered in mailboxes. Dense foliage of coconuts, bananas, breadfruit, and tropical flowers were all around us on our left and the blue sea with small whitecaps on our right. Occasionally we would spot a native fisherman with his nets out on the water in his outrigger canoe.

I have to rate Hotel Bora Bora number-one for peaceful rest and picture postcard vistas. Unfortunately, it is a long way from Texas, and recently it has become rather pricey. We paid $100 per night in 1977, but today the same bungalow is around $600 or more a night. Hotel Bora Bora was the first hotel on the island to introduce over-water bungalows, but today there are several island properties with this type of facility.

# Easter Island

Ever since I read *Kon-Tiki*, Norwegian Thor Heyerdahl's thrilling account of this mysterious island, I had wanted to go there. When we were in Oslo, Norway, we saw a replica of his reed raft on exhibit at the Kon Tiki Museum.

In 1995 my little group of eight boarded the Continental plane at Austin and flew to Houston to connect to Miami. As we arrived in Houston, a terrible storm came in, and our flight was delayed three hours. I was worried that we would miss our Continental flight in Miami to Santiago, Chile. As we deplaned in Miami, a Continental representative was standing there and advised that we had indeed missed our flight, but that they had booked us on American Airlines leaving in thirty minutes.

"What about our luggage?" I inquired.

"No problem. I will see that it gets on the American plane." So much for Continental's assurance.

Well, there was indeed a problem, for when we arrived in Santiago, not one bag arrived with us. I filed a lost baggage claim, and American said they would deliver them to our hotel as soon as they arrived. This seemed fine, as we were to be in Santiago for three days prior to going out to Easter Island.

Each day I checked several times with American, and they had not located our bags. Finally, on the third day, after returning from our all-day tour, and still no luggage, I told everyone to go shopping. I advised them to purchase just enough to get by during the four days/three nights on Easter Island. I told them not to buy a new suitcase, but to try and get everything in their carry-on or just a shopping bag.

Our hotel was right across the street from a nice department store, but we only had one hour to make our selections before the store closed. Another problem: the Chilean people are short of stature and the stores do not stock clothes to fit long, tall Texans. Keith had worn his cowboy boots on the plane, and his tennis shoes were in the lost bag. When he sat down in the men's shoe department, the clerk looked at his foot and shook his head.

"*Mas grande,*" he said.

They did not have a single tennis shoe or sandal or *any* shoe, for that matter, that would fit Keith, and he only wears size 10½! As we were pressed for time, we rushed

*We arrive on Easter Island in our ugly wardrobe.*

to the men's department and found Keith some nice-looking Bermuda shorts and two matching shirts. I always travel with a change of underwear and sleepwear for both of us in the carry-on, so we could make out in that regard.

To the ladies department. Certainly bad news here. I am a foot taller than any Chilean woman. The only thing I could find was a terrible-looking pair of red cotton-knit slacks that were too large but were long enough and had a drawstring at the waist. I did find two T-shirts to complete this great-looking wardrobe. By now the store was closing, and we still didn't have any shoes for Keith or any shorts for me. Out we went to the street vendors. Luckily, they sell everything on the sidewalks in Santiago. The quality left a little to be desired, but this was an emergency situation. Here we each bought a pair of flip-flop rubber shoes, and I found a pair of shorts that fit me. We were now outfitted for Easter Island.

The next morning, it was hilarious to see what everyone had managed to purchase. Kay, a small woman, had found a little girl's dress. I certainly could not laugh at her, for I was a sight in those horrible red pants! The men seemed to have better luck and had a little improvement in appearance than the ladies.

It is more than 2,000 miles from Santiago, Chile, to Easter Island, so named by the Dutch sailor Jacob Roggeveen, the first European to sight the island on Easter morning, thus the island's name. Local residents refer to it as Rapa Nui, the name used by Polynesian settlers. The island is only about seventy square miles in size with a current population of approximately 2,000.

What makes this remote landmass out of the ordinary are the numerous mysteri-

*I feel small (for the first time in my life) among the giant statues of Easter Island.*

ous giant stone statues that at one time formed an almost unbroken line guarding the coast. Originally, there were about 245 moai, the name of the statues. They ranged from six to almost thirty feet in height, made of solid stone and weighing thousands of pounds each. All statues depicted the same figure of a man's long torso (no legs or feet), long face with elongated ears. They originally were topped with a round stone made of red-type material quarried in a different location from the main figures. The only variance was in size. The question to this day is: What did they signify, and how were they transported from the rock quarries in the center of the island down to the coastline (several miles) without any mechanical assistance?

The origin of the first settlers is also a mystery. Both Polynesians and South American Indians appear to have made exploration voyages in this area. Rapa Nui legends describe the arrival of two different peoples: the "Long Ears" from the east and the "Short Ears" from the west. It has been estimated that the first settlers arrived around 450 A.D. The western world did not discover Easter Island until 1722, when the Dutch explorer arrived. At that time he reported the villagers seemed to be worshiping at the foot of remarkably tall stone figures. Outsiders did not visit the island again until 1770, when a Spanish party from Peru arrived and claimed the island for Spain. They wrote in their report that most of the islanders dwelt in caves and their only weapons were sharp obsidian knives. In 1774 Captain Cook recorded that the island population was reduced to misery. Many of the stone statues were toppled over and the island was completely deforested.

Today there are very few trees on the entire island. Wild horses roam free, left by the Spanish explorers. Small vegetable gardens are the only sign of farming. The island depends on Chile for everything. A supply boat arrives once a month, a much-awaited event for the residents to replenish their supplies. When we were there, the boat was a week late and they were running short. Television on the island is by tape, coming in by plane from Chile, and is one week late. Obviously, world news is not a very important factor there.

History of the island tells of a war between the Long Ears and the Short Ears, with the Short Ears as victors. The reason for the conflict could have been over population and lack of food. Also, each group had a territory, and the enemy would topple their moai to insult and anger the owners. As there is no written account, we have to rely on stories passed down from generation to generation.

Spain never pursued its interest in Easter Island. Chile officially annexed the island in 1888, and still holds it today. In August 1985, General Pinochet of Chile approved a plan allowing the United States to expand the island's runway to serve as an emergency landing site for the NASA space shuttle. Therefore, we landed on the modern long runway at Mataveri, Rapa Nui.

Our local guide, Alvaro Atan, an energetic young man in his mid-twenties, was an English teacher in Santiago who guided on Easter Island during his off time for extra money. He was a native of the island, and in fact, his grandfather, Pedro Atan, had served as mayor of the island for thirty years. Pedro worked with Heyerdahl in physically erecting the first reconstruction of the moai in the 1960s. They used the pole and rope method, which most historians agree was how the stones were moved. It took Heyerdahl's men and natives nine days to re-erect the moai in this fashion. The reconstruction now stands on a hillside above the Anakena Beach, and Alvaro proudly showed us the commemorative plaque there listing his grandfather's name.

*The only "smiley face" on Easter Island. Someone created this joke.*

When we arrived at Easter Island, Alvaro said, "First thing after settling in the hotel I am going to take you to a fabulous beach, the site of the statues that my grandfather helped erect. There you can have a wonderful swim."

"Is it a nude beach?" I inquired.

"Of course not, we do not have such here," he indignantly replied.

"Sorry, for we told you our luggage was lost, and we did not spend extra money on bathing suits," I explained.

We stayed at the Hotel Hangaroa, a rather austere, motel-type accommodation. The meals could be rated as passing, but that could have been because the supply ship was late. Alvaro took us all over the entire island and told us all the history and legends of the area. Today many of the moais have been re-erected, but many more still lay on their backs on the ground with the topknots (the large red round stone that was placed originally on top of the head) scattered all around. It is thought that the indentations for eyes were formerly painted, and today there is one repainted. It just stands there, staring right back at you. It is hard to explain the supernatural feeling I had as I looked up several feet at these monstrous statues and wondered why they were put there in the first place and how they got down there on the beach!

The rock quarries were mind-boggling. Here, up the side of the volcanic mountains, there were moai all around—some half-buried in the soil so that just the head peeked out at you. Inside the quarries were over 100 statues with work in progress, lying there half chipped out in the large stone. Scattered along the hillside were about fifty or more completed monuments. Alvaro said that 320 finished moais had not been erected, in addition to the unfinished ones, when the work suddenly stopped.

Our guide took us to Oroango, the site of the "Birdman Cult." Ruins of stone living quarters in caves remain near an ocean cliffside. Annually the island inhabitants moved to this area, where they lived in the stone houses during the "Birdman" celebration, and made offerings and held rites to appease the gods. The climax of the ceremonies was a competition for the highest status in the community, the title of "Birdman for a Year." To accomplish this honor, young men would descend from the cliff face and, with the aid of a small reed raft, swim out to the nearby rocks, home of the nesting sooty tern bird. The swimmer had to find an egg and return to the ceremonial site first to be proclaimed "Birdman" for the ensuing year. Historians are unsure if the last ceremonies took place at Oroango in 1866 or 1867. The Birdmen may be gone, but the sooty tern birds are still on the rocks, evidenced by the white droppings everywhere.

We saw a rock wall made of stones placed so close together you could not put a piece of paper between them. We had seen walls made by this identical method at Cuzco in Peru, which gives credence to the theory that South Americans were early settlers.

It's amazing what you can do when you have to. This trip taught me that so many clothes are not necessary, but I surely hope I look a lot better than I did on this occasion. Those terrible knit pants were made of such poor material. Whenever I sat down for a period of time, as on the plane, and then stood up, the pants were permanently creased at the knees. It looked like I had big knots on my knees when I was standing because the slacks remained in the sitting position. I threw them away when I returned home. Keith walked all over that rugged island in those flip-flops—up and down the mountains to the stone quarries—and he seemed to have no problem.

When we returned to Santiago for the final night, there was still no information on the lost luggage. The next morning we went to the airport for the flight home. When we arrived at the airport, the American official said they had located our bags and led me back into the security area for pickup. All eight bags were there.

"Bring them to the check-in counter and we will just check them back to the U.S.," I instructed.

"Wait ... you have to go through customs first. Open all the bags, please." They wanted me to go through customs when I was leaving the country immediately.

"I don't have the keys to any piece except my own. Can't you just put them through the x-ray?"

This took some rethinking on their part, but they finally consented to x-ray the bags and let me proceed. I then rolled the cart of luggage up to the Continental Airlines counter and checked them back to Austin. We had taken an eight-day trip and never opened our baggage.

When we returned home, we filed for reimbursement for our purchases. I had told everyone to keep receipts. The original claim was with American, but it was Continental who lost the bags. We went round and round between airlines for weeks but finally did receive total payment for the clothes from American. Continental generously gave us a $50 voucher good for one year for a future flight. Big deal.

There is no place in the world like Easter Island. It is certainly worth the distance and effort to see the unexplained remains of this mystifying society.

# Asia

Asia, to me, is one of the most intriguing areas of the world. As mentioned in the prologue, the Taj Mahal in India, was one of the top three places I wanted to visit. I tell about our trip to India where I realized my childhood dream, in my first book. Here are some other countries in the region that I especially enjoyed.

## China

The People's Republic of China has always held a fascination for me. For years, tourists were not admitted, but in the 1970s the country started accepting foreign visitors. By the time our Collette Vacations group arrived in 1992, China had luxurious hotels, a well-organized tourist bureau, and the people were acquainted with tourists. We found the Chinese to be extremely friendly, and I loved seeing the children.

Chinese law forbids a married couple to have more than one child as a means of population control. This makes that one youngster, with loving parents, and two sets of doting grandparents, very special. You could sense the parents' pride of their one offspring. As a rule, the children were dressed immaculately and were given everything the parents could provide. When we inquired what happened if a second child were born, we were told that the child could not be registered with the government and had no privileges or health care, which is all state-provided under the Communist government. This leads to many abortions, and the female babies are often given up for adoption. If the first pregnancy yields twins, that is acceptable. Sometimes in remote farm areas, more than one child is overlooked and permitted.

One thing about the children was extraordinary. I noticed that toddlers were walking around with about a six-inch diameter hole in the seat of their pants, with their little bare bottoms shining through. From birth, they do not use diapers; the baby is just wrapped in a blanket. When the newborn wets or messes the blanket, the mother makes a special sound, like "Ohooo." She does this continually, and soon the baby will repeat this sound when he or she needs to go. They have the holes in their pants (boys and girls

*The precious only child in China gets everything that he or she desires.*

all wear pants, never any dresses) so when they need to, they can just go immediately without having to worry about removing any clothing. You would frequently see a little one doing his business along the sidewalk. They also have special pants designed for boys with a hole in the front. This practice worldwide would be disastrous for Pampers and Huggies!

Our local guide in Beijing met us at the airport and informed us his American name was Tom. He stood at about six feet, tall for most Chinese. He was attending the university and wanted to pursue a career in broadcast journalism. He told us that he was an interpreter for CNN during the Tienanmen Square incident, when students rioted.

"Do you have children?" he asked me.

"Yes, I have a grown boy and girl," I replied.

"Why didn't they come with you?" he inquired.

"First, they have jobs they cannot leave, and secondly, I cannot afford to bring them and they certainly do not have enough money to pay their own way."

"If they have jobs in the United States, then they are rich," he stated.

"No, not everyone with a job in the United States is rich. My children are just trying to make ends meet with house payments, car payments, etc.," I explained.

"If they have a house and car, then they are certainly rich," he proclaimed.

Not wanting to argue the point, I let him think as he wished.

We arrived in Beijing around 5:00 P.M. I have never seen so many people on bicycles in my life. China has a population of over one billion, and I think they were all riding bicycles that evening. As far as we could see down the street, it was solid bicycles. Some carried several people each, or things like furniture, live chickens—anything they needed to transport.

You have to be careful not to get caught in the rush of the many cyclists. One evening we were getting off the transfer bus to attend a Chinese opera. When Keith stepped out, a speeding biker knocked him down and just kept on going. Fortunately, Keith suffered only a bruised leg.

We stayed at the Holiday Inn Crown Plaza in the middle of the city. That night at dinner I learned that you order hot tea with your meal, not bottled water. One four-ounce bottle of Evian was $4! Later we went to the market and purchased bottled water (50 cents for 32 ounces).

The next morning I walked outside the hotel and was immediately approached by a young man selling hand-carved wooden ducks, painted in colorful feathery detail. He had one about three inches long and two smaller ones.

"How much for all three?" I inquired.

"One dollar."

*Get out of the way—the bicycles are coming!*

He did not know I was ready to pay $5 or more for them. I quickly produced the dollar bill, and he seemed pleased with the sale. I certainly was. Now every time I look at my little ducks on the table beside my bed, I remember that enjoyable episode.

We had been to Europe many times and were amazed at things that were so old compared to the United States. But China had gunpowder and printing long before it was developed in Europe. By 200 BC, China had a national road network, standardized coinage, weights and measures. Their arts and sciences flourished hundreds of years before civilization was established in Europe.

The Forbidden City in Beijing, formerly the emperor's residence, saw the rise and fall of two great eras in Chinese history, the Ming and Ch'in dynasties, periods of tremendous creativity. The Forbidden City covers 250 acres, contains six palaces with over 9,000 rooms, and was forbidden to everyone except the royal family and servants. It was opened to the public in 1949.

The highlight of Beijing to me was a visit to the Great Wall. Not far from the city, it is one of the Seven Wonders of the World and so massive that astronauts can see it from space. The wall was built in the seventh century and in places is up to twenty-five feet high and fifteen feet across, with watchtowers at strategic points. Built to keep out invaders from the north, the wall stretches for 2,150 miles across northern China. Today it is China's top tourist site and in 1987 was

*The Forbidden City in Beijing, formerly the Emperor's residence, is now open to the public.*

*One of the wonders of the world—the Great Wall of China.*

listed as one of the world's cultural relics by the World Heritage Committee of UNESCO. The section outside Beijing has been refurbished to its original appearance. What impressed me was the width of the wall. It is said that three horses could easily travel side by side along the top of this fortification. We were not the only tourists. This is a top attraction for the Chinese as well, and it was fun to see them taking each other's pictures along the wall.

Our next Chinese city was Xian to observe another of China's wonders, the Terra Cotta Warriors. In 1974, farmers who were digging a well discovered the mausoleum of the Qin Shi Huang, said to be over 2,000 years old. Here 8,000 figures of warriors, horses, coaches, and arms were buried with the dead emperor. The figures were made of clay, but there were also two copper coaches, with statues of two coachmen and four horses. Pictures I had seen of the statues lacked all credibility when I saw them in their environment and quantity.

As I entered the immense building covering the Terra Cotta Warriors, the sheer impact stunned me. There below in trenches in the earth floor stood life-size Chinese warriors in battle formation lined up as far as I could see. What intrigued me was the intricate detail artistry of each soldier. Each had individual facial features and most of the bodies were similar, although the arms would have different positions. They looked as if they could come to life at any moment, glad to be rescued from their burial for so many years. Restoration was still in progress when we were there, and many of the warriors' heads were missing. It boggles the mind to think of the labor required to produce this masterpiece and then bury it under the ground.

*We were happy to be here at this well-known tourist attraction.*

*Smile! You are on the Great Wall, and we will send this picture to your family.*

*A replica of the Terra Cotta Warriors greets you outside a local restaurant in Xian.*

We flew to Shanghai, China's grand port city that has been influenced by western civilization for centuries, and walked down by the sea wall. It was Sunday, and families were out strolling. They had their one child dressed in his or her finest and seemed to delight in showing them to us. Everyone we met was friendly and eager for us to take pictures of their prized possession.

One older man came up to Keith and started talking. Of course, Keith was unable to respond in Chinese. Our local guide acted as interpreter. The man wanted to know if he had fought in World War II. Keith told him he was in the air force then, and in fact, had been stationed in China. This thrilled the old gent, and he wanted to know where he had been, what he did then, etc. It was such a shame that they could not sit down and have a visit without the burden of going through an interpreter, but it was a rewarding experience for both veterans.

The Children's Palace is a school for the gifted and talented. And they certainly were! We observed classes in art, dance, music, computers, math, and language. At a kindergarten class the five-year-olds performed a dance for us and then proceeded to lead each one of our group out to dance with them. The children were such accomplished performers. They put us old folks through the musical routines without any problem. Each child seemed healthy and very happy.

Speaking of health, we stopped at a clinic and witnessed acupuncture. I got sick at my stomach when I looked at the man sitting there with burning incense sticks stuck in his skin all up and down his legs. This was supposed to aid arthritis, but I think I'd rather have the disease than endure such treatment.

Our guide explained that a country compound is where all the residents work in the fields and then share the profits. They are furnished a house, medical care, and schools for the children. Each compound had its own administration officers who reported to the federal government. The proceeds from the farms are divided among the members at the end of the year.

Our last stop was Guilin, on the Li River, which has some of the most unique scenery in the world. Many of the pictures of China you have seen of a river with green mountain mounds are from this area. Our local guide, Phoenix, looked like a Vogue model and was dressed in a striking designer suit. (Apparently, guiding pays better in China than in the U.S.!)

A day cruise on the Li River offered vistas of the green hills resembling camel humps and extraordinary

*These kindergarten children made me feel like Ginger Rogers as they led me through a complicated dance routine.*

lump-like rock formations reflecting on the crystal clear water. Our Collette guide, Jane, had thoughtfully obtained box lunches from the hotel for us. When we saw the kitchen where the cruise lunch was prepared, we were indeed grateful. We stared in horror as the cook dipped cooking water out of the river right in the docking area (with buildings all around, and the refuse went directly into the river). She lifted up fish in a net that obviously had been caught for some time, for they appeared stiff and dead, then plopped the whole fishes in the pot of river water and set the pot on the fire to cook. Our box lunches looked very appetizing at that time.

The river fishermen were an interesting sight. They paddled along in shallow-bottom boats (few had motors), and on the boat with them were two or three cormorant birds with small ropes around

*A cruise on the Li River outside Guilin offered outstanding scenery, just like a picture postcard.*

their necks that were attached to the boat. As the vessel silently glided among fish in the river, the birds would jump into the water and grab the fish in their mouths. Then the fisherman would tighten the rope so the bird could not swallow the catch. He

*Cormorant birds serve as fishermen for the local people. They dive down, catch the fish, and then the boatman tightens the rope around their necks to keep them from swallowing the fish. The fish are retrieved and deposited in a basket.*

would then pull the bird into the boat and extract the fish. I was told that the birds are trained for this exercise and that after a day of good fishing, they too, get to eat some of the catch. They aren't fed until after the day's work so they will be hungry and go after the fish. I was glad to hear that they were awarded something for their efforts.

If you like rice, you will like the food in China, for EVERY meal features it. At first I enjoyed the Chinese food—a little too greasy to my liking, but the many different vegetables were tasty. What they do to a chicken is unbelievable. They take the whole bird and with a cleaver, start chopping, and put everything in the pot. So you may get a piece of a chicken leg, bone and all, the head, or even the feet. I did not care for the dumplings—just seemed like a lot of uncooked dough to me, although they are a delicacy to the Chinese. This white, slick-looking dough surrounded all sorts of things, including many kinds of meat, vegetables, and who knows what else. We were treated to a whole banquet of dumplings, which was too much for me. At one meat market, we saw dogs in a cage.

When asked why the dogs were at a food market, our guide remarked that this is one place you can get a genuine "hot dog."

Each meal had many courses, usually starting with some strange greasy soup, then rice, vegetables, and some kind of meat, ending with canned fruit. We managed just fine supplementing with our snacks from home, but the first thing we did when we reached Hong Kong was head for McDonald's for a

*You can purchase rice and dumplings from the street vendor.*

hamburger. Of course, food is a matter of upbringing and personal tastes. One of our local guides commented that he had gone to school in London and nearly starved because he could not find rice in many of the restaurants.

China is a very intriguing country to visit. Because it will probably be advancing very rapidly socially and economically in the near future, try to see it before its authentic, old world charm is gone.

## Vietnam and Cambodia

When we told our friends and family we were going to Vietnam and Cambodia, we had one response: "Why?"

One reason was we had not been there, and Vietnam had been so much in the news, I wanted to see it for myself. And I have always wanted to see the temples of Angkor Wat in Cambodia. We had an opportunity in 1997 to go on a FAM trip (familiarization tour for travel industry people offered at a reduced rate) with Geeta Tours and Travel of Chicago to these destinations, and I jumped at the chance.

Keith and I were to meet the group in Hanoi, North Vietnam. We planned our arrival one day in advance in order to rest some from the flight of twenty-two hours (plus a six-hour layover in Hong Kong). At the Hanoi airport we lined up for immigration. We had obtained our visas to this Communist country before leaving home, and the documents were securely affixed inside our passports. As we approached the official, he handed me a visa form and said to fill it out and attach a picture. I tried to explain to him we already had our visas, but he insisted that we had to fill out the forms. Thank goodness I had extra passport photos with me. By the time we had completed this, we were the last to clear immigration. I was afraid our transfer person would have given up on us. When I saw the sign "Mr. and Mrs. Brooks," I wanted to jump for joy! The handsome smiling face behind the sign was our local guide. He introduced himself as Fouck. Afraid that I would pronounce that incorrectly, I asked what it meant in English. "Happy," he replied, and I immediately said, "We will call you Happy."

The ride from the airport into the city was a patchwork quilt of rice fields and gardens. Happy explained that all farmers were on the commune system. Each village worked together and shared the three crops of rice a year, but each family could have individual personal gardens for vegetables. In the lush river valley, all farm work is by hand with some assistance of an occasional water buffalo.

Our hotel in Hanoi was the Sofitel Metropole, built by the French in 1911 and totally refurbished in 1995, but retaining its old world appeal. The entire place was attractive, and it felt wonderful to fall into our king-size bed for a rest after the long flight.

We awoke the next morning, refreshed and ready to see new sights. We began with a tremendous buffet breakfast that included everything imaginable. The most beautiful young ladies I have ever seen, dressed in native Vietnamese long, body-hugging gowns, served coffee and tea. I thought the hotel must have hired these hostesses for their looks. When we went out on the street, however, I was amazed at the striking beauty of all the Vietnamese women. Most have long, shining black hair, flawless white skin, and a figure to die for. I did not see an unattractive young native woman the entire time we were in Vietnam.

After breakfast, we decided to explore before the remainder of the group arrived in

*Lovely Vietnamese ladies dressed in attractive native dress travel via bicycles or motor scooters.*

*Slow time at the sidewalk barbershop.*

*A street vendor has loaded her bike with all kinds of merchandise.*

the afternoon. About a block from our hotel we were approached by two men wanting to take us on a "cycle" ride. This is a bicycle with a carriage-type seat for the passenger in front with the driver in back. We made a deal with them for a separate taxi for each of us for a one-hour tour. The total was $5. Our two drivers peddled swiftly as we went into traffic that was very scary. There were hundreds of these "cycle" taxis, motor scooters, regular bicycles, and an occasional truck. In the old town where we went, there were no traffic lights or stop signs. When you came to a four-way intersection, it was just each vehicle for itself. Most of the time they managed to get through without colliding.

Old-town Hanoi was a sight to behold. The merchandise shops were divided into street blocks. There would be a block of small shops selling clothes, then a block of pots and pans, metal shops, eggs, flowers, shoes, you name it. Walking in the streets were people carrying baskets of vegetables, chickens, and household goods via the ox-yoke method across their shoulders with large baskets at each end of the pole. Everyone was very responsive and waved as we passed. We have reflected that this cycle tour was the highlight on our entire Vietnam trip. When we returned to our hotel, we gave the drivers $10 instead of $5, because we enjoyed it so much and felt it was the best $10 we ever spent. The gesture seemed to make the drivers very happy.

Hanoi, with a population of around four million, is now the capital of the entire Communist country of Vietnam since the fall of South Vietnam in 1975.

*Keith is ready for a "cycle ride" to Old Town Hanoi.*

That afternoon at 4:00 we met the rest of the group. Our leader, Molly, announced she had a special surprise for us—a "cycle ride." Keith and I made no indication of our earlier venture. When we went outside to get in the reserved bicycles, Keith's driver from the morning came running over for him to get in his cart (he remembered the tip). I didn't see my former driver, so just sat down in a nearby cycle. As the group of fifteen took off, somehow I was last in line. It was now the rush hour, as if you could tell the difference, and the traffic was dreadful. At one of the "chicken game" intersections, my bike was hit in the back by another bicycle. It was just a sudden bump, but did bend the other guy's front fender. There I sat while the two drivers argued in a language I could not understand. Meanwhile, the rest of my group was completely out of sight. I began to feel uneasy, for my driver did not speak English. We finally started moving again, and was I ever relieved when I saw the others down the street. This drive was not nearly as attention-grabbing as our morning tour. We never went to old town—just stayed in the hotel area.

The next day we went to the Ho Chi Minh mausoleum, where the leader's embalmed body lies in a glass casket just like Lenin in Moscow. They used the same mortician from Russia. The face gives the impression of being carved out of wax, but I believe Ho Chi Minh looked a little better than Lenin, if a dead body can look good. Happy said that the body is boxed up and shipped to Russia for two months each year for an overhaul.

Ho Chi Minh, born in 1890 in Northern Vietnam, left the country at the age of twenty-one and spent some time in the United States as an itinerant laborer. He was in Paris, France, for seven years, where he joined the French Communist Party, and from there he went to Moscow for special training. In 1925 he was sent to Canton, China, where he founded the Revolutionary Youth League of Vietnam and mobilized Vietnamese students. He drifted between China and the Soviet Union in the 1930s, waiting for the right moment to make his return to Vietnam. When the Japanese occupied Vietnam in 1940, he slipped back into the country and founded the Vietminh Front. In 1945, when Japan was about to surrender, he led the revolution that took control of much of Vietnam, and proclaimed the Democratic Republic of Vietnam in September 1945.

The Ho Chi Minh Trail was a route that brought supplies to fuel the Vietnam War by means of a camouflaged roadway from China to Vietnam. This was one of the keys to North Vietnam's success in the north and south war. Ho Chi Minh died in September 1969 and is revered as the force that unified Vietnam as a Communistic state today.

Included on the tour was the president's residence, where Ho Chi Minh died. The current president occupied it at that time. Vietnam has elections, but only registered Communists can vote.

We stopped by the building that imprisoned captured American pilots during the war. The building had originally been a French prison in downtown Hanoi, and when the U.S. airmen were held there it was referred to as the "Hanoi Hilton." In 1994 the prison walls were torn down to construct a Singapore joint venture project of a twenty-two-story hotel and office center called Hanoi Towers. We were there in 1997 and it was still not completed. Happy said construction had been delayed due to a campaign to make it a national monument. It made me sick to think of all the suffering that had occurred in that building by our soldiers.

Vietnam's oldest institution of higher education, the Temple of Literature, dates back to the eleventh century. Here Confucius founded his school that housed 1,000 male students at a time from all over the Orient and managed to break the Buddhist monopoly on education at the time. Confucius died at age fifty-four and had fathered 300 children. "Populate the world," Confucius must have believed.

That evening, after an elaborate oriental meal, we attended the Water Puppet Show. The puppets perform on top of a water stage, while the operators of the dolls stand in waist-deep water behind a curtain. This was a very unusual show for us, especially when all the dialogue was in Vietnamese, but we enjoyed the colorful presentation and the uniqueness of the event.

We flew about 150 miles south to Hue, located in the central part of the country. This ancient imperial city of the Nguyen Kings is on the narrowest portion of Vietnamese land. It is not more than fifty miles from the Pacific Ocean on the east to the country of Laos on the west. The city is located on the Perfume River, largely inhabited by riverboat people who live and die in their boat homes on the water. This environment gives the river a distinct odor, but certainly not what I would call perfume.

Our first tour was aboard a dragon-shaped boat along the activity-filled river.

*Many Vietnamese families live their entire lives on these small houseboats.*

Here we observed families as they went about their daily life on the water—washing clothes, bathing, fishing, relaxing. The water also served as their bathroom and garbage dump. I tossed ballpoint pens to many of the children who were waving as we passed close to their floating homes.

Hue is a small city, with about 250,000 people. The kingdom was established in 1524, when Lord Nguyen Hoang arrived and thought this would be a good place to establish a capital. He built the Thien Mu Pagoda that remains intact today on the left bank of the Perfume River. The pagoda has seven tiers, each representing a different reincarnation of Buddha. An enormous 4,617-pound cast bell was erected in 1701 and is still rung today. Ten feudal lords ruled this area until the Tay Son uprising was put down in 1802. The tenth Nguyen Lord proclaimed himself emperor and founded the Nguyen Dynasty that lasted through thirteen emperors. They controlled the entire country and built the Mandarin Road, now Highway 1. When the French invaded Vietnam in 1883, they found it expedient to maintain the illusion of imperial rule, so they left the emperors in place. During the Tet Offensive in 1968, Vietcong forces marched into Hue and held it for twenty-four days. During this bloody time, it is estimated that 10,000 Hue residents were killed and many imperial buildings destroyed, including the Imperial Palace.

Happy informed us that his grandfather was a member of the royal court in Hue. When the Communists took over, the court was dissolved and his family fled south to Saigon. As his father was educated and could speak English, he became an interpreter for the U.S. military. He worked very closely with the U.S. Intelligence Department all during the Vietnam War. As a result, when the United States Armed Forces departed and Saigon fell on April 30, 1975, Happy's father was captured and sent to a Communist "retraining camp." Happy's mother chose to join her husband in this confinement. They had to work in the rice fields all day and then be subjected to intense Communist interrogation each night. During their imprisonment, Happy and his siblings lived with his grandmother. They could visit their parents only one-half day a month. In 1980 they were released, and today his father teaches English at a Ho Chi Minh University. During the refugee boat people evacuation, Happy's grandmother and aunt were passengers on a bamboo boat that made it to Guam. From there they went to the United States and currently live in Houston, Texas. We told Happy he should come visit his relatives and us in Texas someday.

That evening at the hotel, our group was honored with a Royal Feast. Each member of the tour group was to wear imperial robes and headdresses. We selected ours and were all ready, when it was proclaimed that Keith and I were to be the emperor and empress and had to put on different costumes. These robes were made of very heavy satin and decorated with elaborate embroidery. Also, heavy metal crowns were placed on our heads. The outfit was so heavy, I could hardly walk in it. We were seated at the head table alone and served every dish first. I might have enjoyed this evening of royal treatment if it had not been so beastly hot. The dining room was not air-conditioned, and it had to be over 100 sticky degrees. Those heavy satin robes were clinging to us. Out in the dining area, the rest of the "royal family" were dressed in light satin robes and were under ceiling fans. We had a servant on each side of us with a feather fan, which they very infrequently waved gently, producing practically no air. I hope the real royalty had more enthusiastic fanners!

The dinner wine was served in a blue and white phallic-shaped bottle. Legend is

*Queen Joyce and King Keith were not enjoying the life of royalty.*

that the wine was developed for a king who had 300 children. I never found out how many wives it took to produce these offspring or how many bottles of wine were required, but at least it seems he stayed pretty busy. At my age, I felt safe in drinking the wine! I was glad when the meal was over so I could get out of those hot clothes and become a peasant again.

We departed the next morning for DaNang via bus. This was an interesting drive through the countryside, offering vistas of rice fields, some in the process of harvesting. The harvested rice was then threshed by hand or with a very primitive machine at the side of the road and spread on plastic sheets on the roadside or front yard to dry. In the streams we saw duck herders with many ducks who were eagerly gleaning the remains of the rice harvests. It was amusing to see those herders in a small boat powered by pushing a pole, rushing around in the water to keep "all their ducks in a row."

*It's not easy to keep your "ducks in a row."*

As we drove along the narrowest part of Vietnam, we could see the mountains of Laos in the distance. I had always heard of the jungles of Vietnam, but primarily we saw cleared-out spaces where apparently jungles had been at one time, now depleted to underbrush due to the war. We were told there were still jungles in the northern portion.

We arrived at the South China Sea—the famous resort area where many of our soldiers took R&R. Our hotel in DaNang was the Furuma Hotel, located on the China Beach. This luxurious new resort had been open only two months, and there were very few visitors there. The public rooms, accommodations, and gardens were exquisite. As we strolled down the deserted beach, I thought of how marvelous this must have been for our soldiers to come here and relax after weeks and months of fighting an impossible war. I also wondered how this expensive hotel property was going to make it. Vietnam is not a very popular tourist destination.

A bus ride of less than an hour took us to Hoi An, the ancient port town that is one of the rare places in this country where you can see original Vietnamese architecture. While much of Vietnam was destroyed during many wars, Hoi An survived. As we walked along the streets of the Old Quarter, I felt like I was leafing through pages of oriental history. Many of the buildings have pagoda-shaped roofs covered with moss. Little shops lining the streets offer all types of native handicrafts, and of course, I could not resist a silk embroidery picture and a water buffalo carving. A young boy about five years old ran up to Keith and grabbed his hand. "Tell me about America," he said in perfect English. He was wearing a Michael Jordan T-shirt. We had a nice visit with him.

Next stop was Saigon, now called Ho Chi Minh City, where we stayed at the Hotel Majestic. From our bedroom windows we could see the constant boat traffic on the Saigon River and hear the twenty-four-hour truck, motor scooter, and bicycle traffic on Dong Kohl Street. It is estimated that the city has one million motorbikes and two million bicycles and almost no private cars. The city is home to more than five million people.

When we went to the local market, I think everyone had ridden a motorbike there. I have never seen so many bikes in one place. The market offered everything—food, clothes, hardware, you name it. As we were leaving, a souvenir salesman approached our parked bus. Molly was standing at the door and made a deal with him for $1 for an eye-catching black lacquer miniature fold-up screen. At that point we all had to have two or three, and we depleted the dealer's stock. Tell an American something is $1, and they go wild. (I am included in that group.)

It was intriguing to see the gorgeous Vietnamese women riding their motorbikes attired in traditional, long, tight-fitting native dress, split up the side, sometimes exposing a shapely leg. The ensemble would be complete with a bike helmet, long straight black hair flowing in the wind, a scarf over the lower part of her face to escape the exhaust fumes, and over-the-elbow white gloves to protect her skin from the tropical sun. There were also women in western dress on the scooters, but they still had the scarf and gloves in place.

In the city we stopped at the War Crimes Museum, a place that is very distressing for Americans to visit. Everything there depicts the "ugly American," with horrifying war photos and news articles. As our bus stopped at the museum entrance and we disembarked, a cute little boy about four years of age ran up to me and took hold of my hand. I thought he just wanted to be friendly, but as we started walking, he had his other hand in my pants pocket, where I was carrying some local currency. I managed to grab his hand before he could remove the money. He went running to his nearby mother, and she started loudly berating me as if I were the one who was wrong. When we returned to the bus, she was still there. As I took my seat on the bus, she was banging on my window and shouting. Good thing I couldn't understand what she was saying. I was glad to get out of that place.

We drove about fifty miles out to the Mekong Delta area, where we climbed into small boats for a ride through the canals. Life along the canals displayed very poor living conditions, where the main source of survival was the river or small rice and vegetable plots. But even the poorest of shacks had a television antenna. The weather was so hot and humid, we were too miserable to take pleasure in much of the tour. The native straw hats they put on our heads didn't seem to help much—just made us look silly.

About fifty miles northwest of Saigon are the tourist sites of the Cu Chi Tunnels that the Vietcong used during the war. These intricate mazes go as much as three levels deep and were the primary key to Vietcong success. The tunnels were not visible from the air, and from a concealed trap door the Vietcong could pop up and fire away and be back down the hatch before American soldiers could react. Suffering from acute claustrophobia, I declined the invitation to explore the tunnels. But several brave souls of our group did and reported the amazing revelation of an underground community. They saw kitchens, rudimentary clinics and operating rooms, meeting rooms, sleeping quarters with bamboo beds, storage chambers, and water wells. Reports are that up to 7,000 men, women, and children could occupy the large tunnel system at one time, or up to 16,000 guerrillas. Today they have increased the size of the entrance hole to accommodate "large western tourists," who can view the chambers by stooping down or crawling. It was comforting to hear that the tunnels are sprayed daily to clear out any snakes, scorpions, and spiders. But the spray does not get rid of the bats (another reason I did not want to venture down).

Throughout Vietnam, we had excellent and appetizing food. The fare was primarily what you consider "oriental," but we were served such a wide variety, we never tired of the menu. We probably received such exceptional cuisine because we were travel agents, and the hotels wanted to impress us so we would send more travelers their way. They certainly did a first-rate job.

After seven interesting and exciting days in Vietnam, we regretfully said good-bye to an "Un-Happy" (who cried when we left, and we did, too). As Keith and I approached departure immigration, I went through first and was quickly processed. When Keith walked up to the custom officer, he looked at him and said: "Were you here during the war?"

"I was in a war, but not this one," Keith replied.

The officer smiled and said, "That is good," and stamped his passport.

A flight from Vietnam took us to the bordering country of Cambodia with our one mission—to see Angkor Wat. We first had to fly to Phnom Penh, the capital. Our flight from Ho Chi Minh City had been delayed several hours, and we did not reach there until nearly dark. Our lodging was the Hotel Sofitel Cambodian, a very comfortable overnight stop.

We immediately noticed the difference in appearance of the people of Cambodia from the Vietnamese. Here the inhabitants were larger in stature with darker skin, and looked more Indonesian than oriental. Everyone wore thong shoes. Practically all the

*Cambodian children take care of their younger siblings while their parents work.*

men wore shorts and casual shirts; the women long skirts and blouses. The children were dressed in old and tattered modern-type clothing, resembling hand-me-downs.

Having been deluged in the United States with Vietnam news, I did not know much about Cambodia and its government. After hearing what these poor people have endured, I wondered how they could smile and be so pleasant today. Cambodia's history goes back to the first century. The country flourished in the middle of the twelfth century, when Angkor Wat construction began. The Siamese invaded Angkor in 1431, stripping it of its wealth and destroying its infrastructure. For the next 400 years, Cambodia was kicked back and forth between Siam and Vietnam. In 1864 Cambodia became a French protectorate. During World War II, they were under Japanese occupation. The Geneva Peace Conference agreed in 1954 to a temporary division of Vietnam into north and south and recognized Cambodia's neutrality.

From 1955 to 1965, the small country, was not involved in the troubles that engulfed the rest of Indochina. North Vietnamese troops moved through the mountains in the northern portion of the country, and in the forest a ragtag band of Cambodian guerrillas began forming. This group, referred to as the Khmer Rouge, proved to be disastrous for the people of Cambodia. By early 1970s, the Khmer Rouge army had grown to 50,000 men, led by a fierce commander, Pol Pot. On April 17, 1975, just thirteen days before the fall of Saigon, the Khmer Rouge marched into Phnom Penh and immediately took the city. Everyone was ordered out. Millions of people were sent to the countryside without food or possessions.

Pol Pot had a vision of a peasant nation of agricultural workers. This was to be accomplished without machinery—with only bare hands. The people were forced to work eighteen hours a day in the fields with a minimum of rations. Cities were emptied and destroyed; books were burned. There were to be no medical facilities, no schools, no money, and no communication with the outside world. The primary religion, Buddhism, was forbidden.

It was reported that the army personnel looked at a person's hands. If they were calloused from work, they could live. If not, they were killed. Those who had an advanced education, such as teachers, doctors, technicians, were executed. It was estimated the number killed from 1975 to 1979 ranged up to three million out of a total population of eight million at that time; thus the area was given the name "The Killing Fields."

In 1979 Communist Vietnam invaded Cambodia. It was reported that the American and British governments gave $88 million in assistance to Pol Pot between 1980 and 1986. The United Nations called on Vietnam to withdraw from Cambodia and seated the Khmer Rouge as the controlling government. Cambodia was placed under the jurisdiction of the United Nations Transitional Authority for eighteen months. The country then started repairing the severely damaged infrastructure ravaged from thirteen years of civil warfare and resettling 350,000 refugees. Elections finally were held in May 1993, resulting in unrest and coups. The Khmer Rouge took to the hills, so to speak, and continued to raid villages. When we were there in May 1997, I asked who was ruling the country.

"We have two parties—the Peoples Party and the Communist Party—and two prime ministers and one king," our guide replied.

"How does that work?" I asked.

"Not very well," he said with a smile.

Two weeks after we returned home, I heard on the news that a violent coup had erupted in Phnom Penh. We luckily were there in about a six-week window of peace.

Since our return, I have met a man who escaped the Pol Pot terror. He wore glasses but threw them away, for if you wore glasses, you were executed. It took him three years to reach freedom by walking through the jungles of Cambodia to Thailand. Because he was educated and could speak English, he eventually made his way to the United States and today holds a very high position in Washington, D.C. as a liaison between Cambodia and the U.S. He introduced me to his wife (an American), and she could not believe we had just returned from Cambodia.

We took a short flight to Siem Reap, location of the mega Angkor temples. The area consists of seventy monuments scattered over more than one hundred square miles. All this is usually referred to as Angkor Wat, but strictly speaking, Angkor Wat is only a single temple—the largest and most majestic, and the one you recognize in photos of the area.

The complex was built in the middle of the twelfth century over a period of about thirty years. The Angkor kingdom was the most powerful in Southeast Asia during its time and constructed many palaces and temples, plus cities. The communities surrounding the temples were built of wood and have long since deteriorated. Through time the jungle or rice farmers have reclaimed the area. It is noted that the Angkor kings ruled the region from 802 to 1431, when the Siamese conquered the area. The Siamese armies ransacked everything, carrying off slaves and stripping the palaces and temples of statuary and stone-encrusted ornaments, as well as gold coatings from towers and rooftops. All that remained were the huge stone buildings they could not carry away.

The natural course of time, wind and weather, plus jungle growth, covered the site until 1860, when a French naturalist, Henri Mouhot, found it while hacking his way through the Cambodian undergrowth in search of beetles and butterflies. It is reported that other travelers had passed this way and had seen the temples, but for some reason this went unreported until Mouhot made known his find. The first recorded pictures of Angkor were by John Thompson in 1866, depicting ruined temples emerging from thick jungle vegetation. During the French control of Cambodia, work was started to restore the shrines, but this was hindered by lack of funds and civil unrest. They did manage to clear vegetation from some of the ruins, install hidden drains to prevent water damage, and begin reconstruction of a number of the buildings. This work was stopped when the Khmer Rouge drove out the French in 1970.

Providentially, Angkor survived in spite of the Pol Pot armies that lit fires in the galleries, shot at the bas-reliefs for target practice, and hacked off heads of statues, selling them to finance their war effort. But mostly, the monument was left intact. In 1989 UNESCO coordinated international efforts to restore some of the buildings, and in 1992 Angkor was named an endangered World Heritage Site. Today many organizations and nations are working together to restore and maintain this magnificent masterpiece.

As we approached the main temple, Angkor Wat, I had goosebumps as I stood in awe of this ancient, imposing structure. This is the world's largest Buddhist temple and best preserved of all the other temples in the area. The three-tier pyramidal structure symbolizes Mount Meru, the holy Hindu mountain composed of seven terraces. Keith and I climbed the narrow steps (my feet are much bigger than those of ancient Buddhists) to the top level, about 200 feet high. From there you could see the entire countryside—the lush green jungles and other temples. We viewed a wedding that was in progress by the small lake below and noticed the bride wore a red wedding dress and veil, as is the custom in the country. Being at Angkor Wat is an overwhelming experience I cannot explain. I can just say it was one of my many "all-time highs" of travel.

As we walked around the complex, native children would come up and hold our hands and assist us through the rocks and steps around the temples. Each child also carried a fan, which certainly was welcomed in the 100-degree plus temperature and humidity almost equally as high. This gesture served two purposes: they were able to learn English as they listened to the tourists and guides, plus they received a tip for their services. The tourist gets fanned along the way and has the pleasure of talking to the local children. My fanner/hand-holder said he wanted to be a guide when he grew up, and he already could tell me many things about Angkor Wat. All the children selling souvenirs were very friendly and not overbearing if you did not buy. Consequently, we couldn't resist and bought even more.

After exploring the reconstructed temples, we went to the area that has not been reclaimed from the jungle. What a sight! There were one- and two-story rock buildings with mammoth tree roots right on top of them or coming out between the rocks like monster-strangling fingers. It was a bizarre picture. I couldn't understand how those trees could grow right on, through, and around those buildings. Monkeys were sitting all around, waiting for a food handout.

We were cautioned to always stay strictly on the paths around the monuments and to never veer off due to the possibility of land mines. During the Khmer Rouge regime, millions of land mines were placed everywhere. Cambodia leads the world in

*It is unbelievable that these tree roots could totally engulf the temples of Angkor Wat, but they did.*

mine infestation. It is said that there is one land mine for every two of its 11 million people. Today it is heart-breaking to see so many citizens on the streets missing an arm or leg. A national effort is currently being made to find and destroy the mines in populated areas, but thousands remain buried along the roads and in rice paddies and forests. This was one of Princess Diana's welfare projects.

With all their past troubles, plus the constant fear of land mines, the people seemed to be happy and were very gracious toward us. I would not take anything for my brief time in Cambodia to see the friendly people, become aware of their trials and tribulations, and personally view one of the great architectural wonders of the world, Angkor Wat.

## Indonesia

One of the most diverse and enchanting countries in the world, in my opinion, is Indonesia. The difference lies in the remoteness of the 13,000 to 17,000 islands (depending on your source of information). These stretch along an area of some 3,000 miles encompassing the South China Sea, Java Sea, Indian Ocean, and Pacific Ocean.

Keith and I were privileged to be part of a Travcoa FAM trip to Indonesia in 1998. Our tour visited Bali, Sulawesi, Java, Sumatra, and Irian Jaya. Each area offered a special insight into ancient cultures and island beauty, but Bali, Sulawesi, and Irian Jaya were the most unusual and our favorites.

First stop—Bali. Here we met our tour director, David, who had been a guide for twenty years. He could handle people and difficult situations better than anyone I had ever met. Indonesia is a complex place to coordinate everything, especially when the airlines only run when they wish and are very strict about overweight baggage. The whole Indonesian population appeared to have a laid-back attitude and was not in a hurry to do anything. To add to David's problems, he had a group of travel agents, who of course know ALL about travel and how things should be handled.

Of all the Indonesian islands, Bali is the most popular destination for Americans, Australians, and Europeans. It is a lovely and captivating island with long white

beaches and rice paddies in stairsteps up the side of mountains, just like you see in *National Geographic*. But to me, Bali is remembered for its colorful people. Their religion of Balinese Hinduism governs their daily life. This form of Hindu is similar but somewhat different from the same religion of India. In Bali, each home has a shrine in front and there are temples in every village. Every morning offerings are carefully prepared and placed outside the door to pay homage to the good spirits. As you enter a shop, you will see an offering of a small plate of flowers and fruit at the entrance. Our van driver had a similar display on the dash of his car.

Practically every day there are religious festivals at different temples. The Balinese dress up in freshly ironed and starched multi-colored costumes and parade to the temple. The women wear headdresses of fruit and flower arrangements that can reach two to three feet high. How the headdresses remain in such a perfect display fascinates me, but even more amazing is how the women walk with them on their heads and without using their hands for balance. One day we had to pull off the road as a procession of probably thirty trucks loaded with people singing and playing instruments passed on the way

*(Top) Rice fields climb up the hillside in terraced steps in Bali. (Center) One of the many Buddhist temples in Bali. (Bottom) Daily you will see religious processions to the temples. Ladies are adorned with tall fruit arrangements and men wear white starched robes.*

to a temple. Most of the time, however, they walked to the shrine. You cannot keep from being impressed with the effort and energy put forth by these people for their religion. It is truly a daily way of life.

We had been in Bali in 1994 with a group on a Collette tour, and on our 1998 trip we noticed the size of the fruit and flower offerings were much smaller. Our guide pointed out that the country was undergoing extreme difficulties, and when you have to worry about feeding your family, the offerings to the gods become smaller.

One stop on our island tour was the Monkey Forest. True to its name, there were monkeys everywhere. Jack, one of our passengers, accidentally stepped on a monkey's tail. The animal bared its teeth and attacked him, striking him on the legs. David grabbed a stick and was able to ward off the angry animal before much damage occurred. Due to the baggy pants Jack wore, he luckily only received a bruise on the back of his leg. The poor monkey went up the side of the hill and sat there holding his tail, looking pitiful.

Our group was treated to a special Balinese dinner and a dance program. Vibrant costumes enhanced the graceful dancers as they swayed and made almost impossible movements to the eerie sounds of native drums and other instruments. A special instructor explained the dance to us.

Sulawesi was our next island. After a night at the wonderful Hotel Sedona Makassar in Ujung Padang, the main city in the south of the country, we were to fly north to Torajaland. However, the plane was not flying that day (we never found out why), so we had to go by motor coach for the day's journey to the center of the island, home of the Toraja tribal people. The Toraja culture has held fast throughout the years, even though the Burgis (a tribe from the south) and Christian missionaries tried to change them.

*This youngster performed an intricate Balinese dance for our group.*

The failed attempt at Christian religion is evident in the numerous vacated church buildings.

The first thing you notice when you enter this area is the unusual structure of the houses. The houses are built on raised poles and topped with massive bamboo roofs, built in the shape of water buffalo horns. The bamboo is split and placed in many layers to give a corrugated appearance. The front of the house resembles a buffalo head and horns, the symbol of wealth in the culture. A row of buffalo horns adorns the front

*(Above) Torajaland in Sulawesi is known by its buffalo-style roofs. (Left) A whole village of these un-usual-shaped roofs.*

panel of the homes of the more affluent. Today many modern houses also have this buffalo-style roof.

David inquired around and was elated to announce that he had located a funeral in preparation that we could attend. A funeral was supposed to be one of the highlights of visiting this area. We drove about thirty miles from the town as far as the bus could go on a passable road. Then we continued by foot for about one-half mile across country by a footpath to the home where funeral arrangements were under way. According to tradition, buffaloes are slaughtered at the funeral. The number of animals depends on the man's status. We were told that this man required seventeen buffaloes for his ceremony.

The man had died three years earlier, but the family had only recently been able to financially procure the seventeen necessary sacrifices. All this time, the deceased had been resting in a brightly painted wooden box on a raised platform behind the house. We arrived the day before the actual ceremony. Sitting on a porch area were many neighboring ladies planning who would bring what for the feast. On the burial platform, two people were retouching the painted designs on the casket. Everyone was very sociable, even though we had appeared unannounced at the scene. They offered us refreshments of cake and tea.

Belief is that without proper funeral rites the spirit of the dead will cause misfortune to its family. The huge ceremony and feast will impress the gods with the importance of the deceased, and they will act favorably to the remaining family members. Depending on the wealth and status of the honoree, celebrations last from two to seven days.

A normal diet in Toroja consists mainly of rice and vegetables. They have meat of the buffalo only at funeral ceremonies. Unfortunately, or probably fortunately for my stomach's sake, we were unable to be there for the slaughter of the seventeen buffaloes and the burial feast.

Irian Jaya, the western half of the island of New Guinea, was acquired by the Indonesian government in the 1960s. On an earlier trip to Papua New Guinea on the other side of the island, I was astonished at the men's wardrobe . . . I had not seen anything yet!

We flew to Jayapura, the main city in Irian Jaya, where we stayed two days. Here we saw the mountaintop area overlooking the Pacific Ocean that was one of General Douglas MacArthur's headquarters during World War II. We flew to Wamena, about

*The corpse has been lying in this coffin for three years. Now they have the seventeen buffaloes required for his funeral, and preparations are being made for the celebration.*

eighty miles southwest in the Baliem Valley. In these central highlands the Dani people have maintained their way of life throughout the centuries. The first white men discovered the tribe in 1938, and out in the villages from the town, nothing has changed except that tourists come now and then.

Our lodge was about ten miles out from Wamena, and David announced he had a surprise for us. As our vans pulled into the hotel entrance, out from the trees and bushes along the roadside rushed about forty native men, armed with spears, bows, and arrows. Their entire wardrobe consisted of a penis sheath made from a gourd held in place by a cord around their waist. If you want to have a little excitement in your life, just be charged by a bunch of nearly naked men

*A real shocker to be greeted by a man in body paint, wearing only a penis gourd!*

*Putting on a show for the tourists (which didn't require much time dressing). After a while, you finally get used to the native attire.*

with warpaint on their bodies and pointing a spear at you! They proceeded to have a mock war among themselves, providing us ample photo opportunities. Then they collected a few native women, adorned only with grass skirts hung very low on their hips (how these stayed up I do not know). Dancing and singing followed, and everyone shook our hands and welcomed us to Irian Jaya.

Have you ever shaken hands with a man in public wearing nothing but a gourd penis cover? I had read about these men and their dress, but for this Bible-belt country girl, it was something of an adjustment. But you know, we were there for several days, and it turned out they would have looked out of place if they were wearing clothes. This practice certainly solves what to wear each day and is not a drain on the clothes budget. I wondered where they carried their money, but I guess in their society, they don't need any.

Still it was entertaining to go to downtown Wamena and see the mixture of old and new. We witnessed two men walking side by side. One had on blue jeans, a ski jacket, and wool cap; the other wore a penis gourd—period. (He was definitely the most comfortable, as it was around 85 degrees!) Another man was walking down the street carrying a twenty-foot board and attired only with a gourd.

The gourds vary in size. Some are so long that, when in place, they reach up to their shoulder and may be decorated with feathers on the end. Other gourds may be short and big around or very skinny and curly. We were told that they remove them to sleep. We saw gourds growing on a bush. To make the gourds long and straight, rocks are tied to the end as they grow.

In the villages, the men all sleep in one long house. A husband can have as many wives as he can support. A wife costs about thirty pigs. Women want their spouse to

take many brides, to help out with the work. After seeing all that they do, I certainly would agree with that practice. The women do all the work; the men hunt and fight.

Each family of women and children sleep in a two-layer round grass and bamboo hut with about four feet between layers. Sleeping quarters are on the top. When the husband comes to visit, he and the selected wife for the night occupy the lower level. When a boy is eight years old, he moves over to the men's house and starts wearing a gourd. Up to this time, he is totally naked. Little girls start wearing grass skirts around five years of age.

We witnessed a pig roast, complete from catching the animal and shooting it with an arrow, to dressing it out and feeding the intestines to the dogs. While the men were han-

(Above) Just a normal afternoon—sitting around the yard, with mother extracting lice from her child's head. (Below) The market offered interesting vegetables and interesting people.

dling this operation, the women were building a fire and placing large rocks in a pit about three feet deep. When the rocks were red hot, they were transferred to the cooking pit with long tweezer-type poles. On top of the rocks the women arranged grass and leaves, then vegetables, and finally the pig. This was topped off with another layer of banana leaves and grass. It would take about three hours to cook. I was glad we had to leave before serving time.

The Dani people have certain customs that disturbed me more than anything I have seen around the world. When a blood relative of a woman dies, they cut off a joint from one of her fingers to be buried with the deceased. This means if mother, father, child, brother or sister dies, she loses a knuckle. Women who live to be very old will be missing several finger joints. We saw many old women with nothing but stubs on their hands. As the woman does all the work, they generously leave the thumbs so she can still function. (Isn't that thoughtful?)

*The older Irian Jaya women show the custom of cutting off a knuckle when a blood relative dies.*

Another custom our local guide related is that when it is time for a pregnant woman to have her baby, she must go out in the bush and deliver it alone. She is not allowed to have even another woman with her. Needless to say, this does cut down on the population growth, as many babies die at birth.

I left Irian Jaya saying my blessings that I was born in the United States and not as a woman of the Dani tribe.

# Borneo

For our 25th wedding anniversary in 1999, Keith and I traveled to the Philippines, Borneo, Sulawesi, and Bali. I had always heard the phrase "wild men of Borneo." On this trip we found that there were many wild animals, but certainly did not see men that looked nearly as wild as they did in Irian Jaya and Papua New Guinea. True, Borneo did have headhunters in the past, but thank goodness, this is no longer practiced.

Borneo is the third largest island after Greenland and New Guinea. The landmass is divided into two Malaysian territories of Sabah and Sarawak, the Indonesian territory of Kalimantan, plus independent and tiny Brunei.

Borneo is primarily covered with jungles, inhabited by 9,000 species of flowering plants including the Giant Rafflesia, the largest flower in the world, which grows up to three feet across. The island also is home to 1,000 species of butterflies, 570 species of birds, 200 species of mammals, and 100 species of snakes. We did not see all of these creatures, but were privileged to personally view a large number.

Our first stop in Borneo was at Kota Kinabula, the capital of Sabah, a Malaysian territory, located in the northeast portion of the island. The lovely La Lanjung Aru Resort, on the outskirts of the city and right on the beach, was our home for two nights. From our verandah we could see Mt. Kinabula, the high granite peak that is the focal point of the area.

Our local guide, Mary Ann, led us on an all-day tour of the mountain region, where we took a jungle canopy walk, viewed the hot springs, and had a nature walk through botanical gardens. We stopped at a native market and café along the way. Here they were serving "bird's nest soup." We were informed that the Chinese consider this a special delicacy. In this region there are limestone caves where swiftlets roost, making nests from their saliva. These nests are then collected, washed, and boiled into soup. I was not interested in sampling the soup, but thought the nests would be something neat to bring home. However, you could not buy just one nest. They came packaged, and the smallest package of about six nests cost $98. The price was quoted to be over $500 per kilo. I decided that I could certainly do without a bird nest soup souvenir, and then was informed by the shopkeeper that I could not bring it legally into the United States anyway, so that settled that. Mary Ann said she loved to go to wealthy Chinese weddings, for they always served bird nest's soup.

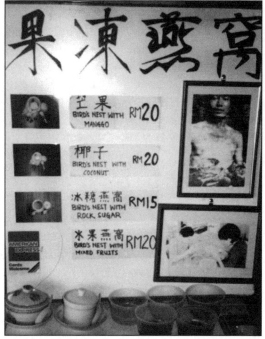

(Above) A canopy walk in the jungles of Sabah on Borneo Island. (Below) The sign advertises the popular "Bird Nest Soup" at a local restaurant.

*The lady wanted to sell me the unusual musical instrument, but all I wanted was a picture.*

At this market, as I was looking over the merchandise, I heard a very unusual noise rising from behind the hanging souvenirs. I peeked behind, and there sat an old woman playing a funny-looking musical instrument. She wanted to sell me the music maker. I told her I did not want it, but would pay her to take her picture. She said that I could take her picture if I bought something. I looked over her offerings and purchased a couple of straw trays. This appeased her into letting me snap her photograph.

Mary Ann, age thirty-four, had two daughters. Her husband was also a tour guide. When she heard that we were later going to the Borneo Rainforest Lodge, she said: "Do you have your leech socks?" We had read in our tour guidebooks that we needed them, but had not seen any opportunity to buy leech socks in the U.S.

"I have some extra pairs from when I was leading tours there," she said. "Just come home with me and I will give them to you." So we went to her home, met her mother, who was babysitting with the two little girls, and acquired the unique socks. Of course, we gave her a nice tip, as we were impressed with her accommodating generosity, plus it was an extra treat to see what Mary Ann referred to as "a middle-class Sabah home." Built in a subdivision, this house was part of a long row of connected buildings, similar to a shopping center. Each quarter consisted of a living room, tiny kitchen, bath, and two small bedrooms. A wire fence separated the family units in the porch area. There was a playground across the street.

Our next stop in Sabah was Sandakan. This city is best known as the site of a Japanese prisoner of war camp during World War II, where over 2,000 Australian and British troops died in prisoner camps and death marches. We visited the home of Agnes Keith, an American wife of a British forestry supervisor. The Japanese captured Mrs. Keith, her husband, and her small son. Her book *Three Came Home* is a heart-rending story of their incarceration for three years in a Japanese prison camp. The book was very emotional to me and personal as I had seen her home and had been to many of the places she described.

During our city tour, our local guide, Avalino, took us to a water village where he lived. The village consisted of probably 100 houses built on stilts over the water, all connected with walkways. You needed to be extra careful with a toddler child here, for that first step off the porch was in the water. Avalino explained that you could own a home much cheaper here, for you did not have to purchase any land. Some of the houses were very nice, and all had electricity and TVs. There was no water or sewer service. The sewage went directly from the home's bathroom and kitchen into the water below. While we were there, I saw a woman throw a plastic bag of garbage out the window. The garbage and sewage are removed when the tide sweeps in and out, but I hate to think what the soap chemicals, plastic, and tin cans do to the sea life.

Outside Sandakan is the Sepilok Orangutan Rehabilitation Centre. Here we were able to get up close to a mother orangutan and her two offspring. We were present for

the feeding of bananas and milk, and numerous orangutans showed up to dine. One large male obtained his handful of bananas first and went off to a nearby cable, where he casually hung by his feet while eating with his hands. The Centre's main function is taking abandoned young orangutans and helping them to grow and slowly be released back to the wild. Tourists who love to take pictures of the animals help fund the project.

*Mother and baby take a rest at the Sepilok Orangutan Rehabilitation Centre outside Sandakan.*

A three-hour ride brought us to our next adventure on the Sungai Kinabatangan River. Our accommodations were basic, but we did have a private bath, which to me is the number-one requirement; everything else I can handle. We were right on the river but had to patch up the windows with my trusty duct tape to keep out mosquitoes. We were the only guests at the lodge when we arrived, so we received special treatment and the food was surprisingly excellent. The cook was a very young man who looked like anything but a chef, but he could prepare gourmet food from native supplies.

Right outside our cabin, we stepped into a motorized dugout canoe for boat trips along the waterways, viewing many species of monkeys, including the unique proboscis monkey. This guy looks like no other monkey. He is rather large, about three to four feet high, has a pot belly, and a long, sad face with a big hooknose. They stay high in the trees, and although we could see one clearly with the binoculars, I was unable to get a good picture.

At one place, as we came along in the boat, a family of monkeys was crossing the river by jumping from the tree on one side into the water and swimming to the other

*Our guide, Avalino, explains the primates of Sabah before we take our jungle river tour.*

side. It was hilarious to see them come sailing out of the tree, hitting the water and furiously swimming to the nearby overhanging limbs on the other side of the river. I tried numerous times to get a photo of this wild activity, but they were too fast for me.

There were numerous bird species, but the most unusual was the hornbill. These birds are large (some up to three feet tall), black in color, with a colorful large red and yellow horn right at the base of a long bill. They also make a prolonged call in various degrees of melody. While we were on the river, we decided we had seen enough monkeys to last us a lifetime, but the experience was very out of the ordinary and a lot of fun.

An overland trip of about two hours took us to Lahad Datu, headquarters for the Borneo Rainforest Lodge. We said goodbye to Avalino and traveled by a lodge van another three hours over a very rough and unpaved road through a logging area to the Borneo Rainforest Lodge. The lodge was located in the heart of the 438-square-kilometer Danum Valley Conservation Area. It was a shock to see this luxurious first-class resort sitting in the middle of a jungle. Everything was included in one price: transfers, room, meals, plus guide service for day and night explorations.

Accommodations were in two-unit structures connected by an elevated walkway to the main dining room and lounge area. We were required to leave our shoes downstairs and wear only house shoes in public areas and guest quarters. This rule was understandable, due to the condition of our shoes after tromping through the wet jungle. Our bedroom was exceptionally large with two double beds. We enjoyed our back porch that opened out to a view of a running stream and many trees filled with various species of birds.

Each couple is assigned a private guide. We were told that we had the number-one guide, Stephen, and I believe it. His native name was Engeri of the Bongalai tribe that had lived in the Danum Valley for thousands of years. In 1970 the area was proclaimed a conservation area and the government relocated Stephen and his people to land farther down the river. Stephen was a child at that time and went to a missionary school, where all subjects were taught in English. Thus he had obtained a superb English vocabulary. He explained that today the Malaysian government operates the school, and all subjects are taught in Malay with only one class in English. Stephen attended secondary school in Sandakan and returned to his village to teach. He became very concerned about the palm oil plantations that were absorbing the entire area. We had noticed that for most of the drive from Sandakan to Lahad Datu, the area was totally covered with palm trees grown for palm oil export. Large companies were cutting down the forests and planting palm oil trees, crowding out the wildlife and causing the rivers to flood from the deforestation. This also affected the villagers in their hunting and food gathering. So Stephen founded a political group and took three companies to court and won.

"This would not replace the jungle and wildlife," he said, but he did get some funds for his village. He worked for a while at a marble factory and while there became ill with malaria. "That is when I started smoking," he said, "for the villagers believe if you smoke, mosquitoes will stay away."

Discontent with his work at the marble factory, in 1997 he heard of a job opening for a naturalist at the Borneo Rainforest Lodge. As this was his native home, plus he knew all about the wildlife and plants and spoke English, he was immediately hired. Today he is the number-one guide and assistant to the manager.

Stephen is married and has six children. The eldest boy, twenty-two, works at a store in his native village. Another son, age eighteen, was the cook at the Borneo Rainforest Lodge (Emeril does not need to worry about competition, but he did make a delicious cake for Keith's birthday that occurred while we were there); two sons, ages eleven and seven, were in school back in his village,

*Our Borneo Rainforest Guide, Stephen, shows us the coffin where his great-grandfather was entombed with his blowpipe made of ironwood.*

and a nine-month-old daughter was with him and his wife at the lodge. He makes 610 ringet (Malaysian money) per month (about $180 U.S.) plus he receives free housing and utilities. From this amount he sends 200 ringet each month to the village to pay for the boys' schooling and he saves about 100 ringet a month in hopes of building his own tourist lodge on land that was granted to him by his grandfather on the river near his village.

During WWII, the Japanese occupied Sabah and frequently came through the native villages seeking food. His grandfather told the Japanese that they would share their food if they would leave his people alone. One night the Japanese came in and stole all their supplies. The next night, the grandfather took his village warriors and with their poison blowpipes killed the entire Japanese raiding party. After that, the village had no more trouble with the Japanese. Stephen said his ancestors were not "headhunters," but if any warriors came to their village with intent to take a head trophy, his forefathers would attack and cut off their ears. The mutilated warriors were sent back to their village with a warning that the rest of the head would go if they returned. He said this tactic was very effective.

Stephen led us up a limestone cliff that looms 710 feet above the river and overlooks the lodge compound. The steep path was difficult as it began to rain. Along the way we encountered an orangutan and a helmeted hornbill, the largest of the hornbill species. He was making his call, which goes something like "*whop-whop-whop*," then gets faster with the *whops* and finishes with a "*ha-ha-ha*," just like a laugh. The natives say that the continuous calls are an indication of rain, and this hornbill had certainly been right, as it began raining very hard. Right before the summit, we veered off to Coffin Cliff, where many years ago wooden coffins were wedged into the crevices of the limestone. Here Stephen showed us his great-grandfather's coffin made of ironwood, the strongest wood in the jungle. Inside the coffin was a blowpipe that had been buried with him. The bones had been removed and placed in a crevice in the cliffside.

A little further up we reached the top-viewing platform. What a picture postcard sight! We were above the massive trees shrouded in a veil of mist, with the river and lodge houses below.

Each evening the lodge guests would climb into the back of an open truck, equipped with benches for a "night wildlife drive." The event was like a meeting of the United Nations. Joining us were guests from England, Germany, France, and Japan. We were the token Americans. Fortunately for us, most of them spoke some English.

During the night drive a naturalist guide would sit on top of the truck cab with a strong spotlight, seeking little red spots of eyes in the dark. The first night, just outside the main building, we spotted a huge wild boar going through the garbage. We all became excited at seeing a wild animal so quickly, only to discover he is a permanent resident of the area, living off the garbage. The night drives did enable us out in the jungle to see owls, deer, black squirrels, leopard cat, civet cat, frogs, and fruit bats.

Day walks in the jungle, early each morning and from 2:00 to 5:00 in the afternoon, produced sightings of several species of monkeys and birds. We could always know when we were approaching an orangutan by the odor it leaves in its nesting place. They spend the night high in the trees, and the area around the base of the tree serves as the restroom. These animals eat so much, producing large, smelly deposits.

Stephen led us along trails or paths he took through the thick growth along the forest floor. One hazard he pointed out: leeches. These creatures are about two inches long and about a pinhead size in width. They attach one end to a leaf and wait, swaying back and forth, for something alive (be it animal or human) to brush against or come near the leaf. The leeches will immediately jump on the body and start sucking blood. We were advised to wear "leech socks," a closely woven cotton sock that goes over your sock and trousers and comes up to the knee, where it is securely tied. Then you put your shoe on over that. (Our guide in Sabah had generously provided us with ours.) Also, you must wear a long-sleeved shirt and have your shirttail tucked in to keep the little rascals from crawling up under and taking a meal.

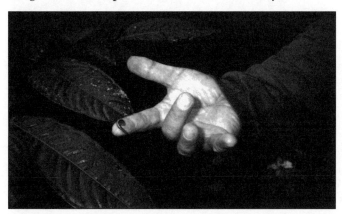

*Stephen extracts a leech from my arm and lets me take a picture of the rascal.*

I was horrified of those things! As we walked along, we kept checking each other and picking them off our clothing. They jumped all around, trying to locate skin to latch on to. In all our walks, I only had two secure themselves to the underside of my wrist at the little opening where the long sleeve buttons. I screamed for Stephen, and he quickly dislodged them before they drank too much blood. A small red spot similar to a mosquito bite remained.

When we asked Stephen how they managed with the leeches when he was a kid, running throughout the jungle without any protective clothing, he explained: "We wanted them to get on us ... we collected them for fish bait."

We were awarded a certificate stating that we had donated some blood to the Tiger Leech and were now an official member of the Danum Valley Blood Donor Society. I was very honored to receive the certificate until I noticed, while going over my lodge bill, that they charged us $3 each for the piece of paper.

Since it is a rainforest, it certainly rains. This area receives an average of 120 inches of rain annually. When we took the jungle walk that day, it had rained all night and everything was slick and soggy. I was trying to be very careful as we made our way on the muddy and leaf-covered path. Suddenly, I slipped and was falling head first on my back down a muddy embankment. *When am I going to ever stop falling?* raced through my mind as I slid down and down. I came to a stop after about a twelve-foot drop on the rocky edge of a stream, with the back of my head in the water. Stephen was down at my side immediately.

"Get the leeches off me!" I screamed.

Stephen sat me up and picked off the intruders. Keith was down there by then, and they lifted me to my feet. Scattered in the mud on the way down were my cap, camera, and water bottle.

As I fell on mud the impact was softened, and I did not break any bones. (What would we have done if I had a broken bone way out there in the jungle?) My injuries included a slight bump on the head, a deep cut, and a bruise on my knee (apparently where I first hit), plus other miscellaneous bruises. I was covered with mud on my backside. After sitting for a while and cleaning up the camera and water bottle, we decided to conclude our little jungle walk for the time being. On the trek of about a mile back to the lodge, Stephen was so solicitous, holding my hand in each endangered place. I was so humiliated. All these years, I have been helping little ladies in my tour group along, and here I was the one who needed assistance.

Dear Stephen. He took my dirty clothes and cap, washed them for me, and hung them in the generator building to dry. The humidity is so high there, they would have never dried and the laundry service could not get them out for me overnight. After resting the remainder of the afternoon, I was able to go the next morning, with just some bruises and a little soreness.

*(Above) I was a mess after my fall down the ravine, but thankful that I did not have any serious injuries. (Below) Keith is all ready for a jungle walk in his leech socks.*

The wildlife sightings were exciting, but in the forest you hear much more than you see due to the dense foliage. To me, the most impressive sights were the tremendous tall trees in the primary rainforest. Some are so tall that you cannot see the tops before they are engulfed in the cloudy mist. Massive undergrowth of ferns and ivy plants seek light around the trees that obstruct most of the sunlight. The forest produces many plants that natives use for medicinal purposes. Stephen told us that scientists have recently announced they had developed what they hope to be a cure for AIDS from a tree in the rainforest.

The first night at the Rainforest Lodge I went to the bar to get some ice for our evening cocktail. I asked the young man at the bar if I could have a bowl of ice cubes to take to my room. He looked rather puzzled, but asked me to wait, and then went over to the kitchen. He returned with a large glass bowl (about three-quart size), in which he placed four ice cubes.

"Could I please have more ice?" I pleaded.

He finally gave me about twelve cubes, and I thanked him, handed him a tip, and picked up the bowl and started to leave.

"Miss," he cried, running after me. "What about the bowl?"

"I will return it at dinner ... or I am in K-2 and you can pick it up."

"No problem, but are you going to drink from the bowl?"

I laughed and explained that I wanted the ice for drinks in the two glasses that we had in our room.

I can highly recommend the Borneo Rainforest Lodge if your interest is wildlife and nature. Here you have great accommodations right in the middle of the jungle. Stephen said that the best time to come is in April and May, the dry season, although no month is totally dry in the rainforest. Also, he recommended his favorite time of September, when the trees are fruiting, as that brings more animals closer for viewing and photos.

Leaving the Borneo Rainforest Lodge, we went by lodge van to the airport at Lahad Datu and boarded Malaysian Airlines for Kota Kinabula. We then transferred to the Royal Brunei Airlines bound for Bandar Seri Begawan, capital of Brunei. Lovely female flight attendants dressed in colorful Muslim gowns welcomed us aboard. Their heads were covered, but not their faces. Brunei is a strict Muslim country. As the plane taxied out the runway, it stopped before takeoff, and over the speaker for several minutes we listened to a Muslim prayer. In all my years of air travel, this was the first time to witness a public prayer before takeoff, but I am all for it. You need all the help you can get. We were handed immigration forms before landing. Again something new. The form requested your race and religious preference.

The country of Brunei is one of the smallest and wealthiest countries in the world. This is all that remains of the empire that in the sixteenth-century controlled the entire island of Borneo. After many wars and series of treaties, Brunei was under the protectorate of the British. In 1984 the current Sultan obtained independence. The country is now totally a monarchy led by the Sultan, His Majesty Paduka Seri Beginda Sultan Haji Hassanal Belkiah Mu'izzaddin Waddaulah, the twenty-ninth of his royal line. No wonder everyone just refers to him as "The Sultan." Due to the massive offshore oil fields and good investments, the Sultan was at one time ranked as the richest man in the world. Bill Gates of Microsoft, at that time, had currently overruled him for this position, but needless to say, the rise and fall of the stock market could change that. Our guide in Brunei said that the Sultan was still the richest, but he just hides some of his wealth from the world.

The Sultan was doing rather well while we were there. He had two wives, and lived with Number One Wife and six children in his palace of over 1,000 rooms. Number Two Wife, a former Royal Brunei Airlines flight attendant, and their four siblings resided in a smaller palace outside the city about thirty minutes away by car. The Sultan did not have to worry about means of transportation, as he was reported to have 153 cars and a private aircraft. His favorite sport being polo, he kept more than 200 Argentine ponies at a private park in air-conditioned stalls.

The palace is closed to the public except once during the year, when it is opened to the citizens for feasting and visitation for three days following Ramadan, the time of Muslim fasting. Our guide said that everyone looks forward to this special time seeing the Royal Family and enjoying an elaborate feast.

The Sultan takes very good care of his population of about 300,000. The country is said to have the highest standard of living in Asia. They pay no taxes of any kind, have free medical care and schooling, and the highest minimum wage in the region. If a promising student wants to go to college abroad, all expenses will be provided if he or she will return to Brunei after completing their graduation and apply their education there. The Sultan has even built an amusement park similar to Disneyland that is free to his people.

As a gift to the populace, he donated the Omar Ali Saifuddien Mosque, one of the most impressive buildings I have ever seen. The golden dome dominates the city skyline. As he is the twenty-ninth Sultan, the building has twenty-nine crystal chandeliers from Austria. The floors are of the finest Italian marble. The stained glass windows are from England, and the lush and colorful carpets from Saudi Arabia and Belgium. The building is decorated with exquisite taste. To enter the mosque, as a woman, I had to slip on a long white robe that reached the floor and had long sleeves. To my surprise, I did not have to cover my head. Everyone had to remove his or her shoes. Non-Muslims can enter the mosque only at certain visiting hours. People of the faith may come at any time to pray. The Men's Prayer Hall will hold up to 5,000; the women's will accommodate 2,000. Throughout the building we saw several people in prayer, and also groups of schoolchildren.

We found the city and country to be very clean and orderly. We were there on July 17, and along the main streets flags were flying in honor of the Sultan's birthday. That night we viewed the birthday fireworks display from our room at the downtown Sheraton Hotel.

*The beautiful Mosque built by the Sultan of Brunei for his people.*

From Brunei we flew to Kutching, Sarawak, a Malaysian province. Unfortunately, our schedule allowed us only an overnight stay there and consequently we saw very little of this area.

We then took a plane to Pontianak, on the western shore of Kalimantan, the largest land area of Indonesia, located in the southern part of Borneo. Here our guide, Sarif, met us. He was a handsome young man, eighteen years old.

"We go to hotel—take short rest and then boat excursion," he said in clipped English. As it was around 11:00 A.M., this was fine with us. At the Mahaka Hotel we were cordially received and directed to our room. The quarters were not luxurious, but certainly adequate.

We were just settling in when the phone rang: "Mrs. Brooks, we are so sorry, we should have put you into our VIP suite," the voice said. We had not paid for a VIP suite, and I told the person we were comfortable where we were.

"No, we insist, as you are special guests from America and this is our gift to you," he replied. So how could we refuse? We moved to a three-room suite, although the furniture was not any more impressive than in the regular room. However, we were on the top floor and did have two television sets. A few minutes later, a bellman arrived with a tray filled with complimentary tropical fruits that sub-stituted for our lunch.

Sarif had said he would meet us at 1:00 P.M. for our city tour. He did not show until 1:45 P.M., which did not set well with me, but I didn't say anything. He said the first thing we were going to see was the Nature Museum, which was one of our prime interests. When we arrived at the museum, there was a sign on the door indicating the hours were 9:00 A.M.–1:00 P.M. It was now about 2:00 P.M. I thought it was unusual for a local guide not to know the mu-seum hours, and was discontented for we could have stopped there when we passed it on the way to the hotel.

We next went to an imposing but run-down palace built entirely out of ironwood. The Kadriyah Palace was home to the regional Sultans when the Brunei Sultans ruled the entire island of Borneo. As we approached the building, an elderly woman was sitting on the steps reading a book aloud, which I was informed was the Koran.

*This woman was sitting on the steps of the former palace, reading the Koran.*

We spoke and she let me take her picture. When she smiled, you could see from the red of her mouth she was a betel nut user. Inside the palace, the only furniture remaining were the two throne chairs. On the wall was a picture of the last sultan and the nameplate read "Sarif."

"That's your name," I remarked to our guide.

"He was my grandfather," he said.

Immediately I began questioning him about his heritage, for I had earlier realized that this kid was not your average tour guide. He said that the Javanese beheaded his grandfather in 1969, when the Indonesians were overtaking the country. His father was born in the palace, but at that time was a plastic factory worker. Quite a comedown for a Sultan heir! And here was the grandson, who if things had been left in place, would be in line to be a Sultan. Instead he was a reluctant tour guide.

We then went to the Equator Monument that began in 1928 as a simple obelisk with an arrow. In 1991 they covered the original monument and erected a twenty-foot-high column on top of that. Here you can have your picture standing on the equator. I realized then why it was so hot.

It was now 3:30 P.M., and Sarif said, "We go back to hotel."

"What about our harbor cruise?" I asked as I showed him my voucher indicating that it was included in the city tour.

"You sure you want to go?" he retorted.

"Yes, our voucher states we get a harbor cruise and I want it."

He saw he had no recourse, so down to the harbor we went. He located a boatman with a very old boat powered by a slow *putt-putt* motor, and off we cruised. This was the most interesting part of Pontianak. The people live in houseboats or in houses

*From our harbor cruise we viewed all kinds of village life. Here a woman is doing the family laundry.*

built over the water. They were actively washing clothes, bathing, fishing, and the children were playing in the water. Great photo ops!

When Sarif delivered us back to the hotel, I reminded him we needed to depart for the airport at 7:00 A.M. Next morning, 7:00 A.M. and no Sarif. At 7:15 I had the hotel call us a taxi. When we arrived at the airport, Sarif was standing at the terminal entrance.

"You were to pick us up at the hotel, not meet us here," I admonished him.

"The car would not start," he said, but I noticed it did get him to the airport.

We proceeded to check-in with Garuda, the Indonesian Airline, and Sarif left. After standing in a crowded and shoving line, I reached the small check-in counter. When I presented our tickets, the agent said we had no reservation, as the tickets had not been reconfirmed. When I bought my tickets in the U.S., the agent stated that it wasn't necessary to reconfirm, as this was our originating flight on this Garuda ticket. I had mentioned reconfirmation to Sarif, and he said his office was taking care of it. To complicate matters, they said the plane was full and there were no seats available for us. I asked to see the manager. I was directed to a small cubbyhole, just wide enough for a small desk, his chair, and a small plastic stool for me. I explained my predicament.

"Who was you local handler?" he asked. Luckily, Sarif had given Keith his card and I handed it to the agent. He called the office and spoke to Sarif. What Sarif said, I do not know.

"I'm sorry, but they did not reconfirm for you and there is nothing I can do," the manager stated. At this moment, he was summoned out of the office on another matter. While sitting there, I looked around and saw an ashtray with several cigarette butts. When he returned, he instantly noticed the package of Marlboros I had placed in the tray. Picking them up, he put them into his pocket. Then he punched something in his computer, handed me my tickets, and said to go to the check-in counter. (Oh, the wonders of one package of Marlboros!)

The counter agent began checking us in only to say that our luggage was overweight and we owed 21,000 rupiah, about $4. At this point I would have paid anything to get on that plane. Keith gave me some local currency, and I ran to pay for the overweight luggage. The Marlboro story must have traveled fast, for when I handed the slip and money to the man there, he said, "For you, no charge," and stamped my tickets. I reached in my purse and handed him a package of cigarettes and was rewarded with a tremendous smile. Back at the check-in, we received our boarding passes and went through customs just in time to board the plane. As we approached the departure gate, the manager whom I had met with was standing there, puffing away on a Marlboro. He handed me his card and remarked, "Use this as a reference if you have any Garuda problems." Again, there is nothing like good old Marlboros when things get sticky.

It was advantageous that I had his card. When we arrived in Jakarta, we were to receive our onward boarding passes to Sulawesi at the transfer desk. Upon presentation of our tickets, they advised us that one wrong coupon had been pulled in Pontianak and one of us did not have the ticket to go to Ujung Padang. I immediately handed them the manager's card. They called him and cleared the matter. All this took considerable time, but fortunately we had about three hours between flights.

We remembered the Garuda Private Club at this Jakarta airport from our previous visit. At this club you can just show your Visa card and for $2 you can relax in comfort, plus partake of the snacks and drinks available to the guests. This is a great way to spend your waiting time in Jakarta, and certainly worth the $2!

## Sulawesi

We collect butterflies, and a search on the Internet revealed that north central Sulawesi was one of the best places in the world to obtain rare butterfly specimens.

The Internet provided us with the e-mail address of The Nature Conservatory in Palu, Sulawesi. We contacted them and received the nicest reply from Duncan, who was from England and the manager of the project there. We conversed frequently via e-mail, and he graciously arranged a five-day tour of the butterfly territory, complete with a guide. He advised that we would be going in remote areas to reach the butterfly farms and that the accommodations were sparse, with only "Asian style bathrooms." We accepted the tour understanding these conditions.

Our first stop in Sulawesi was Ujung Pandang, the great city-port in the southwestern part of the island. We had reservations at the Hotel Sedona Makassar, where we had stayed the year before with the Travcoa group. The manager remembered us, and we were warmly welcomed. We were ushered to an oceanside room with a panoramic view of the harbor and all the boating and people activities. Without a doubt, you can witness the most incredible sunsets in the world from the sea-view windows of this hotel. It's almost worth the trip just to see a sunset from the Hotel Sedona Makassar.

The next morning we flew northward to Palu and checked in at the Golden Hotel. There wasn't a lot of activity around Palu, and the hotel had obviously seen better days. The room did have a small air conditioner, but there was no air conditioning in the lobby area. We met an Australian who was in Palu to sell solar units to farmers who did not have access to electricity. We also talked to a man from England who was there consulting with the telephone company. These were the only other guests we saw at the hotel.

That afternoon we were waiting for our guide, Adri, outside the building because the lobby was so hot. He finally showed up riding a motorcycle, the main type of transportation in Palu. I was wondering if all three of us were going to tour that way, but was pleased to see a van drive up to serve as our city tour vehicle.

Adri, who had been arranged by Duncan, was very eager to be our guide, as we were his first Americans. He spoke English fairly well, and he was thrilled to have the opportunity to practice with us. He worked with the Central Sulawesi Government Tourism Service in Palu, but most of his clients were European or Asian. He said that business had been slow due to the bad publicity regarding the violence in Indonesia, which, he pointed out, did not reach Palu. This was a very quiet area where politics was not a prevalent issue. People here were concerned about where the next meal was coming from, not creating riots.

Our first stop on the Palu city tour was the museum. It was closed, but Adri located the manager and he cheerfully opened for us. The museum had a few exhibits of early life around the area. When we drove out in the country the next day, it appeared to me that not much had changed through the years, for homes and lifestyle were about the same as in the historical museum.

That evening we had an appointment with Duncan and his wife, Rita, for dinner. Again, as we were waiting outside the hotel (cooler than inside, but swatting the mosquitoes), up they drove on a motorcycle. He summoned a taxi to take us to a seafood restaurant. There they had fresh fish on ice, and Duncan picked several to be grilled for our dinner.

Duncan said he had been in Indonesia for ten years—six in Manokwari, in the far northwest portion of Irian Jaya, where he was with the World Wildlife Federation. He met Rita, a native of Irian Jaya, while she was teaching agriculture at the university there. Then they moved to Palu, where he became manager of The Nature Conservatory project. He was working with the natives to help make their natural resources profitable, and at the same time, conserve them. He is dedicated to protecting the environment and helping the natives.

The Nature Conservatory had three projects in Central Sulawesi: bee farms that produce honey, river rafting tours for tourists, and butterfly farms. Each week, Duncan sends someone out to the farms and collects the butterfly specimens that have been packaged individually in wax paper. He then forwards them to processors in Ujung Pandang, who export them to butterfly dealers and collectors all over the world.

When we entered the restaurant, we were the only patrons there. Immediately Duncan and Rita went to the nearby sink in the dining room and washed their hands. I later found out why. When the fish and rice were served, they ate with their hands, a practice of the natives in this area. They were very proficient with it. They picked up a piece of fish with their right hand, dabbed it around in the rice to form a ball, and into the mouth it went. Seemed a lot simpler than the fork I was using, but I am sure I would make a mess if I tried to eat in this fashion.

Adri met us at 7:30 the next morning, and this time he was in a four-wheel drive Jeep (vintage unknown—but old). It looked just like an army issue. The driver and Keith rode in the two seats up front and Ardi and I were on side bench seats in the back with the luggage. The windows were tie-down canvas, but we certainly did not need to close them in the 90-degree-plus heat.

Before leaving town, we gave Adri money to exchange to local currency for expenses. We had given him some $100 bills, and he returned with two, saying the bank would not take them because one was creased and the other one had a small cut in the top. Keith produced two more perfect bills, and that worked. Next we went to a small grocery to buy something for Keith and me for lunch, upon Adri's advice. I selected two rolls with some kind of meat filling and some mango juice.

Keith had been sick for three days with a head cold but was feeling a little better that morning as we started out on our butterfly adventure. Our next stop was to the City Permit Office. We had to obtain a permit to enter the Lore Lindu National Park, our destination. Our research had revealed that this park was a large and remote recreation area that had been barely touched by tourism. There you could see incredible butterflies, some as large as your hand. That little tidbit was the sole purpose of this excursion.

While Adri was obtaining the permit, I noticed several stacks of long poles of rattan. I was told that they had been confiscated from natives who had cut them in the protected park jungles.

Outside the town, the road began to climb upward toward the mountains we could see in the distance. All along the way we saw vegetable gardens, cocoa trees, corn and rice fields. All farming was by hand, and the means of transportation to markets were ox and cart. We stopped at some of the roadside vendors and bought bananas, potatoes and peanuts. As we went higher, the Jeep began to stall. The driver would get out, bang around under the hood, and we would continue slowly on. This happened quite frequently.

At noon we stopped at a restaurant. I then found out why Adri had me buy our lunch in Palu. The eating conditions and cleanliness of the place left a lot to be desired. Adri and the driver were served fish and rice, which they ate native-style. As I made my way to the back of the place to the restroom (Asian-type), I noticed a little boy about two years of age lying on a cot. He was obviously sick. Then I looked in an adjoining open area to the dining room, and there lay two more people who looked ill. I wanted to get out of there before we caught whatever was wrong with them. The people around the place were very friendly and wanted me to take their picture.

As we continued, the Jeep was having more motor trouble. We made it to the park entrance and Adri produced our permit. Inside the park the roads were unpaved, and often there was no road at all. One time we drove right off into a shallow running river, continued down the watery riverbed for some time, and then came out on the other side. I never saw any sign of road, and how the driver knew when to enter the river and exit I do not know. The only other people we saw were either walking or in a wagon pulled by oxen.

Along a mountainside, we noticed a lean-to shack. Adri waved to the man there and said we would go see how palm sugar was made. We walked over to the man's operation. Under the shed he had a pot, about three feet in diameter and about three feet deep. In it he placed palm nuts from the palm trees and boiled them for seven hours. The mixture became caramelized like brown sugar, and tasted like brown sugar. Before it hardened, he poured it into an empty half coconut shell to set. Used to sweeten coffee, tea, etc., palm sugar is sold in the native markets in the shell.

As we approached the place where we were to stay, I noticed several little cottages and assumed that was where we would be, as Duncan had said we would be in a guest house. He had told us to bring sheets and pillowcases. He was very upfront about the conditions and I quote from his e-mail: "You will have an 'Asian Bathroom.' Bathing will be in the traditional way—scooping water out of a tub called a 'bak' for a refreshing shower. I'm sure you know that Asian toilets do not have a part to sit on!" So I was prepared for these listed conditions. What I was not prepared for was what I saw when we arrived.

I had thought it would be just Keith and me in a cottage with those mentioned type of facilities. We drove up to a large building. The stairs up to the porch that sat about five feet above the ground had two broken steps. We entered from the porch into a large room that had two tables with dingy oilcloth coverings and chairs around them. Off this large space were four sleeping rooms, and at the back, the one bathroom (Asian-style) and an open type room for cooking.

Our room was just big enough for a narrow double bed constructed of plywood. On top of the board was a stained cotton mat about two inches thick. (The reason to bring your own sheets!) From the ceiling over the bed hung a mosquito net, which, when lowered, proved to have four or five holes big enough to put your hand through. I didn't think it would be much protection from the bugs that would zoom in through the window and the cracks in the wooden walls. The one window, about two feet square, was the only outside opening in the room, and there was no cover of any kind on it—just an open space. A small desk and chair completed the furnishings. A curtain that moved back and forth from the small breeze of the open-air porch served as the door to the room. This left a lot to be desired regarding security and privacy.

I found out that our guide and driver would be in one of the rooms, and backpackers would occupy the other two. We would all share the one "Asian" bath.

The shared bath was the part that got me. I had been ready to accept any conditions for just the two of us, but cohabitation under these circumstances was hard for me to grasp. I was having difficulty accepting the situation. When you have been brought up with this type of facilities, that is fine, and I realize when you travel you cannot have everything like it is at home. But at my age and with my background, I was having misgivings.

While I was still in shock over the sleeping arrangements, Adri announced he wanted us to take about a two-mile jungle walk to a waterfall. It was now around 2:00 P.M. and the temperature hovering near 100 degrees. Keith said that we had

*I was ready to leave these sleeping arrangements as soon as possible.*

come to this area to see the butterfly farms, and that was what we were going to do first. So off we drove over unbelievable trails (roads were invisible) with the Jeep coughing and sputtering, for about fifteen miles to Kamarora, a small village in the heart of the jungle. There were supposed to be twenty-three butterfly farms in this region. As we entered the hamlet, the makeshift road came to a sudden dropoff where a bridge had been washed out completely. There were no warning signs; I guess they think everyone knows the bridge is gone. A detour trail led around it through the shallow running creek.

Our driver let us out at the first butterfly farmer's house and said he was going to try to find a part for the Jeep. A man and woman came out to greet us, probably around sixty years old. The woman was smoking one cigarette after another. Next to their home was a butterfly enclosure, about 12x14 feet. Some flowering plants and a few butterflies were inside. The farmer said he had more varieties about a half-mile away. So off we went, over streams, through thick jungle growth, in about 100-degree temperature and equal humidity. I was carrying my big purse with all our valued possessions and Keith had my camera case. As we walked through the jungle, my head became congested, I assume due to the tropical mold and pollen.

At this butterfly enclosure, which was about the same size as the one at the house, a

*We saw some butterflies, but none of the hand-size variety.*

teen-age girl met us, waving a large butterfly net. Apparently her job was to catch the butterflies in the jungle and bring them to the caged area. Inside the enclosure were more butterflies, as well as jars with various stages from caterpillar to cocoon to new butterfly. But there were not any different types from the ones we had seen at the farmer's house and certainly not any of the hand-size variety. As we made the trudge back to his house we met his wife, who was carrying two buckets full of water that she had run down to collect from the stream about a half-mile away.

The farmer brought out the butterflies he had for sale—two types which had been dried with the wings together and placed in wax paper. We explained that we could not use that kind, for they would crumble when we attempted to separate the wings for mounting. He said to inject them with alcohol and they would become pliable and suitable for mounting, something we were not inclined to try. Adri suggested that we go see what other farmers had to offer.

The old man escorted us around. He told us that there were twenty-three butterfly farmers around Kamarora and that during the previous year they as a group shipped 17,500 butterflies and received 1,000 rupiah each (about fifteen cents). If you calculate that out equally, each farmer made a little over $100 that year on butterflies. It's good that they grow their own fruits and vegetables, and that rice is cheap. They do also grow cocoa, which Adri said recently had been a good money crop.

As we walked through the town we saw some children playing ball and others playing with rocks along the side of the road. We met one group of small girls, around five or six years old, returning from the stream where they had apparently bathed and brushed their teeth, for they were carrying towels and their toothbrushes. When we reached the stream, we saw women washing dishes and clothes. As I looked at them, carrying their pans full of dishes back to their house, I felt very guilty that I complain when sometimes the dishwasher is not working. We in the United States take so many everyday luxuries for granted.

As we walked along the streets, the natives were fascinated by us. Children would come up to Adri and ask if I would take their picture. One woman asked Adri: "Where are they from?"

"America." (Seems no one knows the term United States.)

"What are they doing here?" she continued.

And I thought to myself: *What ARE we doing here?* I was feeling worse by the minute. My head was stopped up, I felt like I had a temperature, and my back was killing me from walking for a long time lugging that heavy old purse.

We continued to stroll along in the heat from one house to another, seeking butterfly farmers. Apparently they were out of business or out of town. We finally came to one in operation, but he had the same kind of butterflies as the first man. Everyone had said that only one man had any specimens for sale, and he was gone for the day. However, if we waited, he should be back anytime. "Anytime" to them could mean days! His wife said she could not show us what he had for sale. At this point, we had been going around on foot for about three hours, and I was feeling terrible. Plus we had not seen any unusual butterflies, much less one the size of your hand!

"Adri, I have to sit down for a while," I murmured.

"Just sit here on the road side and I will go find our driver," he said and took off.

Keith and I plopped down on a concrete culvert by the side of the road. Sitting there in the hot sun with my back killing me, I knew I was coming down with Keith's cold and that I was running a temperature. The more I thought of feeling the way I did and staying at that place for the night, I could not endure it.

"I have reached a stage of my life at age sixty-five that I should not have to stay in a place where I will be miserable. And I don't know what we might catch by eating food prepared there. I want to go back to Palu tonight," I told Keith.

I think he was happy that I was the one to make that decision. When Adri returned with the Jeep and driver, we told him our plans. I felt sorry for him, but I could not bring myself to continue on our schedule. The more I thought of the lovely hotel in Ujung Pandang, the more this spoiled American wanted to get out of this area.

Around 10:00 P.M. we arrived back at the Golden Hotel, and this time, it looked as good as the Waldorf Astoria—private bath, good bed, air conditioning, and a door that would lock. Also, the thought of some ice for our drinks (an impossibility in the jungle) sounded heavenly. We had ordered ice the other night we were there without any problem. I called down to the front desk and told them we would like some ice (they did not have room service per se), and shortly a young man knocked at our door and said he was there to pick up the Thermos.

"We do not have a Thermos here in the room. What we want is some ice cubes," I stated.

Later he appeared with a Thermos filled with ice water. Keith took the Thermos back and told them we wanted ice cubes. Still no results. So I went down to the restaurant to explain what I wanted, and finally I was able to make them understand. I returned victorious with a bowl of ice cubes. That vodka gimlet and the air-conditioned room with a private bath helped immensely in soothing my ailments.

Much to Adri's distress, and also upsetting to me emotionally for I liked him so very much, we were able to change our flight from Palu to Ujung Pandang. It was a tearful moment when we departed. He had so wanted to be our guide and had made lots of special arrangements. I felt so sorry for him, but I just could not face any more of those sleeping arrangements, especially while sick. If this had happened in my younger and more adventuresome days, I might have given it a try. But at this stage of my life, no way.

As a going-away gift, Adri presented us a hand-painted bark cloth mat made by his relatives in his home village. He was such a dear and gentle man, and this job had meant a lot to him. We paid him in full, as if we had taken the complete tour. When asked who he wanted to lead their country, as this was in the midst of the new leader election, he replied: "Just a person that will keep the country and my family safe." He had a wife and three children—two boys and a girl.

Once home, I mailed him a package of T-shirts and six little girl dresses plus some of the photos of our stay there. Even though I sent them airmail, it was *six months* before he received them. This was a lesson. Next time I will send via UPS, so it can be tracked and will cost about the same as the U.S. mail. When I spoke to our postmistress about it, she said: "Anyone knows better than to send a package to a third world country!"

Back in Ujung Pandang and looking out our ocean-view room of the Sedona Hotel, I started feeling much better. Adri referred us to Jimmy, an associate travel agent there. With Jimmy we were able to go to a butterfly area outside the city and bought fifty-three butterflies, each properly preserved in plastic bags, just what we were looking for up in the jungles of Palu (with the exception of the hand-size variety).

We couldn't change our flight from Ujung Pandang to Bali, so we spent three days touring the area with Jimmy, seeing the mountains and farmlands. The highlight of each evening was sitting at our hotel window and watching the brilliant-colored sun sink into the blue ocean, with the silhouette of boats forming shadows on the horizon. I must have taken fifty pictures of this incredible sight.

Our last stop on this twenty-three-day tour was Bali. We needed to go there to connect with our Continental flight home, and we had loved the island so much on our two previous visits. Our reservations were at the Nusa Dua Beach Hotel, where we had stayed on our first visit five years earlier. Today the Sultan of Brunei owns it, and he has really spruced up the place. It was a beautiful hotel right on the beach to begin with, but was now totally redecorated. We were in the Palace Club section, which offered private check-in, free valet pressing of garments, and free video rentals. The rooms opened out to a tropical garden. All this plus a complimentary full breakfast in the morning, high tea with goodies at 4:00 P.M., and cocktails and buffet from 5:00 to 8:00 P.M. Due to all these freebies, we never paid for a meal while we were there, which, regrettably, was for only two days and one night.

With all the amenities, I can heartily recommend the Nusa Dau Beach Hotel and the Palace Club if you plan a trip to Bali.

# Africa

As I mentioned in the Prologue, "those wild animals in Africa" were on my list of top-three dream destinations. In Around the World in the Middle Seat I recorded our experiences in Kenya and Tanzania. I also reported on our cruise to the Canary Islands, Maderia, and Morocco.

## South Africa

In 1984 our group of twenty-four began our journey "From Cape to Cairo" in Johannesburg, South Africa. This country is filled with outstanding scenery and wildlife, and has a very colorful history. At the time of our visit, the country was looked down upon by many nations for its government's practice of racial apartheid and white supremacy. Today things have changed in this respect.

It was an eighteen-hour flight from Houston, Texas, to Johannesburg, South Africa, with one stop at Cape Verde Island. On this hour stopover, we were eager to disembark and stretch our legs. We were ushered into a small tin building that served as the terminal, and they locked the door. I don't know where they thought we could go in the middle of the pitch-dark night out on the stark, desolate island.

Every seat on the plane was full, with many screaming children. I had one youngster behind me (of course, I was in the middle seat) who continuously kicked the back of the seat. Johannesburg was a welcome sight, and the comfortable Carlton Hotel looked even better. After a champagne reception, we all retired to our rooms for some much-needed sleep.

The next morning we exchanged our dollars to South African rands. Our local guide, Sue, explained to us on our way out to a gold mine that there were 600,000 black workers in Africa, mostly working in the mines. Many had come from adjoining African countries, and the number of them had created deplorable living conditions. We passed a "shanty town" where illegal squatters were living in cardboard or old tin lean-to shacks with no sanitation or water facilities.

At the mine we were informed that gold was discovered here in the 1800s. They recover only about 8 grams of gold from one ton of rocks and dirt. A demonstration revealed the method of melting and then pouring gold into a mold to make gold bars, at that time worth $300,000 each.

To prepare for descent into the mine, we put on yellow raincoats, boots and hard hats with a headlight. We also strapped on belts that contained heavy batteries for the

light. A shaky elevator ride delivered us 790 feet below the surface. Some mines are more than 2,000 feet in depth. A few workers were using jackhammers to make holes in which they would load explosives to extract the gold. It was obvious this area was for the tourist to see and not a full working mine. I have claustrophobia and do not like to be underground, so I was glad to get out of there.

*We are all outfitted to go down in a South African gold mine.*

After a native dancing demonstration, we had time to shop. I bought a bushman rock art painting on a real rock that weighed about five pounds! This was not too smart to have to lug it around in my tote bag for the next twenty-four days.

A short flight south the next morning revealed Capetown, one of the loveliest cities in the world. It sits right on the sea, with the famed flat Table Mountain as a backdrop. This city was established by the Dutch in 1652 and became a place for ships to stop on their way from Europe to Asia. British convict ships bound for Australia used it as a place to restock their ships and buy livestock. Later British settlers came, which led to conflict between the British and Dutch. This resulted in the Anglo-Boer War in 1899, with the British as victors. The country was part of the British Commonwealth until 1961, when it became an independent state of South Africa.

Ninety miles from the city lies the Cape of Good Hope. Here the Atlantic and Indian Oceans meet, creating many shipwrecks. You can actually see the undercurrents and swirls of the water where the two seas collide. As I stood there with the fiercely strong wind in my face, I could visualize the tall sailing ships battling the forces of nature on these wild seas. All ships had to come around this horn to go from the Atlantic to the Pacific Oceans prior to the construction of the Panama Canal, which opened in 1914.

Returning, we passed through a game preserve and encountered many ostriches and baboons. At one place, the monkeys crawled up on our bus. Sue said that ostrich eggs are edible, and one is equal to twenty-six hen eggs. Now, that would make some omelet! Early Bushmen used the shells to store water when they traveled from one waterhole to the next.

This southern portion of South Africa is known for its excellent wines and vegetable gardening. A wine tasting at a local winery proved their savory flavors. At the university town of Stellenbosch we saw many Cape Dutch houses and an Anglican church, all adorned with Protea blossoms, the national flower. Since I returned from South Africa, I now notice this large, lovely pale pink blossom in many floral arrangements. We passed "Neerbust," the house where James Michener stayed while writing the historical novel about South Africa, *The Covenant.*

The next morning was bright and clear, perfect for our cable car ride to the summit of Table Mountain, so flat on top that it indeed looks like a table. Many times the clouds hovering over it resemble a white tablecloth. From the viewing point at 1,907 feet, we could see the city below and the beautiful harbor. Sue pointed out, a few miles from shore, Robben Island, where at this time Nelson Mandela was being held prisoner. The only comment she made when we asked about the prison was that the island was a place for political radicals. Mandela was released in 1990 and in 1994 became president of South Africa and was awarded the Nobel Peace Prize. He retired from office in 1999.

All around were comical little furry animals called "rock rabbits." They looked like guinea pigs to me, and they loved to eat anything the tourists would give them.

Capetown had marvelous seafood. We feasted on calamari, lobster, prawns, mussels, plus succulent vegetables and fruits. One evening our group was divided into pairs to have dinner in a Capetown home. The Capetown Overseas Hospitality Club consists of forty-five dedicated women. Their purpose, through personal contact with visitors, is to show the South African way of life and hospitality with the hope of removing prejudice and providing information regarding their country. The hosts were concerned about how other people of the world felt about them and their segregation policies. They were hoping to work out something amenable for all races, but believed that the news media had been unfavorable to them. We had an enjoyable evening of cultural and political exchanges.

Our route back to Johannesburg was aboard the legendary Blue Train that ranks right up with the Orient Express for comfort and opulence. The train was officially introduced in 1937, when the twelve new all-steel blue luxury sleeping coaches arrived from England. The train was out of service during World War II, and was named the "Blue Train" in 1946 when operation resumed. This epitome of train travel will accommodate 107 passengers.

Upon entering our compartment with private bath facilities, we were delighted to see a bottle of champagne and two souvenir Blue Train wine glasses as a gift. The meals were indescribable. When we sat down at the white linen covered dining tables, the first puzzle was which silverware to use - there were a total of 12 knives, forks and spoons at each place setting. Mother always said start at the outside and work in, and that is what I did. Lunch was a five-course gourmet event, followed a few hours later by a seven-course dinner. The only exercise was to walk back to your compartment or the lounge and watch the interesting countryside slide by. That night, after dinner we returned to the compartment to discover our day couches had been converted into inviting beds. As we sped northward through the country that night, we slept peacefully in the almost total silence of the train. (Guess one reason we slept so well was the welcome champagne and all that food.)

After a sumptuous breakfast the next morning, we pulled into Johannesburg station, where Sue greeted us. That afternoon we toured Soweto, a township of ninety square kilometers and home of two million black people. At this time, blacks had to live in this area by law. Unemployment was high and so was crime. They had their own schools, soccer stadium, beer halls, stores, hospitals, and churches. All houses were small, square boxes that had recently acquired electricity and water. The residents cooked with coal. It was a very depressing place. The day we toured Soweto was August 23, 1984. One week later, riots there started the breakdown of apartheid that eventually led to the freeing of Mandela and his election as president ten years later.

A visit to South Africa is not complete without visiting a diamond mine, one of their primary sources of revenue. Diamonds were discovered in 1868, and the largest found was the Cullinan Diamond that weighed 3,106 carats. It was presented to King Edward of England on his birthday. The huge rock was cut into smaller stones, some of which are in the British crown jewels today displayed at the Tower of London. We toured the Premier Diamond Mine and saw pictures of the Cullinan Diamond that is now gracing Her Majesty's jewels.

Pretoria, the capital of South Africa, is located north of Johannesburg. Nineteen miles of city streets are lined with lavender jacaranda trees that bloom in October and November. They were just forming buds when we were there in late August. This whole area is adorned with monkey pod trees, hibiscus of all colors, and bougainvillea.

Outside the city is the tall memorial dedicated to the Voortrekkers, the early Dutch settlers. A ring of sixty-four wagons cut in stone surrounds this imposing monument, and a stone frieze inside depicts the history of the people and relates the bloody war between the Dutch and English.

The Overseas Visitors Club in Johannesburg invited us to dinner at the local country club on our final night there. The evening began with cocktails and conversation with about thirty club members. In the dining room we were divided into four Texans and four South Africans at each table. Spirited dialogue ensued at each venue during the delicious dinner, complete with local wines. As we were having dessert accompanied with a South African orange liqueur called "Van-der-Hum," one of the women in my group rushed up to me.

"Joyce, come quickly!" I followed her, and to my horror and chagrin, I found that one of my group had slipped out of her chair and was completely under the table. You have heard of drinking yourself "under the table." Well, she had accomplished that feat, bigtime!

With the aid of Keith and another gentleman from our group, they pulled her out and I immediately saw that she was unable to walk. We sat her down in a chair, and the men carried her out in this fashion. I kept trying to keep her dress down as she flailed her legs around. She kept mumbling incoherently.What to do? Here we were in a foreign land, guests of these people, and we set this kind of an example for Texas and the United States. I was mortified! I instructed Sue to bring the others back to the hotel when they finished. Keith and I would take the embarrassment to the hotel in a cab. I quickly expressed my apologies to the hostess chairman, and we made our getaway.

When we arrived at the hotel, she still could not walk. I rushed in and asked a bellman to bring out a luggage carrier or dolly, the kind that has two wheels. We manhandled her out of the cab and stood her up on the luggage cart, strapping her on like we were moving a refrigerator. All this time, she had no idea what was happening. I had the bellman open the door to her room, gave him a good tip, and Keith and I sat her on the bed. I sent Keith on to our room. I undressed her down to her underwear and put her in bed. She was still out like a light. I sat there with her until her roommate arrived.

"We need to get her to go to the bathroom, for in her state of semi-consciousness, considering all she has drunk, she could wet the bed," I told her.

Between the two of us we drug her to the bathroom and sat her on the commode. "How are we going to get her to go?" the roommate asked.

"Turn on the water," I said. She turned the tap, and *presto!* Mission accomplished. We then took her back to bed.

I couldn't understand how she could get that intoxicated with just the beverages we had been served at the party. I looked around the room, and on the floor of the closet were two empty wine bottles. That was the answer. She had been half bombed when she arrived at the party, and the drinks there just completed the process.

*What am I going to do?* I wondered. We were only one-third the way through our twenty-six-day tour, and I had an alcoholic on my hands. I hardly slept a wink that night.

The next morning I went straight to her room and knocked on her door. To my surprise, she opened it, fully dressed, and said in a cheery voice, "Good morning, Joyce. Am I running late for breakfast?" Although she did not look too perky, there was no indication of what had happened the night before.

"Oh, no," I replied. "I just wanted to remind you that we fly out this morning and you need to have your luggage outside the room at 8:30. I failed to tell you last night."

For the remainder of the trip, I kept a close eye on her, and as far as I know, she never took another drink. Neither she nor I ever mentioned the incident.

# Zimbabwe

Our next country on this tour was Zimbabwe, just north of South Africa, formerly called Rhodesia. In 1970, Rhodesia proclaimed itself a nation independent from Great Britain, but the United Nations would not recognize it due to its policy of political apartheid. In 1980 apartheid was overthrown, and the country was renamed Zimbabwe. Over 94 percent of the country's population is black, and they were able to establish a Black African-ruled republic.

Our guide, Greda, met us at the airport in Harare. Her family emigrated from the Netherlands and had been manufacturing clothing there for many years. She said she would like to leave Zimbabwe, but you could only take $1,000 with you if you left the country. All your other possessions would become property of the state. As they were not ready to leave their home and financial security, they had to remain. She said she had sent her children to South Africa to go to school.

We drove through very arid country. This was in 1984, during the terrible drought in Africa. There was very little vegetation. An extraordinary sight in this vast expanse was several baobab trees that look like they are growing upside down. Legend is that God ripped the trees up and shoved them back into the ground top first, leaving what looks like the tree trunk and roots exposed and no leaves. The tree bears a seedpod that is used to make cream of tartar.

We arrived at the government-operated Victoria Falls Hotel. When we were in

*The baobab tree in Zimbabwe that looks like it is upside down.*

South Africa, the people at the country club had told us we would love this hotel. Obviously, they had not been there recently. It was apparently a lovely old colonial property at one time but had received no care or maintenance in several years. Our room had holes in the window screens, rips in the bedspread, and the curtains were badly faded.

A boat ride on the Zambezi River offered views of impala, elephants, and water buffalo grazing, but they were too far away to get a good photo. The magnificent sunset made up for everything. As we sailed back to the hotel, the sun cast its rays on the river, forming incredible shades of red, orange, and pink as it sank into the horizon.

Our reason for coming to this area was to see Victoria Falls. As this was during the drought, the falls were not at their best display, but it was still a very majestic sight. The falls are the largest in the world in width, divided in five separate waterfalls. Therefore you cannot see the entire falls at one time except by air. They exceed 350 feet in depth in places, and their spray can be seen shooting into the air from a mile away.

When he discovered the falls in 1855, Dr. David Livingston called them "the most beautiful sight— the most wonderful sight that I have witnessed in Africa." And I have to agree with him. A statue of him commemorates his discovery at the falls. The

*Dr. Livingston, I presume? This statue is located at Victoria Falls in Zimbabwe.*

falls had not been overly commercialized at this time. No carnival atmosphere that you find at Niagara Falls. When we were there it was pretty much the same way Livingston found it, with the exception of a bridge that has been built as a walkway over a portion of the falls, and the hotel. It is truly one of the great Seven Wonders of the World.

We returned to the hotel for lunch that was served outdoors under large shade trees. Romping around above us in the trees were many monkeys. What made these monkeys different from any others I have ever seen was that the males had blue testicles—a bright turquoise blue. Their bodies were gray all over, but the males had this added distinction. The monkeys were not friendly. After lunch, we were all sitting around enjoying a leisurely afternoon out under the trees. I was reading a book, and one monkey came right up to me and slapped the book out of my hand. Vanessa, of our group, was sitting not far from me, also reading. She had her little cloth tote bag in a chair next to her. The bag was open at the top and contained some more books

*These active monkeys disrupted our lunch, and then filled Vanessa's tote bag.*

and her sweater. Suddenly, we heard *plop!* A monkey in the tree overhead had pooped right in the bag. A perfect hit! All of it neatly fell into the bag and nowhere else.

"Joyce!" she screamed. "What am I going to do?"

"Throw it all in the trash. I have an extra tote bag for you."

The rest of us could not keep from laughing, but we decided we needed to move inside, despite the fact that there was no air conditioning in the hotel.

# Egypt

Following an eight-day safari in Kenya, we flew to Cairo. I wouldn't take anything for my visit to Egypt with all its ancient wonders, but I could not tolerate the way the souvenir peddlers stalked us, even when we denied eye contact (which usually works). They continued to pester us by holding the merchandise right in our faces. In all our travels, we have encountered all kinds of "trinket hawkers," but usually when you say a firm "no" or turn away, they will leave you alone. Not the case here. They were so persistent that we could hardly enjoy the sights as we toured Cairo.

However, the pyramids, and the Nile cruise were worth the hassles. When we arrived in Cairo, our guide, Raoul, told us that this was one of Egypt's newer cities, only a little over 1,000 years old, compared to Thebes and Memphis, which date back to more than 3,000 years. I was appalled that the city was so crowded and the poverty so bad that people were living in tombs originally built for burial. Raoul said that Cairo had over 17 million people—about the same amount who lived in the entire state of Texas at the time.

When I looked at the Pyramids of Giza, a short distance from the city of Cairo, I was surprised. Enormous blocks stacked in a slant form the pyramid, making the surface up close look like steps upward. From all the pictures I had seen, taken at a distance, I thought the surface was smooth. When I commented about this to Raoul, he said that originally there was an outer casing of smooth white limestone, but it has all deteriorated through the ages. He said that it took 100,000 workers twenty-five years to build this monument without any cement or mechanical equipment. The Great Pyramid covers about thirteen acres and originally was 481 feet high. Today thirty-one feet has worn off from the top. It was a magical moment to stand back and gaze at another of the Seven Wonders of the World as it has stood for over 4,500 years. I started to go inside the Big Pyramid, but when I approached the small passageway to enter, my claustrophobia took over and I immediately backed away. I was content to view the pyramids from the outside.

The poor old Sphinx has suffered the ravages of sand, wind, and time and the details are almost all gone. It was exhilarating, though, to actually be looking at something I had seen only in pictures for many years.

A camel and driver were nearby for tourists to have their pictures taken. I could not resist the opportunity. The camel was kneeling down, and the driver helped me into the saddle (which was very dirty and smelly). Upon command from the driver, the camel first stood up on his front legs and nearly threw me off the back, and then I tumbled forward as he rose up on his hind legs. I had no idea he was so tall! I felt like I was twenty feet from the ground. I had ridden horses during my younger years, and there was no resemblance. I told Keith to quickly take the picture so I could get

*My camel ride in Egypt was very brief.*

off the thing. I sensed the camel knew I was not a happy rider, and he turned around and tried to bite me. I screamed for the driver to stop him, and as I got off, the beast spat at me. The camel and I did not have a great rapport.

Our city tour included a papyrus paper plant, where we saw demonstrations of how in ancient times they made paper from the plant that grows in the river Nile. Of course, I had to buy a couple of pictures.

We lunched at the lovely Mena Hotel, built in 1869 by the government when the Suez Canal was under construction. The treaty to declare World War II against Germany was signed here. King Farouk, Egypt's last monarch, lived in the hotel until his death in 1965.

As we drove along the crowded streets of Cairo, we noticed that the men wore a "*galabea*," which is a long white shirt of Egyptian cotton that reaches the ground. The women wore long black dresses if married. All women had their head covered in the Muslim style. The day we were there was the religious holiday called Bairam, and all along the sidewalks were ceremonial lambs for sale.

You could spend days at the King Tutenkhammon Museum, but our guide directed us to the most celebrated items found in the tomb. King Tut's tomb was discovered in 1922, and it took eight years to remove and catalog the more than 2,000 relics. It is estimated that King Tut was only ten when he became ruler, and he died at the age of nineteen. What made the discovery of his tomb so important was that it was found nearly intact, not robbed or opened by thieves as so many other tombs of the Nile area. The young king's inner coffin was made of 242 pounds of solid gold. A beaten gold mask concealed the face of the mummified body.

We had to rise at 2:00 A.M. after a short sleep for our flight to Abu Simbel. As we approached Abu Simbel from the air we could see the Aswan Dam, the largest and highest in the world that formed Lake Nasser from the Nile River. The plane flew over the temples of Abu Simbel, guarded by the four colossal statues of Ramses II, the greatest pharaoh of ancient Egypt.

Next we were transferred to the Ramses monument. The sandstone statues, each almost seventy feet high, stood at the entrance. The temples are impressive, but what is inconceivable is that when the Nile was dammed to form Lake Nasser, these 3,200-year-old monoliths were going to be underwater. A project of UNESCO financed by Egypt, the United States, France, and Belgium raised $36 million to move and reconstruct everything. The temples and statues were cut into thirty-ton blocks and reassembled on dry land. As you stand in front of these monuments, it is unbelievable that they had been moved. There is no obvious evidence that the statues have not stood in that exact place for hundreds of years.

A short flight took us to Aswan, where we boarded our Sheraton *Golden Boat* for a five-day cruise down the Nile River to Luxor. The ship was comfortable and the crew accommodating. Our guide was Abdulla Amin Abdullah. He said to call him "Triple A," which we certainly did! He was very knowledgeable of all the ruins, temples, and gods. We took a ride on a small sailboat called a *feluca* to the other side of the river to see the mausoleum of the Aga Khan. AAA said the Khan was crippled with rheumatism so badly he could not walk, so he took a series of treatments of putting his legs in the hot sands of the Nile and was cured. Lovely botanical gardens landscaped the mausoleum, and AAA knew the name of every plant.

Daily we had many stops, including temples of Edfu, Esna, the Valley of the Kings (where we saw King Tut's tomb), Karnak, and Luxor. At each monument AAA would expound on the history of each king and the legend of the many gods. As this was the end of a twenty-six-day tour, all that information was too much overload for this tired old brain. It was interesting, but I was getting confused about Isis and Horus and all the others.

What Keith and I enjoyed most about the cruise was sitting on the top open deck and watching the parade of activity along the riverbank and on the water. The children bathing, women doing laundry, men fishing, grain being harvested, donkeys pulling loads, and people on bicycles captivated us. They would return our wave as we passed. The final night featured an Arabian foods buffet. I had no idea what some of the items were, but they were delicious.

Upon arrival at Luxor, 250 kilometers from our departure at Aswan, we flew back to Cairo to prepare for our flight home. We arose at 4:30 A.M. and rushed to the airport. Our passage through customs went very smoothly, and we were to take the bus to ride out to the KLM plane that was some distance away from the terminal. There was not enough room for my entire group to get on the first bus, so I went first and left Keith with the remainder. When we arrived at the plane, many soldiers with machine guns were all around. We were told to board the plane. I explained I needed to wait outside to see that the rest of my group arrived safely. The soldier did not take my request very well, and indicated with the machine gun I should get on the plane immediately. Somehow a gun pointed at your body tends to change your mind. Inside the plane we were advised the president of the country was departing soon, and when he makes a move, all traffic stops, delaying us about forty-five minutes. In the meantime, Keith hoped we had not left without them. Finally, the presidential party made its exit and the others were transferred to the plane. This was a rather dramatic climax to a very eventful tour from Cape to Cairo.

## Madagascar

I had always wanted to see lemurs in the wild, and the only place to do that is in Madagascar. We went to Tanzania in 1998, and since we had already flown that far, it was an excellent opportunity to visit the land of lemurs.

Madagascar, the fourth largest island (after Greenland, New Guinea, and Borneo) lies 250 miles off the east coast of Africa. It is about 1,000 miles long and 350 miles at the widest part.

The first people to arrive in Madagascar were from Indonesia and Malaya around the first century. A few Arabs settled in the ninth century. The Portuguese discovered the island in 1500, and for the next 200 years there were many unsuccessful attempts to establish French and British settlements due to disease and hostile natives. By the early 1700s, the island became a haven for pirates and slave traders. Our guide said that the slave boats loaded up in Africa, sailed to Madagascar, and at that point culled out the sick, too young or too old, and left them here. Thus the black population in the southwestern part of the island developed from this event. The northern inhabitants are primarily Malaya.

Andrianampoinimerinandriantsimitoviaminandriampanjaka. Yes, that was a real name of the man who led the rise of the powerful Merin Kingdom in 1794. He succeeded in conquering and uniting all the island's tribes, and his descendants ruled until the French took over in 1896 and the monarchy was abolished. The French controlled until 1960, when the country achieved independence. From 1975 to 1991, the country was under Communist power. Our guide said that she remembers, as a child of nine, that there were no presents at Christmas during this time.

We flew from Nairobi, Kenya, stopping in the Comoros Islands. A varied assortment of people boarded the plane—women in colorful India-type saris, other women in African Masi attire, men in long white shirt/gowns (Egypt-style), plus the usual western dress. Keith and I were certainly the minority.

We arrived at Antananarivo, Madagascar. As you can tell, they like long names. However, everyone refers to the capital as Tana, thank goodness! The city is built on two levels. The lower portion features a lake and the top part was where our hotel perched on the mountainside.

Our guide, Wangi, welcomed us. I had read an article in a travel magazine written by some travelers who had just returned from Madagascar, and they commented that Wangi, their guide, was very good. So I requested her to be our guide when making our reservations. This was a wise move. She was our constant companion the entire trip, which was a comfort, because there were times we did not feel very safe. She ate every meal with us and stayed in a nearby room when we were traveling throughout the country. Her knowledge of the flora and fauna was remarkable, and she made our trip very informative and delightful.

Upon arrival in Tana we went to the Hotel Colbert. Apparently they were not crowded at this time, for they gave us a three-room suite when we had only paid for a standard room.

The next morning Wangi took us on a city tour. Poverty is very prevalent, but the markets did offer nice-looking produce. We saw meat hanging in the open air, though, adorned with flies. I noticed a large number of people standing outside a storefront window.

"What are they doing?" I asked.

"Watching TV," she explained, "for many do not have a set of their own and this is the only way they can see television."

We flew to Fort Dauphin on the southwest tip of the island. From there we went west via private car of the seventies vintage. Our driver could spot wildlife at the same time he tried to miss the enormous potholes in the road. The French constructed the asphalt roads, but there had been little or no maintenance since their departure in 1960. As we drove along, we would come to a sudden stop and he would point out a chameleon lizard or a tree frog. We got a big kick out of one lizard, about a foot long, that was crossing the road. He moved in a back-and-forth motion that reminded us of a pro football player's dance in the end zone after a touchdown.

After about fifty miles of dodging holes, sometimes driving in the ditch, we arrived at Berenty Reserve, known for its tame lemurs. I can attest to that claim. When we arrived at the reserve headquarters and motel, about twenty lemurs ran out to greet us and jumped up on the car hood. I assumed we would have to tramp through the jungles to see them, and here they were as a welcoming committee, practically knocking us down!

Our accommodations were clean, but basic. We were awakened at 4:30 the next

*Cute, bug-eyed lemurs are everywhere in Madagascar.*

morning with sounds of jumping on the roof overhead, plus various high-pitched screams and noises. I first thought it was some kind of bird, and then I looked outside. Many, many lemurs, all sizes, filled the trees by our room and in the yard. The protected reserve of Berenty is known for its population of ring-tailed and brown lemurs. They are lovable creatures with bright round bug eyes and fluffy long tails, about the size of a medium monkey, and definitely as active.

A young woman with a clipboard was standing among our visitors outside. She was from England conducting a five-year research on the habits of lemurs for her Ph.D. This was her third visit. She travels to Madagascar for two months the same time each year to study the life of the lemur. She had named most of them.

"This family consists of thirty-seven members, dominated by two females," she explained. "Lemurs are territorial and mark their property, which can cover about fifty meters, with scents of musk secreted from the wrist and anal glands. The female is the dominant ruler of the clan, and she is receptive to mating for only one week in April or May. This leads to much competition between the males for this once a year treat. The babies are born in September, and for the first few weeks cling to the mother's stomach, and then later climb on her back for riding jockey style. Lemurs eat fruit, flowers and insects, plus nearly anything that you will feed them."

Our breakfast offerings were custard apple juice that tasted terrible, toasted French bread, honey, and a pot of tea. It was served in the motel's open dining room, attended by many lemurs, wanting a handout. There certainly was not enough food there to share! Afterward we took a walk through the reserve forest, and saw many lemurs and birds, but not as many as we had experienced right outside our motel window.

That night we took a walk in the reserve seeking the Mouse lemur, the smallest one of the species. It was spooky as just Wangi, Keith, and I tramped through a jungle in the dark with only Wangi's spotlight for illumination. There were trails to follow. We were fortunate to see three of the little rascals with their beady eyes shining from their nests in the hollow of a tree. As we started walking back to the van, we heard singing and drum music. I couldn't imagine where it was coming from. As we reached the entrance of the park, there, in total darkness, sat a group of natives chanting away. We figured they came out to serenade us for a tip, so we obliged. I was glad to get back to the motel.

Nearby was a sisal plantation and factory. It was interesting to see how they take a plant that looks a lot like a skinny century plant cactus, strip the spike leaves with a machine, and then put the pulp on racks to dry in the hot sunshine. It is then sorted in bundles to be made into twine or rope. Sisal has become one of Madagascar's top exports, with more than 30,000 hectares then in production.

The ride back to Fort Dauphin offered many changes of scenery, from forests with cactus to palm trees. One unique tree was the bottle tree, its trunk shaped like a Coke bottle. The villages, occupied by black people, were extremely poor. A one-room wooden shack about eight feet square had only a dirt floor for sleeping. Cooking was by an open fire outside. There was no water or electricity. Their diet consisted mainly of rice and sweet potatoes. Even though they are not far from the sea, they do not fish. They derive their meager living from cutting the trees and making charcoal, which is offered for sale along the road. This activity is consequently totally deforesting this area. The children were either naked or dressed in tattered clothing. I had some writing pens to give them, but Wangi said not to, because they had no paper to write on and they don't go to school.

Back at the city, we spent the night at the Miramar Hotel. In our room we were alarmed to see the following posted notice: (This is verbatim.)

*Sisal, a rope material made from a cactus plant (shown here drying in the sun) has become a profitable export for Madagascar.*

*Poor villages are found on the southern portion of Madagascar. Their only means of income is making charcoal from the trees and therefore deforesting the area.*

Owing to nuisances undergone by tourists, we like to inform our kind guest:
—To be very careful when you walk by foot, especially in all zones where there are no or few circulation.
—Take care of your objects. When you're followed by people who're interested by, but who finally wait you to pass in the remote place for tearing away your camera, bags, etc.
—By these alive examples, any object stealing was neither found nor gave back despite of the official complaint deposited.
—To avoid begging and for respecting the peace at the hotel, we wish you not to buy shell necklaces, etc. in the front of the hotel.

After reading this, we certainly did not go outside the building without Wangi.

We flew from Fort Dauphin back to Tana, changed planes, and then continued north to Nosy Be, a small island just off the northwest coast. We chose this destination because it is the place to see the rare black lemur. Wangi had arranged for a local guide, John Robert, to take us to our hotel about fifteen miles from the airport. We stopped at a gasoline station at Hellville (appropriately named). The driver put in only three liters, about ¾ of a gallon of gas! I certainly hoped his car got good gas mileage. The car was a funny little French model, and to shift gears he pulled a lever in and out.

Our hotel/motel was in the village of Belle Rye, and destitute conditions were all around. The residents wore bedraggled clothes and even looked hungry. The property was on an enclosed compound right next to all this poverty. The rooms were right on the beach, and that is about all I can say it had going for it. The beds were hard, the shower provided only a trickle of water and the area around the plumbing was all rusted. An air conditioner made all kinds of noise, but did produce a little cool air.

Wangi had planned a day excursion to a nearby island, Nosy Komba. John Robert (apparently he had bought more gas) picked us up and we traveled several miles to the eastern side of the island. We were instructed to take our shoes off and walk out to a long dugout outrigger canoe for our journey across the bay. I fully understood the wide influence of American television when I saw the boat captain's three-year-old son with his cap on backward! We were in one of the most remote places in the world, and the backward cap craze had reached even that place.

After about an hour's ride, cramped in the dugout canoe, and bailing water all the way, we had to stop about 500 yards from the village shore due to the low tide. We walked in on the soggy sea floor. The villagers were ready for us with their handmade cutwork tablecloths swinging from clotheslines in the wind, shells, and woodcarvings displayed around the trees. This was a typical Malagasy Village consisting of small wooden houses with palm leaf roofs and dirt floors. These handsome people seemed to be a cross between Malay and African heritage and their skin was light chocolate color. The village apparently existed from tourist trade, as some cruise ships stop at Nosy Be.

After refreshments of fried bananas and Coca-Cola, we embarked on an "Indiana Jones" jungle walk. This was truly a jungle walk—no trails—and the guide had to hack our way through with a machete. It was a rewarding wildlife trek. We saw the black lemurs, plus brown and gray ones, as well as chameleons, a tiny poisonous frog with an orange belly, and many snakes. I was supporting myself as I went along the slick and uneven path by catching hold of the nearby trees. As I grabbed around one tree limb, right above my hand was a snake coiled around the branch. I nearly had a heart attack! The guide assured me that it was not a poisonous snake, but I couldn't care less. To me a snake is a snake!

The jungle contained all types of plants: pineapple, jackfruit, the essence tree for making perfume, vanilla trees, pepper plants, and mango, all growing wild. After about three hours walking in the humid, hot jungle, I was ready to return to the village. Out on this remote island, we were served one of the best meals we had in Madagascar. We feasted on shrimp, beef on skewers, fish, crab and rice, all prepared by the village women over open fires. Bananas and mangos completed the delicious lunch.

When we returned to our hotel that evening, passing through that pitiful town, Keith and I agreed we would like to cut our visit short at Nosy Be. We did enjoy trading for shells with the native girls on the beach. But we never felt safe at that hotel. Wangi was able to change our airline tickets to return to Tana a day earlier than scheduled.

The lovely Hotel Colbert looked like a wonderful secure haven when we returned. That evening at dinner we visited with a woman from the United States. She said she was making a survey of Madagascar's population, environment, and economics. When I inquired how her report might benefit the local people, she stated she was not sure.

Our last excursion in Madagascar was to Perinet, a special reserve for the Indri Indri, the largest of the lemurs. This was about a four-hour drive east from Tana, and to our relief, the road was paved and without the many chug-holes we had experienced in the south of the island.

Our hotel was the new and comfortable Vakona Forest Lodge. Individual bunga-lows encircled the main lodge, where appetizing food was served in a large open din-ing area. We were elated to encounter a birdwatching group from Austin, Texas, run-ning around with their cameras on tripods, seeking sights of rare specimens. Wangi

*The horrible-looking fruit bat—not something you want to meet or eat!*

said that a large percent of Madagascar's tourists are bird-watchers due to the abundance of rare bird life on the island.

A walk from the hotel on a gravel trail was very thrilling. As we ventured into the jungle, we began to hear an eerie, wailing sound that our guide said could be heard for up to two miles. This was the roundup call of the Indri Indri. This lemur stands about three feet with barely any tail. The long tail was the most distinguishing feature of the other lemurs we had seen. This species is black and white and resembles a panda. It can propel itself up to thirty feet between the forest trees. The calls were spine-tingling. We would just stand still as they came leaping through the trees overhead. Their heavy weight caused the tree limbs to swing violently back and forth, and they would appear right above us, usually in groups of a family of five. An incredible sight! Madagascar has thirty species of lemurs, and we were victorious in seeing twelve of them.

On the return drive to Tana we stopped at a Butterfly and Reptile Farm where we added to our butterfly collection with some special purchases. Here we saw in enclosures many species of butterflies, lizards, frogs, snakes, and the horrible-looking fruit bat. It has a body about one foot in length, large head and ears, sharp teeth, and a wingspan up to three feet. It hangs upside down from the trees during the day and hunts at night. A terrifying sight!

Our last night was back in Tana at the Colbert Hotel. One thing we noticed about Madagascar: no McDonald's or Kentucky Fried Chicken. The only American influence we saw was Coke and very little television.

It was now time to leave Wangi and continue our trip to the Seychelles Islands. I travel with a pocket video poker machine to pass time while waiting in airports and other places. Wangi was fascinated by it. She had never seen a video game before, and did not know how to play poker. I showed her how, and let her play with it for the last few days of our trip. When we left, I put the poker machine in the envelope with her tip. I think she was more thrilled over it than the tip we gave her. She may have started a video game craze in Madagascar!

# Seychelles Islands

The Seychelles Islands are promoted as a paradise and Garden of Eden. As we were so near when we were in Madagascar, I wanted to go see for myself. Unable to get a direct flight from Madagascar to the Seychelles, we stopped overnight about midway on Mauritius Island. We stayed at the elegant LaPirogue Resort right on the Sugar Beach. This was a perfect place to catch our breath after hiking through the jungles looking for lemurs. We were so excited when room service brought us a big bucket of ice—something we had had difficulty obtaining in Madagascar.

A gigantic buffet was served at a lovely outdoor beach location. I was so ecstatic over all this luxury and wide selection of gourmet food after our recent austere experience, I walked away from the table, leaving my purse with our passports, airline tickets, money, credit cards, everything necessary to our travel. It was the first time in my life I had ever done such a careless thing. When we returned to the room, as I was getting ready for bed, I looked for my purse to get my contact lens case. Then it hit me. I rushed back to the dining room, explaining my loss to the waiter. Some nice man had seen me leave the purse at the table and had turned it in to the headwaiter. Everything was intact, but my blood pressure. This was another example that there are many honest and wonderful people in the world.

Mauritius, one of the Indian Ocean islands, centers on an imposing extinct volcano that monopolizes the skyline. The island was settled by the French and is now independent, but English is spoken everywhere. It is densely populated, with more than 850,000 people living in 720 square miles. They derive their living from small fields, salt export, and tourism. We had requested a tour the morning before our late afternoon flight. Our guide did show us some of the island attractions but became very upset when we did not want to go the diamond showroom or buy a sailboat in a bottle. Apparently these are the two most important items to sell tourists on the island, and I am sure he would get his cut from the sale. He seemed very unhappy when he delivered us to the airport.

Over 100 islands make up the Seychelles, but only a few are inhabited. It was dark when our plane landed on Mahe, the most important of the group. We finally found

*Mauritius has a beautiful beach and many wonderful resorts.*

transportation to our hotel, the Sun Resort. Everything is very expensive, and we chose an off-beach property that was very nice and not so pricey. We were on an airport transfer bus that made stops at several hotels. Arriving at the Sun Resort, I jumped off to register and thought Keith would get our luggage. He picked up everything except my roller bag, which is always my responsibility. After our luggage was delivered to our room, I discovered my bag was missing. Keith thought I had my bag, and I thought he had it. In that bag were my cameras, our "ditty bags" with all our necessary toiletries and medications, plus the vodka, which at this point, I certainly needed. I called the woman in charge of the hotel and explained our problem. She contacted the transport company, who said the driver had already gone home in the bus. I could not sleep worrying about my loss. Last night my purse, and today my bag. It was time to go home! The next morning, about 8:00 A.M., there was a knock at our door. There stood the hotel manager with my bag. I wanted to kiss her! Everything was there, including the vodka!

The Sun Resort was very comfortable. We had a bedroom, sitting room, and small kitchen, complete with ice in the refrigerator. We hired a car and driver for an island tour of Mahe. The Seychelles Islands are the only mid-ocean group of granite islands in the world, as most islands are volcanic and coral. The granite forms striking designs along a dramatic coastline, with occasional exquisite white sand beaches. The island has luxuriant foliage of all types of tropical plants.

*Granite boulders and sand form a striking beach in the Seychelles Islands.*

The Seychelles were settled by the French in 1770 and changed hands many times until ceded to Britain in 1814 and in 1976 obtained their independence. Even though they were under British rule for a long time, French remains the primary language; in fact, it is difficult to find anyone who speaks English. Most of the tourists are from Europe, primarily from France. We were the only Americans everywhere we went in the Seychelles. However, one Frenchman told me he was surprised to see us at a moderate-priced resort, for most Americans stayed at the more expensive ones. Maybe that was why we never saw anyone from the U.S.

After two nights on Mahe, we flew Air Seychelles (small plane with two propellers) twenty-five miles to Praslin, the second largest island. We chose to go there because this is the location of the Vallee de Mai, home of the 100-foot-tall coco de mer palms that bear the largest fruit in the world. Legend has it that this valley was the Garden of Eden, where Eve gave Adam the forbidden fruit.

We stayed at Maison Des Palmes, recommended by my agent in the U.S. who knew the owners and said that they spoke English. In reality, the wife was the only one on the place who spoke our language! But the resort was perfect for us. We had a private bungalow about twenty feet from the ocean. When we arrived, colorful fresh flowers were adorning the bed, lights, pictures, and even on the commode in the bathroom. Breakfast and dinner were included in the room price. Everyone was so hospitable to us, and we managed without verbal communication most of the time.

The meals were typically French and the food very good. One night they had what they titled a "native food" buffet. Little nametags accompanied each dish. We approached one rather unappetizing container entitled "fruit bat stew." After seeing those ghastly looking things up close and personal in Madagascar, I could not imagine anyone eating them. I am usually game to try new foods, but I certainly passed by this one.

Our package included day tours. The first day it rained (really poured) all day long, so we were forced to remain inside. The next day the weather cleared, and we were able to go to the Vallee de Mai. In our tour group of fourteen, we were the only English-speaking passengers. Even though our guide was multilingual, she first explained in detail everything in French, and then commented a few sentences to us in English. We did get to walk through the Vallee and see the tremendous coca de mer palms and the fruit. It takes twenty-five years to produce fruit from a seed. A mature plant will produce a nut at seven years from pollination. The fruit can range in size up to two feet in length. Because this is the only place in the world that has these trees, the Seychelles government regulates the fruit. To bring one home, the fruit has to be bought from a registered agent and have the proper stamp affixed. The fruit from the inside is removed, so it is permissible to bring to the United States. We did find one, and paid way too much for it, but we now possess a genuine coco de mer. For some reason, when I show it off, people do not seem to be impressed. Guess you had to be there to fully appreciate its rarity.

*Keith holds the rare coca de mer fruit, found only in the Vallee de Mai on Praslin Island in the Seychelles.*

We visited a small coconut plantation and had the opportunity to eat all the coconut meat we wanted (not good for those with high cholesterol). Next came another rain shower. At lunch, our guide came to me and said she had located another English-speaking couple from another tour, and had arranged for us to sit together. They were from London, and regretfully, we could hardly understand them. They certainly had difficulty understanding our Texas drawl. We eventually mastered each other's accent and had a pleasurable meal.

The next day the rain came again, and being at the end of an extremely long trip that had begun in Tanzania, and taken us to Madagascar, Mauritius, and now Seychelles, we were tired and wanted to go home. We canceled our tour over to the Bird Island and flew back to Mahe. Unable to change our tickets, we rested an extra day in Nairobi before we embarked on that long flight back home.

The Seychelles Islands were pretty, but I was a little disappointed. I had read so much about their unique beauty, but I feel that Bora Bora or even Hawaii equals or surpasses them. Perhaps my view is clouded because we were tired at the end of the trip, or that we had such difficulty with the language. If you are in the area, be sure to visit the Seychelles, enjoy their beautiful beaches, and see the one-of-a-kind coca de mer fruit.

# Europe

As a rule, the first trip abroad for people from the United States is to Europe. Years ago, it was fashionable for the rich to send their young graduates for a "tour of Europe," and later it became a place for young backpackers. I agree that this is probably the best first foreign destination for Americans; however, I advise to go first to the British Isles—England, Scotland, Wales, and Ireland. Here you have no problems with the language. Just remember to drive on the left and look first to the left when you are crossing the street.

Europe is like a colorful collage—many different cultures and traditions so closely blending together. Today, with the Euro currency in most of the countries, traveling between them is much simpler. Europe is steeped in history, and most Americans can trace their heritage to some part of this continent. I think one thing that impresses me about Europe is that everything is so old, compared to the United States. I am also amazed that many speak several languages, where the majority of Americans know only one, and that is in the dialect of the region where they live.

I recommend visiting one or two countries completely instead of the "eight countries in seven days" tour. You will have a more rewarding trip, plus you will be able to remember what you saw and not spend all your vacation time on the bus going from one country to the other.

We have been to all the European countries and to some part of Europe eighteen times, and I loved every country. However, Paris, France, was the first place I wanted to go, and I was forty-two years old before I accomplished that dream. I tell of this city in my first book. Paris still is my favorite city in the world. There is no more beautiful place than this city illuminated at night.

I am going to share with you some less traveled destinations on this remarkable continent.

In August 1988, a year before the fall of the Berlin Wall and decline of Communism, I led a group to the "Capitals of Eastern Europe."

# Czechoslovakia

Maupintour offered a tour in 1988 of the leading cities of the Communist Block Nations. I received notice from one of my favorite guides, Jan, that he was going to be leading this tour, so I immediately booked it. I had fourteen in my group, and we joined thirteen other members from the U.S. and Jan at the origin of the tour in Prague, Czechoslovakia.

My Austin passengers changed planes at JFK Airport in New York, where we were to meet Ruth, one of my group, from Minnesota. Her plane was late, and she did not make the connection. All during the flight over, I kept worrying about her, an older woman, and how she would manage on the trip across the Atlantic alone. At Prague, our local guide, Kay, asked the airline to check on Ruth, and they confirmed that she would arrive later that afternoon.

Another member of my group, Millie, did not receive her bag when we arrived in Prague. The airline gave her an emergency kit to tide her over. Millie laughingly told us that the kit contained a toothbrush, toothpaste, a comb, some aspirin, and a condom. (I guess they wanted to cover all emergencies.)

Kay and I went out to the airport to meet Ruth and pick up the delayed luggage. She drove a little Czech car. When she came into the airport, somehow she drove in the wrong way and immediately a policeman stopped her. She was terrified that they would take away her driving permit. But when we explained we were there to pick up a stranded American, the policeman let her off without any trouble.

My first impression of Prague was what a charming city it was, containing many architectural splendors, some of which are of the finest Baroque and Art Nouveau styles in Europe. The buildings have remained in their original elegance because the Czechs allowed Hitler's troops to take over the city without any violence.

Kay stated that everything was arranged in Czechoslovakia according to plan by Russia. The schools were free and compulsory for eight grades, followed by two years of technical school. After that, college was for those chosen on scholarly ability and family position in the Communist Party. The country had one of the largest sports complexes in the world, and they concentrated on gymnastics

*The Church of Our Lady Before Tyn located on the Old Town Square of the beautiful city of Prague, Czechoslovakia.*

from the age of two. The Russian language was compulsory, plus the student could choose one other language (such as English, French, or Spanish). They had total freedom of religion, but it was not encouraged and citizens received better jobs if they did not attend church.

All commercial goods were made in Czechoslovakia and the Soviet Union. In the market we saw fresh watermelons, peaches, tomatoes, and cucumbers. The group reported that the beer was excellent. As I am not a beer drinker, I can vouch for the delicious wines.

Prague is a beautifully preserved ancient city on the river, and the Prague Castle high on the hill is the centerpiece of the area, commanding attention at night with its full illumination. The food was good and the cultural entertainment outstanding. I saw no billboards in the city.

My notes on Prague: "On the surface the city looked very attractive with clean streets, and the people were well dressed in modern western clothes. They appeared happy and healthy. Many of the old buildings had scaffolding on them, but we did not see anyone actually working, and there was practically no new construction."

## Poland

Our next stop was Warsaw, Poland. Upon arrival at the airport, we had to fill out a currency form indicating how much money we were bringing into the country. If you were not on a pre-paid tour, such as ours, you were required to spend $15 per person per day (certainly you wouldn't be living very high on that amount). Driving into the city, the only billboard I saw was one advertising Hatachi televisions.

The 700-year-old city of Warsaw was totally destroyed by the Nazis in World War II. Before the war, Poland had 380,000 Jews, as this country was one of the best places to flee Hitler's wrath. During the war, all the Jews in Warsaw were confined in the Jewish Ghetto and suffered starvation. Many were sent to concentration camps or shot in mass executions on the street. In 1944 the remaining Jews were killed when they staged an uprising against the Germans. Hitler gave orders to totally destroy Warsaw to set an example for all cities of Europe that would go against him. It took two months for the soldiers to burn and dynamite all the buildings that had taken 700 years to build. Today on the city square you can see a movie depicting this appalling destruction.

The country has tried to reconstruct some of its statues and buildings to look like the originals, using whatever pieces could be recovered. But most of the architecture is the typical Soviet square or rectangular gray block buildings, making the city very unattractive.

We drove about thirty-five miles outside the metropolis to Chopin's birthplace, a quaint cottage in a park. We were honored with a private piano concert of the master's music. Chopin was born here in 1810 and gave his first concert at the age of eight. He died in France in 1840 and was buried there, but his heart was

*The pianist who performed our private piano concert shown here at Chopin's birthplace in Warsaw, Poland.*

brought back to Poland and interred in the Warsaw Holy Cross Church. There his heart would always remain—in Poland.

Our guide said that it could take up to twenty years to obtain an apartment in downtown Warsaw. Most families have refrigerators, but they have difficulty finding meat and a variety of fresh vegetables. When we were there, fruit was plentiful in the markets, but the offerings did not seem to be of very good quality. We were advised not to drink the water, and the purchased mineral water tasted terrible. Opportunely we had a refrigerator in our room and could drink chilled vodka (makes the old, ugly buildings look better).

My impressions of Poland were: "All the buildings were gray concrete blocks and look the same. Everything in Warsaw had been rebuilt since 1945. The people were not as well dressed as in Czechoslovakia, but more in an older European manner. They seemed healthy and happy. They had lots of Fiat cars. Petrol and meat were rationed. If they wanted more than the allotment, they could purchase it at a very high price on the black market."

## Union of Soviet Socialist Republics

I grew up during the cold war, and had been brainwashed to fear the Russians and the possibility of their attacking us at any moment. When I visited their country, I was totally unprepared for what I saw. In my mind, here was a country that had put men in space, had tremendous military power, plus the atomic bomb, so I expected to see a very advanced country. Granted, they have accomplished the previously mentioned things, but their poor people have suffered greatly. When we were there in 1988, Gorbachev was introducing his political and economic reforms, but they had not come into effect. When we visited St. Petersburg in 1990, we could see some improvement. But in 1988, the average Russian was standing in long lines for very poor-quality merchandise. They were working in state-appointed jobs, all at the same rate of income and still living in an atmosphere of fear. Fortunately, these conditions have improved during recent years.

In 1988, the USSR was the world's largest unbroken stretch of landmass consisting of fifteen republics of more than 150 nationalities that spoke over 67 different languages plus numerous dialects. The country was ruled by the czars from 1613, when the sixteen-year-old Mikhail Romanov began a dynasty that was in power until the revolution in 1917. This was when Lenin seized control and immersed the country into Communism until 1988, when Gorbachev reduced repression that later led to the independence of the fifteen republics. A new confederation of independent states emerged in 1991, with Yeltsin as president of the newly formed Russia state.

But back to 1988 when we were there. We flew from Warsaw to Leningrad (now changed back to the original name of St. Petersburg). Located in the north on the Neva River that flows a short distance to the Baltic Sea, Leningrad is Russia's second largest city and was the capital until 1918. Peter the Great founded the city in 1703 (thus the name St. Petersburg) to give Russia "a window looking on Europe," as it is just across the Gulf of Finland. Because royalty built it, many wonderful palaces and museums abound.

We arrived at the Leningrad Hotel around 10:00 P.M. and had to wait a long time in a very dark and dreary lobby for our guide to obtain our room assignments. The only lights in the place were at the registration desk. Everything else was dark. When we finally received the card indicating our room numbers, a very slow and small elevator took us to our assigned floor. There we presented our card to the floor attendant (a very solemn-faced lady), and she gave us a key without uttering a word. Our room had one window with a view of an ugly purple building and a small pond covered with green slime, created from some excavating for an addition to the hotel. It looked as if the project had been abandoned. The furniture consisted of two narrow beds with a thin mattress on a board, a small chest of drawers, and one chair.

We were instructed not to drink the water. The only place to buy bottled water, since we arrived at night, was in the bar. Up to the bar we went. The bartender stated that we could purchase bottled water only with Russian money (rubles), which we had none of as we had just arrived. They wouldn't let us charge it to our room or use a credit card. So, without water, we did the next best thing: We brushed our teeth with vodka! Not bad—you should try it. (The next morning we exchanged some money for rubles, and after we bought the water, I wanted to stick to the vodka. The so-called mineral water had rusty-looking flakes in it. We had to strain it through a handkerchief before we could drink it.)

We finally retired at 1:00 A.M., and it still wasn't totally dark outside. Being this far north, the sun never fully sets during the summer in Leningrad. In contrast there are very few hours of daylight during the winter.

The next morning we gathered in the dining room as a group for breakfast. (In Russia, everything was done as a group.) Tables had been set aside for us. At the end of each table were some opened, room-temperature Pepsi Colas. I can't stand Pepsi when it is cold, much less this way, but I found it was a good alternative to the terrible mineral water. Breakfast consisted of some watered-down egg mixture, fresh tomatoes, and a hard roll.

Each meal we had the same waiter. Word got around that he would exchange money at a much greater rate than we could get at the bank or hotel. This is the way his system worked: He would serve the bowl of soup (which, incidentally, was the only thing fit to eat at that hotel) and then would say (in perfect English), "Exchange money." If you wanted to do so, you nodded your head and then put the U.S. bills under the bowl. When he came to remove the empty bowl, he picked up the money. When he brought you your entrée, the rubles would be under the plate. He gave us about five times the number of rubles we could receive at the hotel exchange, and it was such a smooth operation.

Some people in our group wanted to buy caviar. He was obviously stealing it from the kitchen. Anyway, the purchase of the caviar worked the same way as the money exchange, and he was selling a tin of the fish eggs for about one-half the price in the hotel gift shop. Many of our group did business with him, but not being caviar enthusiasts, we did not participate in this event. We noticed at our last meal we had a different waiter. When we asked where Boris was, we were told that he had been fired for stealing caviar from the kitchen!

Our local guide, Helen, had been Nancy Reagan's personal guide when she had visited the city earlier in the year. She was fabulous. Her English was flawless, and she knew all the history and culture of the country. She worked for the Russian State as a

*We had some fun at a party in Leningrad as the waiters dressed up in Russian military costumes.*

guide. Helen declared that she was not a registered member of the Communist Party, and to our surprise she said that the majority of the population of Russia were not members of the party.

The most important attraction in Leningrad is the Hermitage, built as the czar's Winter Palace. Today six buildings of the complex serve as the museum. I wanted to see the art collection at the Hermitage because I had read that its collection was comparable to the Louvre in Paris and the Prado in Madrid. From what I saw—no way. It appeared to me that they were doing nothing to preserve these valuable art masterpieces. Helen informed us that the Hermitage had three million items of art. At that time the Hermitage was not climate-controlled. Windows were open, and the humidity coming in from the sea was very high. The lighting came only from the open windows, so it was difficult to see many of the art details. They also did not restrict flash photography, which many tourists were using with great rapidity. It was so hot and crowded that the Hermitage visit certainly was no pleasure.

The most impressive attraction to me of the czar reign was the Treasury. Here we saw many of the royal jewels and ancient ornaments. I was particularly interested in the intricate and lavish Fabergé Egg Collection. When Lenin took power in 1917, he requested all the royal buildings and furnishings be protected for the people.

A hydrofoil took us forty kilometers across the Gulf of Finland to the Summer Palace, a magnificent castle with fountains and gardens that rivals Versailles, French King Louis XIV's palatial edifice. Peter the Great wanted his building to be as splendid as the castle in France. At the beginning of World War II, the palace had 92,000 pieces of art. Only about 7,000 of them were saved from theft or destruction by hiding them in the Ural Mountains in Siberia. The Nazi soldiers made the palace their headquarters during the 1,000-day Siege of Leningrad and they destroyed most of the buildings and furnishings. When we were there, the Russian government was in the process of restoring the palace to its original beauty. Each room had a picture of before and after, to show how they were progressing with the refurbishing.

Our next royal building was Catherine the Great's Palace (Peter the Great's wife—glad to know she was also Great) at Pushkin, a short drive from the city. The Germans used this palace as a barracks during the siege. The mansion was built in 1710. The main floor had fifty-five rooms, twenty-two of which had been restored by the time we visited. In many places, the original walls were of amber gemstone. It was reported that the original sheets of amber were last seen being loaded on a train by Nazi soldiers, and it is still a mystery what happened to them. When we were there they were working to put up sixty tons of new amber on the walls and hoped to have it completed by 1990.

Helen said that Hitler was planning to use the czar's palaces as one of his retreats when he defeated Russia, but we all know how that turned out.

That evening our dinner consisted of hot Pepsi, fairly good soup, some indescribable meat with cabbage and tomatoes, plus lovely-looking dessert pastries, which tasted like cardboard.

Afterward Keith and I went walking by the River Neva, which faced our hotel. A young man who wanted to "trade pins" approached me. Jan, our Maupintour guide, had told me to bring lapel pins from the U.S. to trade with the Russians, so I had some Texas pins with me. I was eager to exchange my Texas pin, and did so, for one with a picture of the *Aurora*, a ship that was now a monument in the harbor in front of our hotel. It was from this ship that the first shot in October 1917 was fired in revolt against the Hermitage.

When we went to a local food market, I was shocked. On the shelves were brown bags of sugar, flour, coffee, salt, and all types of staple foods. There were no brand names; pictures indicated what they were. No meat was available. The only fresh produce were some tomatoes (must have been the season for them), three half-rotten lemons, and some terrible green grapes. Cheese, milk, and eggs were also in plain containers. The outside store windows displayed pictures of produce, meat, and other items that should be inside, but when you entered, there was hardly any merchandise for sale. I wished that these Russian housewives could have one day in our bountiful supermarkets. They wouldn't believe it.

As foreigners, we were eligible to shop in the "dollar stores" that only took hard currency (U.S. dollar, French franc, German mark, British pound, or Japanese yen). The store did not accept the local ruble, and only tourists and high-ranking members of the Communist Party could shop there. The inventory was mostly souvenirs, but they also had electrical appliances and a small selection of grocery and beverage items.

Helen requested that instead of a tip, she would prefer a food mixer, which we could buy in the dollar store but she could not. So we collected enough money and Jan purchased it. She was thrilled when we presented it to her.

Reminiscing on Leningrad: "The general shopping areas had no merchandise displays in the windows, just pictures of what should be inside such as clothing, food, and the like. Entrance was by just one door, and people lined up outside with their shopping bags in hopes of buying something. The only thing they have to show the tourist was from the czar nobility era. The food and mineral water were terrible. We saw no single-family dwellings. Everyone lived in an ugly apartment building constructed of the typical Russian gray concrete blocks and all about the same height, three or four floors. The grounds around the living areas were un-maintained, and we never saw children playing around the buildings. Everyone seemed unhappy. Practically all natives wore western clothing of poor quality—the older women usually had a kerchief over their head. We never saw anyone laughing; no one smiled at you when you smiled at him or her. A very depressing sight."

*In Communist Russia, everyone had a job, even though it might not be what they wanted to do (as the lady street cleaner demonstrates).*

We flew on Aeroflot, Russia's national airline, to Moscow. We were informed that the entire fleet could be transformed into military planes in twenty-four hours. And I believe it. The uncomfortable airline seats looked like the ones I've seen in pictures of military transports. Once airborne, a flight attendant came around serving "leemoonaid," at least that is what it sounded like. A small paper cup held some yellowish-looking liquid that might have had one drop of lemon flavor in it, but even that was questionable.

Arriving at the Moscow airport, once again we had to proclaim how much money we were bringing into the country (even though we had already gone through this act in Leningrad) plus list any jewelry in our possession and cameras, video recorders, etc. Our Moscow guide was Linda, a college girl dressed in very modern clothes. She wore blue jeans and a T-shirt with the English words "Anything Goes." I asked her where she purchased her clothes and she openly stated, "From the Black Market." She was a sweet girl but had only been a guide a few months and after having the experienced and talented Helen, she was very lacking in comparison.

The first thing we learned is the correct pronunciation of Mos-co, not Mos-cow. It is a pretty city with a river that meanders through the metropolis for about eighty kilometers. The streets are very broad, lined with enormous buildings.

We were taken to the Cosmos Hotel on the north side of the city. The view from our hotel room was the Space Monument and a communication tower that was said to be the third largest in the world. When we reached the hotel, we were advised that the hotel was overbooked and that the single women in our group would have to double up. Millie and Ruth were my two single women sharing a room. They put Mrs. E (not in our Texas group) with them. During the tour we had realized that Mrs. E. had acted a little strangely, such as not dining with the rest of the group and going out on the street and buying things to eat.

The next morning Millie and Ruth rushed up to me. "We can't stay with that crazy woman any longer," they said.

It seemed that she slept in the nude (something that these sixty-plus-year-old ladies did not think too highly of), and that she was sick all night, throwing up and continually talking in her sleep. I am sure her illness was due to eating food from street vendors. I told Jan that if they could not move Mrs. E, that Keith and I would give Millie and Ruth our room and we would go to another hotel, or sleep in the lobby, anything to keep them from having to endure another night. When Jan went up to check on her, he ascertained that she was very ill. He took her out to the airport and put her on a plane homeward bound.

After noticing we didn't have any soap in our bathroom, I went out in the hall and found a maid, but had no luck trying to explain what I wanted. I returned to my room and took two of the lipsticks I had brought as gifts. I went to the hall lady, who spoke English, and had her write down the word "soap" and our room number in Russian and gave her one of the tubes. Then I took the note to the maid and handed her the other lipstick. I've never seen a woman so grateful. I thought she was going to kiss me! When we returned from our city tour, we had ten bars of soap in our bathroom.

Moscow was founded in 1174 and in 1988 had a population of 8.8 million. We noticed many buildings had "CCCP" on them, which means "USSR" in Russian. To me their alphabet is very unusual, with letters upside down and backwards, but I am sure our alphabet is strange to them.

Our first stop on the city tour was Lenin's Mausoleum. Linda told us to leave our purses and cameras on the bus, as we weren't allowed to carry anything into the tomb and couldn't even put our hands in our pockets while in the area. Soldiers checked us at the entrance. We queued up in the long line packed mostly with Russians.

Once we reached the tomb, a rectangular, unadorned building, everything was dark and we had to go down steps. (I thought of the lawsuits that could be made from falling down here if we were in the U.S.) Then my eyes were drawn to a light shining on the body in a dark suit lying on a marble slab. His skin looked like wax. I was ready to get out of that ghostly place as soon as possible. Looking at dead people is not my favorite thing.

Outside the Mausoleum were statues of all the Russian premiers except Khrushchev (apparently not in favor with the right guys). The only ones I could recognize were Stalin and Brezhnev. On the wall were square black plaques listing names and dates of birth and death of high Communist Party members. Vases of red carnations were on the ground below each plaque.

The most important sight in Moscow in my opionon is Red Square, dominated by the colored, ornate, onion-shaped domes of St. Basil's Cathedral. This is always the background for TV reporters broadcasting from Moscow, and it is truly an extraordinary building, unlike anything I have ever seen. St. Basil's was commissioned in 1555 by Ivan the Terrible to be built on the edge of Red Square. The cathedral was constructed to commemorate Ivan's military defeat of the Tartar Mongols. The victory came on the feast day of the Intercession of the Virgin, so the czar named his new

*A long line forms outside Lenin's Tomb in Red Square in Moscow to view the former leader's wax-like body.*

church the "Cathedral of the Intercession of the Virgin on the Moat" after the moat that ran beside the Kremlin. Later the church was nicknamed "St. Basil's" after "Basil Blessed," who was popular with the people of Moscow at that time.

This Russian masterpiece has eight pillar-like towers crowned with multicolored domes, plus a ninth tower with a tall tapering top whose composition has no parallel in the entire history of world architecture. The final and ninth addition was erected in 1588 to hold the tomb of the church's namesake, Basil the Blessed. The glazed tile inserts of brilliant colors and gilt iron coils and roof spirals achieve a festive appearance. I bought a painting of St. Basil's from a street artist and always enjoy looking at it, fondly remembering our times in Russia.

St. Basil's has had its narrow escapes throughout history. In 1812 Napoleon was so impressed with the building that he wanted to take it back to Paris with him. Unable to do so, he ordered it be destroyed when the French retreated from the city. Miraculously, a rain shower distinguished the fuses the Frenchmen were trying to light, saving it from destruction. During the Communist regime in 1819, the cathedral was closed down. Later it was suggested that St. Basil's be knocked down to create space for public parades on Red Square, but Stalin rejected the idea. Today the country continues to renovate the most beautiful ecclesiastical building in Moscow.

St. Basil's Cathedral is at the end of Red Square; the home of the Kremlin is behind nearby stone walls. While we were standing in the Plaza admiring St. Basil's, five black Mercedes cars suddenly came roaring out at top speed from the Kremlin. People had to run to get out of the way.

Across from Red Square is GUM's, the largest department store in Moscow. The store is enormous, covering several floors. The building was erected in 1893 and is a large open structure with a glazed roof. As we walked through, we noticed many completely bare shelves. The fur coat department seemed to be the only area with ample merchandise. The shoe department contained only very poor-quality footwear. We came upon a long line of women. I inquired what they were waiting for, and someone said that a shipment of bedspreads had just arrived. Although they didn't know what the bedspreads looked like, these women wanted one regardless. The guide said the reason the women always carry shopping bags is that they never know when they might be able to buy something.

*All Russian women carry a shopping bag in hopes of finding something to buy.*

While browsing through GUM's, we found some souvenir nesting dolls we wanted to buy. The Russian method of shopping was new to us. First we selected the items we wanted that were displayed behind a counter. The clerk gave me a slip of paper with a number. Then I went to another desk and stood in line to pay. The items were totaled up on an abacus! This ancient apparatus was the only method of addition at the finest department store in a country that has put a man in space. After payment in rubles, I was given a receipt. Then I had to stand in another line at the pickup area and give the receipt to the clerk. Another saleslady wrapped the dolls and handed them to me. This process took about thirty minutes. There is no fast shopping in Moscow.

I had the best time trading with the youngsters for pins. Jan had told me to bring bubble

*My souvenirs of Russia: the many pins that I traded bubble gum for, my painting of St. Basil's on Red Square, and three sets of nesting dolls.*

gum, and I know the kids must have smelled it. Every time I was out on the street they approached me to trade pins for bubble gum. By the time we left Russia, I had thirty-six different pins. I now have them proudly displayed in a frame as a special keepsake.

All the pins depict Soviet leaders or symbols of Communism. One even has Lenin's baby picture in a red plastic star frame.

A circus performance at Gorky Park was very much out of the ordinary. There were trained camels, cats, dogs, porcupines, kangaroos, pelicans, monkeys, elephants, horses, and birds. Afterward we drove by to see Red Square illuminated at night and then stopped at the new nearby Baskin-Robbins for ice cream. The shop accepted only hard currency, so we paid for it with U.S. dollars. I thought how sad it would be if you were a Russian grandmother with only rubles and couldn't buy your grandchildren an ice cream cone in your own city with your own currency.

We were told that the average Russian had quite a bit of money, but nothing to buy. We commented that in the United States we have too much to buy and not enough money.

Inside the Kremlin walls we strolled past government buildings and five cathedrals. We were told that Ivan the Terrible founded the Kremlin area that was later inhabited by Napoleon and now served as headquarters for the Communist USSR government. We were admitted to the Armory, a museum filled with royal clothes, carriages, jewels, valuable icons, all types of armor and weapons, plus more Fabergé eggs, dating back to the czar's reign.

One thing that caught my attention was the lemonade dispenser along the sidewalks. These resembled a Coke machine, but there was an indentation that held one glass (real glass). You put your ruble in the machine, picked up the glass, and held it under the spigot for the lemonade. You drank it, and replaced the glass back in the holder for the next customer. I stood back in shock as I watched people drinking from these communal glasses. Perhaps it's too cold here for germs to grow, but I certainly didn't want to partake of any street-side lemonade.

Our farewell dinner in Moscow was at the Georgian Restaurant, a well-known café located downtown. Our tables, set in a private dining room, contained one liter of vodka and a bottle of wine at every other place setting. We were served the best meal that we had in all of Russia. Many of our group did not care for or drink vodka. However, one couple among us seemed to enjoy it very much, so the unused bottles were passed on to them. They were not members of my Texas group, and because I was sitting at the other end of the table, I was not aware of what was happening. The man became so smashed that when we started to leave, he could hardly walk. He used a cane to walk anyway, and in this condition he certainly needed it. As he approached the doorway, which had a small step, he fell down and broke the cane in three pieces. (Yet another time I wanted to crawl into a hole because of the actions of a tour member.) Jan and Keith picked him up and carried him to the bus. I certainly was glad he was not a member of my group or my responsibility.

When we asked about religion in Russia, we were told that since 1917, citizens eighteen years or older have total freedom of choice in religion. Obviously, if you have not had any religious training prior to age eighteen, it is unlikely that you will start going to church; thus mostly older folks attended the churches. They said that there was complete employment, although not everyone had the job they wanted.

My notes on Moscow were: "St. Basil's Cathedral and Red Square are very impressive. I would not take anything for the opportunity to stand in their midst. I had the most fun trading bubble gum for pins. The people dress more fashionably than in

Leningrad, but everyone still seems very unhappy. Vodka is drunk straight without ice, sometimes chilled, sometimes not. Workers go about their jobs very slowly and without any enthusiasm. They stand in line for everything. The subway, which was very fast and efficient, looks like a museum with colorful art on all the walls. Calculating the purchases on an abacus in GUM's blew my mind."

I am overjoyed when I read and see on the news that conditions appear to have improved since 1988, when we were there on this tour. I felt sadness for this educated race that had financial means for a better way of life but were unable to obtain it, and for the unhappiness that seemed universal throughout the country.

## Romania

The first thing we noticed when we landed in Bucharest, Romania, was the difference in climate. Here it was 86 degrees, while the weather had been so nice and cool in the previous countries. The Hotel Intercontinental provided much nicer accommodations than we had experienced in Russia. Our spacious room had a balcony, providing a view of the skyline that was crowded with building cranes. From our vantage point we counted forty building cranes!

The Communist dictator at the time, Ceausescu, had destroyed the old city and attempted to create a new one of Paris grandeur. He did not achieve the appearance of the French city, however, instead building monstrous, Stalinist-type buildings. He had had difficulty finding funds and experienced workers, and the project was less than half completed when he was overthrown and executed in the December 1989 revolution. These people had every right to revolt. What we saw when we were there in 1988 was a hungry and obviously very discontented population.

I have read that since the revolution, Bucharest has neither the will nor resources to tear down or complete the buildings, resulting in a city of half-constructed monuments and decaying facades.

Our guide related that Romania was a country of 23 million people divided into three parts: Bucharest, Moldavia, and Transylvania. We, of course, asked about Count Dracula, and were informed that Dracula is purely fictional. However, many say that the character was patterned after Vlad the Impaler (sometimes known as Dracula). Vlad was Romanian and was known for his fondness for impaling enemies on a stick. Residents of Transylvania have capitalized on the Count Dracula stories for tourist purposes, offering special Halloween tours.

After World War II, the country became a People's Republic under the Communist rule. Bucharest had two million people at the time of our visit. The city was first referred to as Bucharest in 1459, when Vlad the Impaler issued a decree.

In 1977 the country suffered a terrible earthquake: 8 points on the Richter scale. The United States sent aid, and included in the shipments was a carload of Kent cigarettes (certainly a necessary item for quake victims). Anyway, the poor Romanians had been smoking those horrible Russian cigarettes, and when they inhaled the Kents, they were hooked. When we were there Kents were the top-selling cigarette brand, but very expensive and difficult to obtain. Jan had told me to bring a carton of Kents, and at the time I did not realize their importance.

We had lunch at an old café called "Beer Wagon," established in 1879. With the exceptional superior lunch, beer was served in very old and attractive beer steins. I asked Jan if I could purchase one of the steins for a souvenir.

"You can try, but wait until everyone is out of the room, for all the group will want one," he advised.

When the room was cleared, I asked the manager (who spoke English) if I could buy one of the steins.

"Yes," he replied. "It would be ten lei" (their currency, amounting to less than $1), and he started to hand me the stein. Jan had advised us not to exchange any money because all our meals were prepaid and we could only buy souvenirs in the state stores that took dollars. I explained that I did not have any local money and tried to hand him a dollar bill. It was against Communist law to accept foreign currency, and he shook his head.

Then I remembered the Kents. I reached in my bag and took out one pack of cigarettes. This traumatized the manager; he just stood there. When I did this, all the waiters gathered around us to witness the incident. At this point, I took out another pack, and *presto*—that did it. In a matter of seconds, one waiter rushed up to the manager, put 10 lei in his hand, took the stein, handed it to me, I gave him the two packs of Kents, and Keith and I quickly exited. Not one word was exchanged. I acquired a unique souvenir, plus a very good story as well.

Romania is known for their spas and anti-aging pills and creams. We stopped at one spa and every woman on the tour, including me, purchased some cream, but I haven't seen any overwhelming results.

Meditating about Romania: "All those building cranes and no one working on the buildings. The poverty and unrest of the people. Children were begging on the streets. The power of Kent cigarettes. I tipped our local guide and driver with the cigarettes, and I had never received such appreciation."

## Bulgaria

Sofia, Bulgaria, was our next Eastern Block country. We stayed at the Sheraton Sofia Hotel Balkan. Behind the hotel were city ruins said to be 7,000 years old. Bulgaria's colorful history had many rulers, but after World War II, it, too, was part of the Communist regime. However, Todor Zhivkov, the country's leader from 1954 to 1989 (fall of Communism), allowed the farmers to have private plots and industrial growth to prosper. Thus this country fared better for the Bulgarians than their Communist republic counterparts.

This was evident as we ventured around the city. The fruit and vegetable market revealed plenty of quality produce. I bought a bottle with a wooden sculpture inside it from an old woodcarver. He explained that they used the bottles with the wood-carvings to store their plum brandy, as the wood aids in the aging process. I was delighted to have it because of its authenticity and because the date of June 10, 1988, is inscribed in the woodcarving.

Bulgaria is known for its rose and rose oil production, used in all fine perfumes. Rose petals are picked from 4:00 to 7:00 A.M. for the rose oil. It takes 3,000 kilograms to make one kilogram of rose oil, and they export seventy percent of the world's production of this product.

Memories of Bulgaria: "The people have much more food and merchandise than in previous Communist Block countries and appear happier. Bucharest is the oldest settlement in Western Europe. Many of the ancient ruins have been excavated for viewing today."

# Hungary

Our last city of this Eastern Block Capital tour was Budapest, Hungary, located right on the romantic Danube River. After being in the previous Communist Republics, it was refreshing to come to this colorful country with its beautiful landscapes and rich folk gypsy heritage reflected in food and music. Even though this country was included in the Russian Communist Block, they seemed to have thumbed their nose at the Soviets and gone about their own way of producing farm products and having updated commercialism. When we questioned our local guide about this, she replied that Hungary was the farthest country from Moscow and bordered the free country of Austria, therefore making it easier to trade with the free world.

We could look out from our hotel window at the famous blue Danube River, although at this time it was not blue but muddy brown. The city is divided into two parts by the river: Buda, the old city on the hilly side, and Pest, the new city located on the flat side of the river. The Allies bombed all six of the city bridges during World War II. The bridges have been rebuilt, so it is easy to travel from one part of the city to the other. Budapest has attractive old buildings, and we did notice a red star perched on top of the Parliament Building, which was the Communist headquarters.

Budapest is known for its Turkish baths. In fact, there are 123 pools in the city. (We did not have time for a dip). A cruise on the river offered wonderful vistas of the picturesque metropolitan area. The last night of the trip, we had our farewell dinner in the dining room on the top floor of our hotel. From the windows we could see lights on the mountains up on the Buda side, plus, something I thought a little ironic, a bright neon LEVI sign.

Hungary reflections: "This country is by far the most progressive and free of the Eastern Block countries. The people are a proud race, and this is mirrored in their folk art and food. If I had to live in a Communist country (and thank God I don't), I would certainly want it to be Hungary."

On the flight home, we had a plane change at Frankfurt, Germany. In the departure lounge we found some bananas at the duty-free shop. We paid $1 each for them, and it was worth every cent. We had just spent twenty-two days with hardly any fresh fruit. There is nothing like a trip such as this to appreciate the good old United States of America!

# Switzerland—Italy—Germany

On our first car trip through Europe in 1976, Keith and I drove in Switzerland to St. Nicholas, where we left our rental car and boarded a train for Zermatt. This enchanting Alpine hamlet does not permit cars within its city limits, thus adding to the allure and old world ambiance. Horse-drawn carriages meet the train to transport you to your destination.

*The only means of transportation in Zermatt—horse and carriage.*

Our hotel, the Romantica, looked just like a picture postcard of Switzerland. The building, an A-frame, had a balcony laden with flower boxes overflowing with bright blossoms. I had selected it because they offered separate guest cottages that were like a "Heidi" house. (I'm partial to this because my daughter is named Heidi, and I had read the book many times to her.) Our cottage was apart from the main building. It consisted of a tiny sitting room with a loft for the sleeping area and an even tinier bathroom, complete with a small sit-down tub. We could just make it up the narrow stairway to the loft, but I loved the atmosphere and uniqueness of the place. That evening we took advantage of the local dishes, enjoying a flavorsome dinner of cheese fondue and white asparagus soup.

When you arrive in Zermatt, you are immediately drawn to the stunning view (hopefully it is a clear day) of the Matterhorn, rising 10,170 feet. You can take the cogwheel train up to near the top. Disney did a good imitation, but nothing can compare to the real thing—breathing in the crisp, clean air with the snow-roofed triangle mountain so close to you. Skiing is possible all year round, as the snow never melts near the peak.

As we walked back down to the train station to depart the next morning, I had to get just one more look at the famed Matterhorn. I was walking backwards along the street when I stepped into a hole and, I thought, sprained my ankle. It swelled up and was very painful, but this was my first trip to Europe and I was not going to let anything like an injured ankle ruin it. So I kept going, bearing the pain. Nine days later, when we returned home, the soreness was gone and I just had a little puffiness around my ankle bone, which never went away.

About ten years later, I was playing tennis and fell. I thought I had broken the same ankle. We rushed to the doctor. When he examined the x-ray, he commented: "Well, you do not have a broken ankle this time, just a bad sprain. But at some time you have chipped a bone and it is suspended in the ankle area, causing that swelling. However, since it is not bothering you, I advise to just leave it alone."

To this day, I still have a puffed-up ankle, my souvenir of the Matterhorn.

I always wanted to return, and several of my "faithful followers" were interested in attending the Oberammergau Passion Play in Germany in 1990, so I decided to design a trip to that area of Europe to include many places I had always wanted to see.

Our group landed in Milan, Italy. For the city tour, our guide was an old woman, with not a tooth in her mouth. She had snuff drippings on her white tour guide's uniform. She had been a tour guide for thirty-two years, and she knew her stuff (and, I assume by her appearance, dipped her snuff). We saw the original painting of *The Last Supper*. It was awe-inspiring to actually view the real masterpiece after looking at copies on Sunday school cards as a child. The next day we drove through scenic northern Italy to Lake Como, to stay at a hotel I had read about and dreamed of one day visiting.

Listed as one of the top ten hotels in the world, Villa d'Este is opulent with old world charisma. It is located in one of the most beautiful spots in the universe, right on the banks of Lake Como in northern Italy, not far from the Switzerland border.

Lake Como, only two miles wide and thirty miles long, is surprisingly one of the deepest lakes in Europe, at 1,235 feet. The depth creates the brilliant aquamarine color of the water. Lush, dark green foliage grows right down to the water's edge, and in the background you can see the blue-tinged foothills of the Alps.

*The opulent Villa d'Este Hotel on the banks of Lake Como, Italy.*

This piece of paradise originated in the mid-1500s as a summer residence for a cardinal and passed to various aristocratic families of Europe's nobility. In 1815, Princess Caroline of Wales, wife of King George IV of England, fell in love with the place and bought it. She gave it the present name of Villa d'Este. Reports were that she and the king were not getting along very well, and she wanted to get away from London. She lived at Villa d'Este until 1820. Afterward it was home to various elite, until 1973, when a group from Milan purchased it and transformed the property into a lavish hotel. The Droulers family of Europe managed it when we were there.

Throughout the years, the Villa has undergone complete streamlining in order to provide beauty and up-to-date service. The facade has been left intact, and none of the old-fashioned allure has suffered. The guest rooms have the intimacy of an elegant private home, and no two are exactly alike in either color or décor. The main fabric in draperies and wall coverings is silk, as this area is known for its silk production.

The gardens, some areas developed over one hundred years ago, are beyond description. It is a renaissance-style park, highlighted with elaborate mosaic walls, columns of mythical figures, fountains cascading into reflecting pools, and an artist's

*The view from our window at the Villa d'Este revealed manicured gardens, fountains, and statuary.*

palette of colorful flowers everywhere. Carefully shaped shrubs line graveled walks and stairways.

Along with the splendor of the building and grounds, amenities abound. There is a unique heated swimming pool floating on the lake, a children's pool with a private sandy beach, an indoor swimming pool with an ultra-modern sauna and gym, eight tennis courts, plus water sports (with instructors available). Our group enjoyed the leisurely boat trip on the lake, stopping at some of the picturesque villages for an ice cream cone or a glass of local wine.

Dinner that evening was in the Verandah Dining Room, an enclosed area with electrically controlled glass screens that can instantly turn the space into outdoor dining enchantment. We had a separate section of the dining room, and special menus with our group's name printed on the cover. Our pre-ordered meal consisted of homemade noodles and salmon, veal chops with vegetables in mozzarella cheese sauce, concluding with orange mousse with strawberry sauce—delectable! After dinner we enjoyed our coffee out on the terrace. The September evening was perfect to view the lake, with shimmering lights from the villages, and even the moon cooperated by reflecting full on the mirror surface. In the background, strains of a piano in the bar soothed us even more. We had only two days and one night in first-class grandeur, but it was heavenly. I recently noticed that rates for the Villa d'Este ranged from $600 to $1,300 per night, including breakfast. Aren't we glad we went when we did!

Following the included gourmet breakfast the next morning, we began our spectacular ride over the Alps to the area where we caught the train to Zermatt, Switzerland. Here, where no cars are allowed, we walked up to our hotel, while our luggage came by carriage. That evening Keith and I went down memory lane as we found a restaurant that served white asparagus soup, and stopped by the Romanitica Hotel, where we had stayed fourteen years earlier. The flowers were still blooming profusely.

We awoke to a glorious morning, with the sun shining brightly on the magnificent Matterhorn. Our group rode the cog train up to the mountaintop restaurant, where we enjoyed fantastic views and lunch. The train ride down the mountain was exceptionally crowded. One European couple had their Scottish terrier with them. The dog kept sitting on one of my group member's feet. Suddenly, she felt something warm through her canvas shoe, and we all noticed a very unpleasant odor. The dog had pooped right on top of her shoe! The embarrassed owner tried to clean her shoe as best he could, but she still had a brown stain—a special souvenir of Zermatt.

The next morning we boarded the *Glacier Express* train for our ride through the alpine country of snow-covered mountains, picturesque old-world villages and farm people waving along the way. We arrived at St. Mortiz, a French winter resort for the rich and famous, nesting 6,000 feet high in the Alps. Our hotel was the Schweizerhof, which offered a splendid view of the lake. When we ordered ice for our evening cocktail, I handed the delivery boy my usual $1 tip. He said it was not enough—the price was three Swiss francs ($2.40) for about six ice cubes. In all our travels, this is the first time we were charged for ice. Welcome to the jet set resort!

We traveled through eastern Switzerland and Austria to Ettal, Germany, located in a narrow mountain valley of the Western Alpine foothills. The centerpiece of this village is the Abbey of Ettal, established as a monastery in 1330. Suffering

The impressive Matterhorn as seen from the village of Zermatt below.

through many trials and wars, the abbey has continued to maintain its Benedictine monastery, where monks study and also brew up some excellent beers and liqueurs they sell to the public. We stayed in Ettal to attend the Oberammergau Passion Play, located just three miles away.

It was early September, and the morning we attended the play it was overcast and very chilly. The venue that seats 5,000 is in a semi-building, with many areas open to the outdoors. We had bundled up, but the cold air was rather uncomfortable.

Every ten years since 1633, the residents of Oberammergau present the Passion Play, performed the first time when they were spared the plague. The play has become a worldwide attraction. Actors speak in German, but translation booklets are handed out in all languages. I didn't need an interpretation, having known the story of Christ since my childhood days in the Baptist church. The actors were brilliant; live animals helped in the realistic portrayals. I was horror-struck as I witnessed Judas' hanging, and could not look when Christ was nailed to the cross. The sound of the nails being pounded into his hands and feet were very realistic. It is impossible to explain the soul-searching feeling of witnessing this spiritual event. I can highly recommend attending this once-every-ten-years spectacular. However, the play is very long; it lasts all day with a break for lunch. This provides you with time to stroll around the storybook town, with its fairytale paintings on houses and dazzling flowers in window boxes. On the down side, many of my group developed colds from sitting all day in the uncomfortable weather.

Another highlight of this tour was a visit to Mad King Ludwig's castle, Neuschwanstein, the one that inspired Walt Disney in the creation of his Magic Kingdom's centerpiece. I had thought the Disney World and Disneyland castles were something, but I had not seen anything yet! The real thing is overwhelming in size, located right on a lake with the snow-covered mountains as a backdrop. The interior décor of royal blues, reds, greens, and gold is lavish. Every surface is intricately decorated.

King Ludwig built three elaborate castles, all located within close proximity to each other, but my favorite is the "Disney original."

The next stop was Salzburg, Austria, where we stayed at the Golden Hirsh Hotel, located in the heart of the city. As we boarded the bus for our city tour, our guide was playing a tape of *The Sound of Music.* He said we were going to see the places were the film was made, including the house, lake, bridge, and beautiful rose garden. I could envision Julie Andrews and the children skipping through the grounds as we drove through the area. Later we visited Mozart's home.

A short drive took us to another place I had always wanted to see—Hitler's Eagle's Nest, located in the Bavarian Alps near the town of Berchtesgaden. Special tour buses brought us up the steep and hazardous climb on Germany's highest road to the entrance of the Eagle's Nest at 6,000 feet. We entered a tunnel that led to a brass-plated and green leather elevator, decorated with mirrors. Reports are that Hitler had claustrophobia, and the mirrors helped him feel better while in the enclosure. The elevator rises 300 feet through the mountain to reach the Tea House, Hitler's private mountaintop resort that was presented to him by the Nazi regime on his fiftieth birthday in 1938. Our guide said that Hitler did not like the place, fearing

*The entrance to Hitler's Eagle Nest outside Berchtesgaden, Germany.*

he might get stranded up there, but Eva Braun loved it. Today it is a restaurant and tourist attraction with superb views of the surrounding mountains. Somehow, it was completely missed by repeated air raids during World War II.

# Mediterranean

In 1989 my group had an overnight flight to Barcelona, Spain, where we boarded the *Royal Princess.* Keith and my documents stated that our room had a partially obstructed view. As group tour leaders, you do not have a choice of your accommodations—sometimes they are great, and other times not so great. Upon entering the cabin, Keith and I noticed that there was just some low equipment in sight and were pleased that we could see out so well. As the ship readied for departure, we were horrified to see the gangplank pulled up and stored right in front of our windows! The only thing we could see outside by peeking around the blockage was if it were daylight or dark.

From Barcelona we sailed for a day, and the next scheduled port of call was Cannes, France, with an excursion to Monte Carlo. The wind was so high the captain announced that we could not go into the Cannes port. I was so disappointed to miss Monte Carlo, since I had always wanted to "break the bank at Monte Carlo."

Some years later I led a group to France with a day excursion to Monte Carlo. Although I did not break the bank, and gambled a very small amount of money, I came out with more than I invested in the slot machines. One emotional experience in Monte Carlo was the visit to Princess Grace's tomb inside the Monaco Cathedral. The inscription on the tomb does not refer to her as "princess" but as "prince's wife," which is traditional in the House of Grimaldi.

*Princess Grace's tomb in the Monaco Cathedral.*

But back to the Mediterranean cruise of 1989. Instead of Monaco, we stopped at Livorno, Italy. There wasn't much to see there—just some clothes and souvenir shops and a large open market. The ship overnighted in the port there. The next day buses took us into Florence, about a two-hour drive.

Florence, the Italian city that abounds with history and art, grew wealthy from wool and banking from the thirteenth to the fifteenth centuries. A profusion of poets, painters, and sculptors created a ceaseless stream of exquisite works of art. To name a few: Dante, Boccaccio, Giotto, Donatello, Botticelli, Machiavelli, Michelangelo, and Leonardo da Vinci.

Through my research I knew what Keith and I wanted to see, so we elected to try it on our own instead of joining the ship's guided tour. We were afraid we would spend more time getting on and off the bus than actually seeing things plus being trapped for two hours at an Italian lunch. Unfortunately, we had only one day, and to fully savor this city of art, you need days or weeks.

We bounded off the transfer bus and rushed to the Piazzale Michelangelo for a panoramic view over the city and a stop at a public toilet that cost 200 lira. Then we rushed downtown to the Uffizi Museum, encountering a line about a mile long (the ship excursion people). Not wanting to waste our precious time standing in a line, we went to the Duomo (Cathedral). Arnolfo di Cambio designed this building with its freestanding Campanile (bell tower). Construction began in the thirteenth century and continued for 140 years before it was finally consecrated. This is a cathedral to end all cathedrals. It can accommodate over 20,000 people and is the second largest in the world, after St. Peter's. It is known for the mighty cupola that is 138 feet in diameter and surpasses the domes of St. Peter's in Rome and St. Paul's in London. The interior is decorated with multicolored marble. The baptistery is covered with magnificent mosaics, and the bronze doors are intricately worked scenes from the Old Testament. In Europe, where there are so many "ABC Tours" (Another Bloody Cathedral), this one was outstanding. Nearby is the Palazzo Vecchio, also designed by the Duomo's architect. This townhall was completed in 1314 and is still Florence's city hall. Here in the courtyard we viewed the famous fountain, the Dolphin Boy.

We returned to the Uffizi Museum and were able to walk right in without any waiting. The paintings here cover the best of Italian and European art from the thirtieth to the eighteenth century. I was excited to see the only work by Michelangelo here—a round panel entitled the The Holy Family, his earliest known painting, dating to 1503. The most publicized treasures of this museum are the sculptures of Venus de Medici and the Dancing Fawn, classical Greek works, and Botticelli's paintings, Birth of Venus and Primavera. The museum is small in comparison to the Louvre or Prado, but the quality is exceptional. From one window in the museum you have a perfect view of the Ponte Vecchio, the oldest bridge in Florence over the Arno River. This was the only bridge in the city spared in World War II. Built in 1345, the covered passageway was constructed so that the Grand Duke Cosimo de' Medici could go from the Pitti to the Uffizi palaces without getting in the rain. Today it houses many shops.

Lunch was a quick pizza and Coke, and then we were off to inspect the glorious Michelangelo's sculpture of David. I was disappointed to find out that this was a copy. The original had been moved to the Academia in 1873.

At 3:00 P.M. we met the ship's transfer bus for the ride to the Leaning Tower of Pisa. It really is leaning! At that time it was fourteen feet off perpendicular, and they were working on it then to save this one-of-a-kind attraction. Built in 1172 as a bell tower, plans were for a ground floor, six stories of open area, and then the bell chamber. By the time they constructed the third floor, it became obvious that the foundations were inadequate and the project was leaning. The white marble structure of about 180 feet high insists on toppling over. It was reported that it slants about eight millimeters every year. Tourist-wise, this is a good thing! No one would come to see a straight tower.

We returned to the ship about 6:00 P.M. with the only regrets of not having enough

*I was standing straight; the Leaning Tower of Pisa is not.*

time to casually absorb the beauty and history of this extraordinary area.

The next day we took a launch from the ship docked at Portofino around the scenic coast of Rapallo. We sailed past beautiful houses and villas, perched along the cliffs above the calm blue-green waters of the Mediterranean. The excursion called for a stop at the beach of Santa Margherita, a popular resort. As we approached the village, a downpour of rain greeted us. It was coming down so hard, the launch did not attempt to go into land.

Amazingly, we cruised just around the Portofino peninsula and the rain stopped. Here we disembarked at the foot of the mountain in a sheltered cove at the charismatic fishing village of Comogli. During the mid-nineteenth century this seafaring community had a fleet of over 700 vessels. The fishing business declined, and today only a few fishermen remain, but its multicolored houses of past sea captains along the sea cliff, combined with brightly painted fishing boats moored in the harbor, give the place a most picturesque appeal. From the dock we climbed up the hill dotted with interesting little shops and side-walk cafés emitting wonderful aromas. We selected an inviting little restaurant and feasted on seafood pasta, accompanied by a local wine. From our outdoor table we could see the harbor below filled with small fishing boats and out to the glorious Mediterranean Sea.

Following the gratifying luncheon experience, we continued walking up the crooked road to the top of the mountainside and discovered the Hotel Cenobio Dei Dogi, the former residence of the Genovese Doges. From its elegant lobby and out on the terrace we could see the harbor below and miles out to sea. This was one place we vowed we wanted to return and stay several days. (Regrettably, so far, that has not come to pass, but it's something we look forward to.) Departing this captivating little community, I realized why this area of the Italian Riviera is referred to as the Paradise Gulf and is the home to many of the rich and famous.

Next stop—Rome. This is one of the most interesting cities in the world, and we had *one* day to see it all! To quote the ship's literature: "If you have never been to Rome, here is your chance to see enough in a day to encourage you to return for a longer stay." Well, I can certainly agree with that! We docked at Civitavecchia, and it was an hour-and-a-half drive into the city—so three hours were shot right there for the round trip. Our local guide's name was Yola, probably in her sixties. I loved to hear her talk, "lika Italiano."

Our first stop was Vatican City, a nation in the middle of Rome covering 108 acres, and the residence of the Pope and the world's largest church. The elite corps of Swiss guards has protected the Vatican since 1506. Their original uniforms of red, yellow, and blue pantaloons were designed by Michelangelo but have been replaced with a blue Vatican guard costume. St. Peter's Basilica was consecrated in 1626 and covers more than three and a half acres. The interior is breathtaking with its array of gold, mosaic, marble, and gilded stucco. A highlight was the supreme masterpiece of Michelangelo, *Pieta,* the superb marble sculpture of Mary and the crucified Christ. I couldn't believe I was standing inside St. Peter's Cathedral in Rome. I've been in many, many cathedrals, and justifiably, this was the most outstanding in every way.

The Sistine Chapel, private chapel of the Popes and the site of the secret conclaves at which cardinals elect new leaders, was an extra delight. When we were there they were

restoring the ceiling artwork, *The Creation of the World.* Michelangelo, working totally alone, and lying on his back on scaffolding, completed this unbelievable work of genius in four years. Our guide said that the current restoration was financed by $3 million from Japan in exchange for all the postcards and film concessions of the Vatican in the future—a pretty sweet deal. At the end of the chapel is the acclaimed *Last Judgment* painting that Michelangelo started seventeen years after completing the ceiling. This one took more than eight years to finish.

Next on the schedule—the two-hour Italian lunch. What a waste of time! Outside that restaurant was ancient Rome, and we were held hostage inside a dull dining room consuming food that we certainly did not need, since our ship had superb Italian chefs who served us four or more times a day! Finally, we were back on the bus and to the Coliseum.

It was amazing how this construc-

*The magnificent Coliseum in Rome where man battled beast for the pleasure of the audience.*

tion has withstood time since it was inaugurated in 80 A.D Stone tiers surround the oval arena that would seat 50,000 cheering people as they watched the lions devour some poor soul. The masses thronged through the eighty arched passageways (many still standing today) to watch all-day shows of beasts and gladiators fighting to the death. (Guess this gene in mankind makes wrestling so popular today.)

We did not have time to stop at the Forum, where Julius Caesar was killed. The whole city of Rome is virtually a museum with ancient ruins everywhere. We had twenty minutes to "shop," and Keith and I ran about ten blocks to see the Spanish Steps, probably the most magnificent flight of steps in the world. Built in 1725, they lead into the Villa Borghese from the west. At the bottom of the steps is one of Rome's renowned fountains, in the shape of a boat. At the top is the house, now a museum, where Keats died in 1821.

The bus did stop at the celebrated Trevi Fountain. However, it was closed and the sculptures were covered with plastic for renovation. I threw a coin in the fountain anyway and promised to return to Rome when I could take the time to experience this captivating city.

We had a day at sea to relax and catch our breath after the vigorous sightseeing. As we sailed past the coast of Sicily, we witnessed the smoking Stromboli Volcano. That night in the dining room they served Baked Alaska in the shape of the volcano, and the waiters marched single-file into the darkened room with the desserts flaming.

Greece—next stop. The ship docked at Itea, on the Bay of Corinth. Once an important shipbuilding center, today it is a peaceful port and serves as a gateway to Apollo and Mount Parnassus. As this was our first time in this country, we wanted to see as much as possible, so we booked a morning and an afternoon tour. We started at Delphi, considered by the ancients to be the physical and spiritual center of the Earth. The road to the sacred site of the Temple of Apollo wound inland through a forest of olive trees and up into the green hillsides 4,000 feet above sea level, where we enjoyed magnificent views of the Gulf of Itea and the surrounding mountains. Legend is that in this area a shepherd found a spring with sulfur vapors, which he said made him speak prophecy.

Our sixty-year-old guide, from Athens, told us she could trace her family heritage back to the Greek fifth century. She explained that temples were erected by the springs, and within those temples a priestess would sit on a tripod—the throne of Apollo. Drugged by the intoxicating sulfur vapors from the springs, she would mutter incoherent phrases, which the priests interpreted (very vaguely) as holy words from the oracle. From about 200 B.C. until 300 A.D, even the most intelligent men of Greece believed implicitly in the responses of the oracle. In the fifth century zealous Christians initiated the destruction of this holy place and later earthquakes polished it off. Excavations began in 1892 and continue to this day. Treasures from the site are seen in the Delphi Museum.

We were concerned that we would miss our afternoon tour that was to begin at 12:45, as we did not get back to dockside until 12:40. When I mentioned our concern, the guide said, "No problem ... I am the guide for the afternoon tour. Just stay on this bus and we will leave in about twenty minutes." Seeing a restaurant across the street, I left Keith on the bus so they would not depart without me.

"I need a quick sandwich to go," I said to the old man sitting outside the diner.

He took me inside. "Taka your pick—watza cooked," he said, pointing at a glass case with several dishes inside. I saw clams, fish in some kind of sauce, and then I noticed some round things.

"What's that?" I inquired.

"Moussaka ... maka witha eggplant, lamb, cheese." (I could see this was no McDonald's.)

I took two moussakas and two Cokes. He fixed it all up with wonderful hard Greek bread, and I made it back to the bus just as we were ready to leave. The food was fantastic—even better than all that fancy stuff we had been having on the ship.

The afternoon tour, "Scenic Drive on Mount Parnassus," was appropriately named. We drove up 2,000 feet in the mountains past groves of olive trees. Our guide said that Greece had four million olive trees and was third in production of olives and olive oil after Spain and Italy. We stopped at the mountain village of Archova, famed for its multicolored hand-woven rugs produced by the local women during the harsh winter months. Of course, we had to have one.

The bus continued up the mountain to 5,000 feet, where the landscape was very rocky, barren, and dry. On the drive back, the guide pointed out some small buildings on the side of the mountain. "Shit sheds," it sounded like she said. Then I saw several sheep and realized she was saying "sheep sheds"! When we returned to the ship at 6:00 we were thoroughly fulfilled with our excursions to Delphi and Mount Parnassus.

The next port of call was Corfu, which was not very impressive. Our tour took us through narrow dirty streets with houses in disrepair and yards unkempt. We toured the Achilleion, a mansion built by Empress Elisabeth of Austria and later owned by Kaiser Wilhelm II. As palaces go, this one was nothing to write home about. It had been converted to a casino.

Our cruise continued on to Dubrovink. In 1989 Dubrovnik was in Yugoslavia. Today, through civil strife, that country has been split, and the city of Dubrovnik is now in the country of Croatia. When we were there it was a living museum, one of the most well-preserved medieval cities in Europe. Around 550 people lived within the walled city. We entered via the Pile Gate, adorned with an arch carved with numerous statues of St. Blaise, the city's patron saint. Legend is that his miraculous warning staved off a Venetian attack thousands of years ago.

*A special travel high was walking on top of the ancient walled city of Dubrovnik, Yugoslavia—now damaged due to civil war.*

The entire village is surrounded by an imposing medieval fortification. The wall varies in height and in some areas reaches all the way down to the sea. It's about one and a quarter miles in circumference and in some places is up to eighteen feet thick. These stone defenses were first constructed as early as the seventh century. Ray and Kay (of our group) joined Keith and me on our walk atop the city walls. The walkway around the city took us up and down steps from one section to the other. On one side we could see people fishing, swimming, and playing in the deep blue sea. On the other side we looked down on the red tile rooftops and courtyards for an intriguing and intimate view of their daily life. People were tilling their tiny gardens of leafy vegetables and vibrant flowers and hanging the day's wash on the line. Children were running and playing among the dogs, cats, and chickens. The sounds of radio and television rose from the small houses. The walk around this awe-inspiring ancient city was invigorating. I can add this experience to my growing list of all-time favorite events.

We awoke the next morning at 6:30 and went out on deck (as our window was blocked by that gangplank). The fog was so thick we couldn't see to the front of the ship. We were to sail into Venice that morning, but visibility was so bad, the ship was unable to move. The captain announced that he did not know if we would make it into Venice.

This was a place I had read so much about and was anxiously looking forward to seeing. Disappointed, I did what most everyone else on deck was doing: I ordered a Bloody Mary. As I was sipping the spicy drink in the fog, I thought, *This is certainly a Bloody Mary Morning.*

Around 2:00 P.M. the fog cleared some, enabling the launches to take us through the Grand Canal to St. Mark's Square. Finally, I stood on this famous site—and all I could see were people and pigeons. The fog covered the Campanile (bell tower) that rises 322 feet. Apparently the weather had grounded the pigeons also, for hundreds of the birds were bumping into each other in the plaza, battling for the morsels of food the tourists were flinging on the ground. What goes in must come out, of course. *What a mess!*

I herded my group to the Doges Palace to see this elegant Gothic basilica of San Marco, architecturally one of the most colorful and unusual buildings in the world, combining Byzantine, Romanesque, and Gothic styles in incomparable splendor. There had to be thousands of people trying to see the same sight at the same time. We did manage to see some of the great rooms that featured colorful art frescoes and golden mosaic murals. As we passed through the corridors, on our way to the dungeon, the guide pointed out the window for the view of the Bridge of Sighs, so named because the bridge spanning a narrow canal was the last thing that prisoners saw on their way to execution.

All my life I dreamed about a romantic ride in a gondola in Venice. Keith wasn't too excited about the

*Our gondola ride wasn't too romantic, but the city of Venice is awesome.*

escapade, but agreed just to please me. At that time, the cost for a forty-five-minute ride was $65, which Keith thought was a big "rip off." I still wanted to go, regardless of cost. As this was our last day in Italy, Keith made a "deal" with the gondola man: 830 lira (all the remaining Italian money we had) and $20 U.S. for a twenty-two-minute ride. Obviously, the boat captain wasn't happy with this arrangement. We took off through the ugly, back water streets, and all we saw was dirty water and what the boat driver said was Marco Polo's house. No gondolier singing—no romance whatsoever. In eighteen minutes he returned us to the departure place. I have now had a gondola ride, but it was more of a nightmare rather than one of my pleasant dreams!

## Black Sea Cruise

When I threw that coin in the Trevi Fountain in Rome, I vowed to return. My wish came true in 1990, when I had a group cruise that began in Naples, Italy.

Keith and I took this opportunity to see Rome before we joined the group in Naples. We had a pre-cruise package offered by Princess Cruises of three nights in Rome at the Boston Pullman Hotel. I cannot recommend it for the rooms, but the location is excellent, just a short distance to the Spanish Steps and fabulous shops. We discovered the terrace at the top of the hotel that provided a panoramic view from the Vatican to the Spanish Steps. We went up there every afternoon for our cocktail and to watch the sunset over the mystical city.

This time we saw Rome in our own time, missing very little of everything the old city had to offer. We returned to the Trevi Fountain, and it was still under restoration. I threw another coin in just for good luck.

The cruise line provided a transfer bus to Naples, where we boarded the *Royal Princess*. This time we had a room with a verandah—very nice. I located all my passengers and saw that they were situated in their cabins.

The first port of call was Messina, Sicily. A motor coach took us thirty-five miles through the mountainous countryside, passing through twenty-five tunnels. We arrived at Taormina, now a famous resort, nearly 700 feet above sea level. From there you could see the coastline and across to the snow-capped Mount Etna. There wasn't anything really unusual about the town; it had many bakeries, fruit stands, and the typical stores.

After a day at sea, we docked at Izmir, Turkey. From there we drove south, past cultivated olive groves, vineyards, tobacco and cotton plantations. In a little over an hour (about fifty miles), we arrived at the Mangnesia Gate, the entry point to the ancient city of Ephesus, with ruins dating back 4,000 years. A guide directed our walk through ancient, biblical times. Two thousand years ago, Ephesus had 300,000 inhabitants. Now only ghosts and crumbling buildings remain. It was very moving to walk where biblical characters had trod.

The city has been rebuilt four times. What remains today are ruins of the third city, built in 200 A.D. We sat in the amphitheatre, where St. Paul preached, and saw the remains of the Temple of Diana, one of the seven wonders of the ancient world. Also, we saw the amazing Celus Library. We even got to sit over one of the holes in an ancient public outdoor toilet! Earthquakes in the area have taken their toll, but it was amazing to see the remarkable standing structures that linger despite ravages of time.

(Above) The ruins of Ephesus, Greece. Note the excellent condition of the library at left, which has stood for over 4,000 years. (Left) Not too private, but I guess you could catch up on the local gossip as you sat on this public toilet in Ephesus.

Once a port city, it is now five miles from the sea. Legend claims that the Virgin Mary spent her last years and died just five miles outside the city.

"It's Istanbul, not Constantinople," according to the old song, and I could not believe that I was really standing on my verandah and seeing the city appearing before my very eyes. The only city astride two continents (Asia and Europe), Istanbul, Turkey, sitting on seven hills, has dominated the Bosphrus Strait for over twenty-five centuries. Constantine selected it as the capital of the Roman Empire. When it fell, the Byzantine Empire took it over, to be sacked by the Fourth Crusade, then captured by the Turks, who adorned the city with hundreds of mosques.

Our local guide, Rosie, told us there are 5,000 mosques in Istanbul. To enter the prominent Blue Mosque, we had to remove our shoes. This imposing structure has six minarets instead of the usual four to match the number gracing the Kaaba Mosque in Mecca. Rosie explained that Muslims pray and wash five times a day as she pointed out many washing facilities about town. On the streets many women still wore the traditional Muslim black dress with their head and face covered. However, frequently

*As our ship sailed into Istanbul, this sign was posted at the harbor.*

young women were seen in western dress with just the hair covered, or some without any Muslim attire whatsoever.

A dazzling, eye-popping experience was the Grand Covered Bazaar. As far as you can see, glittering gold shops beckon you. There are 4,000 shops under one roof and twenty entrances—an excellent place to get lost. Other than the dominant merchandise of gold, there are shops for leather, furs, shoes, and carpets. You name it, and you will find it there. Rosie suggested that we offer half the price quoted and then settle with the merchant for about 75 percent.

Topkapi Palace, the imperial residence of the Ottoman sultans for nearly 400 years, was incredible. Overlooking the Bosphorus, the Golden Horn and the Sea of Marmara, Topkapi was the administrative center of the empire. Priceless collections of Chinese porcelain and artworks abound. Rosie told us the third largest collection of jewels in the world (behind the British Crown Jewels and Iran's jewels) were displayed here. Included were an 87-carat diamond and a solid golden throne. These guys lived high on the hog!

Regrettably, we sailed too soon from the glistening city of Istanbul, arriving the next day at a totally different environment, Yalta, Soviet Union. The launch ride to the city was lovely, with the Crimean Mountains in the background. Yalta is built on the lower hills that come down to the Black Sea. During the czar's reign, this city, with its excellent climate, served as a summer retreat for royalty. After 1917, Lenin declared

*You can't leave Istanbul without going to a carpet showroom. Many travelers come home with beautiful hand-woven rugs.*

the area to be a sanitarium for sick peasants. We found it to be a bleak city, with no individual homes—only Soviet-type concrete block apartments.

Yalta is best known in the western world as the site of the 1945 conference between Roosevelt, Churchill, and Stalin at the end of World War II. We visited the site of the conference at the White Palace, built in 1911 by Czar Nicholas II, and saw the room where Roosevelt stayed and the table where the treaty was signed. At the Yalta Conference, according to our guide, Germany was to pay $20 for damages, the USSR got three old ships, and the United States got "zero." I don't know how accurate that report was. When the *Royal Princess* pulled out of Yalta, citizens gathered on shore and waved to us while a band played.

As our ship approached Odessa, USSR, on the northwest corner of the Black Sea, all we could see were loading cranes and container boxes. The city is Russia's second largest port (St. Petersburg is first). Our city tour, led by a lovely Russian girl who spoke impeccable English, began with the monument to the Russian poet Alexander Pushkin, who spent a year in exile here. The guide pointed out the Odessa Hotel as the city's best (it looked horrible) and then the Opera House. She said the Opera House was one of Europe's finest, built along the classic-baroque lines of the Vienna Opera House. It was closed for renovation, so we could not go inside. Our guide alleged that this was Russia's finest building, but I disagree. I think St. Basil's in Moscow outshines it, at least from outward appearances.

We were told that the city had one million people, but very few people could be seen along the streets. The only activity we saw were a few elderly women with shopping bags and a few other old women sweeping the streets with weed brooms. The guide stated that the schoolchildren were on collective farms for the harvest season. The rest of the population must have been working or sleeping.

On the whole, the city looked like all the other Russian cities I had seen—dull, drab, stark, and dreary. There were no individual homes and no yards, although Odessa did have many green park areas. Twenty-five miles of sandy beaches surround the city, and this is the location each summer of the Premier Children's Camps. At this camp they have special sports programs and classes in Communism for all children of the country.

When we asked the guide how Russians were responding to the new policies under Gorbachev, she stated: "Many do not like Gorbachev's way of not having enough food, tobacco, and vodka. In the olden days, here in the Ukraine, we used to have plenty of these items."

On the way back to the ship, we stopped at the feature attraction of Odessa, the Potemkin Steps, and Keith and I opted to walk down all 192 of them. An Italian architect, Boffo, completed the steps in 1841. Although the steps appear to be built on parallel lines, they are nearly twice as wide at the bottom as at the top. The steps are so named because during the people's revolution of 1905, city workers joined mutineers from the battleship, *Potemkin,* and this was really the beginning of the unrest that led to the Civil War of 1917, changing the rule of the country from the czars to Communism.

After two days at sea, we arrived at Athens, Greece. During our last cruise we had seen some of Greece, but had not gone to Athens, which dates back to 2000 B.C. The center of the city is four miles from the sea. It was so exciting to see an area containing so much history.

As if a crown, the Acropolis and its legendary Parthenon are visible as you look up to the hills. The Acropolis is a ten-acre rock rising 300 feet above the city. The Parthenon, a miracle of marbled harmony, was inspired by Phidias, an artistic genius of classical Athens. Work began on the building in 447 B.C. It was so moving to stand in the place that I had seen in pictures. I was amazed that it was built to such perfection during ancient times, and is still partially standing today.

(Nashville, Tennessee, has an exact replica of the Parthenon, complete with the gigantic statue of Athena in full color and gold decorations. If you can't make it to Athens to see the real thing, stop by and see the Nashville offering of what the magnificent structure looked like originally.)

Back to the cruise. That evening we attended a sound and light show. The Acropolis lighted at night transports you out of this world into the past. Readings for the presentation were by Richard Burton and Lawrence Olivier. Unfortunately, the sound did not come through clearly on the speaker system and marred the presentation. This was in October, and it was so cold, everyone was shivering as we sat out in the open. We had taken blankets from the ship, but were still miserable. However, to see this piece of art history illuminated was worth the uncomfortable time.

The next scheduled port of call was Mykonos, but due to high winds, we docked at Santorini instead. The city of Thera sits on the top rim of a volcano that had its last eruption in 1956. You have a choice of ascent: cable car, donkey, or walk up the 586 steps. We were told that the cable car had been in existence only about two years. Before that time the only way up was by donkey or foot. We chose the cable car.

To our surprise, street after street of shops and restaurants were on top of the mountain. It was great fun to explore the cobbled stone pathways from one store to another. Keith even found a *Wall Street Journal* only one day old, an item he had not been able to locate since we left Rome. The view of the aquamarine Mediterranean with the elegant *Royal Princess* anchored in the distance was spectacular. To return down the mountain, we decided to walk. It was an easy stroll down the many steps; we just had to be careful to sidestep the donkey dung!

This cruise took us again to Dubrovnik. We were eager to retrace our path around the city from the top of the wall, as we had enjoyed it so much before. Frequently, when you return to a place that was so impressive the first time, it is not as rewarding the second time. But that wasn't the case with the Dubrovnik Wall. The colorful sights were still in place—the sea lapping against the wall on one side of the city and the active townspeople on the other.

I was upset to hear that in 1991 the federal army moved against Dubrovnik and damaged the wall. The troops pounded the old city with artillery. When the shelling stopped in 1992, 382 residential, 19 religious, and 10 public buildings plus the wall were damaged. Reports are that 92 lives were also lost.

Restoration efforts have been made since that time, but progress is slow because they want to keep it as original as possible by using construction techniques that are centuries old. Despite all that, Dubrovnik is still a functioning renaissance city where people live much the same way that they have for centuries. It will be impossible now to relive the two extraordinary times we walked on top of the unmarred ancient walls of Dubrovnik. I am so thankful we were able to stroll along this site of history in its original form before the damage.

Last port of call for this cruise was Venice, Italy. The night before arriving, the ship's comedian said: "I did not care for the Venice Street Walkers—guess it was the flippers and scuba mask that turned me off."

Having "done" the gondola ride last time, we chose the vaporatti (their city water bus). For a few lira we traveled round trip from St. Mark's Square the entire length of the Grand Canal, the main street of Venice. We sat on outside chairs and could see everything. This method of viewing the city was so much better than our previous "gondola fiasco," and certainly the price was right.

Some 200 palaces built between the twelfth and eighteenth centuries stand along the Grand Canal banks. Some are meticulously restored; others are sadly crumbling. Grand aristocratic families once lived in the villas, and a few are still inhabited by their heirs. Others are currently municipal offices, hotels, and museums. On the return, we stepped off at a famous landmark, the Rialto Bridge, for some shopping. We walked back to St. Mark's Square, and the pigeons were still in great supply (in fact, I think they had increased in number). A Coke at a St. Mark's Square sidewalk café was $6.

*The pigeons are permanent residents at St. Mark's Square in Venice.*

As this was our last night on the ship, I hosted a cocktail party for my group. I told them how wonderful they had been: I had not had a single problem and no complaints. Everyone seemed to enjoy this exceptional Black Sea Cruise.

I knew I had probably spoken too soon. The next morning, as my group sat in the departure lounge, scheduled to disembark at 9:00 A.M., it was announced that the charter plane we were to take from Venice to Newark would be delayed and we would be transferred by bus to a Ramada Hotel. There we sat for four hours before finally being able to board the plane. We were told that our chartered plane had been required by the military to go to Kuwait, and the company had to obtain a new plane and crew, creating the delay. This setback caused us to miss our scheduled Continental flights from Newark to Houston. When we arrived at Newark, it was after 9:00 P.M. A Princess representative was there to arrange hotel rooms. I finally had everyone settled at midnight. At 6:00 A.M. I put my group on shuttle buses back to the airport. I had changed our tickets for a 9:30 A.M. departure, but we had to get all the tickets and boarding passes re-issued. It sure felt nice when the plane finally arrived in Austin, Texas—a day late, but safe and sound.

## Elbe River Cruise

Collette Vacations offered this new itinerary in 1992. The Elbe River was the former border between West and East Germany and had just become freely accessible for tourists after forty-five years along a divided country. The Elbe River played an important part in German history. Germanic peoples settled west of the river in the

*The storybook villages along the Elbe River in Germany.*

fourth century, and in the eighth century it was the eastern border of Charlemagne's empire. The brochure proclaimed: "From the observation lounge, sundeck or cozy bar you will cruise by former East Germany's splendid cities, fairytale castles, palaces and medieval villages." That sounded good to me, and to thirty-six of my clientele.

We flew to Vienna, Austria, for one night and then by motor coach crossed the border into Hungary to revisit lovely old Budapest, located right on the Danube River. From there we drove to Prague, Czechoslovakia, the centuries-old city that is one of Europe's best-preserved jewels.

On Day Seven we crossed the border into the eastern part of present-day Germany to Bad Schandau, an historical spa town. We were ready to board our riverboat, the MS *Clara Schumann,* and cruise down the "fairytale stream." Operated by the KD River Cruises of Europe, the ship accommodated 150 passengers and was specifically constructed to maneuver the shallow river waters. Regrettably, it did not have shallow enough draft to sail the Elbe under its current conditions. There was a drought in the area, and the river was too low for the ship to navigate. We were told "not to worry, for water from a dam upstream will be released tomorrow, and we will sail then."

The accommodations were basic but comfortable. The staff was attentive, and the food, leaning toward German fare, on the whole was first-rate. Complimentary excellent German wines accompanied both lunch and dinner. (Maybe that was what made the food so appealing.)

The next morning, I peeked out my cabin window, and the river looked the same level to me. The announcement was made that the water had not been released yet, and we would go by motor coach to Dresden.

My first impression of the former East Germany area was that the roads are horrible. Apparently there had been no or minimal maintenance since the Soviet takeover forty-five years earlier. The farms and small houses along the road appeared to be abandoned.

Dresden is a contrast of the old and new. From 1694 to 1783, the city was called the most beautiful city in Europe and was referred to as the "Florence on the Elbe." Today the ravages of war are very evident in many of the bombed-out ruins. Dresden suffered heavy damage during the World War II air raid of February 13-14, 1945. Our guide said that the Allies, presumably in an attempt to crush the morale of the Germans (and some say it was in retaliation for the bombing of London), dropped phosphorus and high-explosive bombs on this great city of art. A devastating firestorm engulfed the area, destroying most of the buildings, and it is reported that at least 35,000 people were killed. The Communists restored some of the Old Town, adding their typical gray rectangular architecture. Our guide stated that she was afraid all restoration would be hampered now that they were a united Germany, for there were too many things that needed to be done in the former East Germany. She said roads and factories had priority over the huge expense of restoring Dresden's monumental buildings.

The next morning, still no water had been released, so back on the motor coach for a tour of Meissen, called the "City of White Gold." The world-famous Dresden pottery has been produced here since 1710. (I never realized that Dresden china was made in Meissen.) As we entered the city, we could see the dominant cathedral and Albrechstburg Castle, proving that there were indeed castles along the Elbe River; we just hadn't had an opportunity to sail past them. At

*Dresden, Germany, suffered greatly during bombings of World War II. Some have been rebuilt, but many ruins remain.*

the Staatliche Porzellan-Manufaktur, we saw how the centuries-old manufacture of Dresden china is still in progress, and in many instances, using the same designs from the past. It was fascinating to see artists applying touches of gold to a plate or a cup. China dishes and figurines that had been made in Meissen through the ages were displayed at the Porcelain Museum. Outside the city we could see terraces of vineyards in the Elbe Valley, which has been producing fine wine for over 1,000 years.

After breakfast the next morning, the captain announced: "The water we were expecting will not be released due to the farmers upstream needing it for their crops. We are going to try to sail this morning and see how we fare."

At last, after all this time, we would finally sail down the Elbe—for about three hours before the captain decided the water was too shallow to safely continue. They bused us to the area we were supposed to cruise through—the Saxon Alps, known as "Saxon Switzerland." Here the land has eroded over the millennia into fantastic rock formations, accented with dark green foliage. From trails in and over the rocks, there were panoramic views of the river and mountains, a truly enchanting and lovely region, and it was easy to see why they call it the "Switzerland of Germany."

On Day Five of the scheduled cruise, it was time to leave the ship (where we had slept and dined, but only sailed for less than half a day). On the way to Berlin we stopped at Wittenberg, the ancient university town made famous by Martin Luther, who lived and preached there. In the center of the town, statues honor Luther plus another of the city's celebrated sons, humanist Philipp Melanchthon. A Protestant reformer and scholar, he was a friend of Luther's and later of Calvin's. At the Luther Museum we toured part of the monastery in which Luther lived and also the parish church where he preached. History of the Reformation led by Luther is chronicled here. We saw the door of the church where Luther pinned his ninety-five theses.

Later in the afternoon, we arrived in Berlin. A tour of both West and East Berlin were the highlights of the next day. Now with the wall destroyed, you can easily go from one part of the city to the other, but it is still very obvious which part was under Communist rule. When we were there, all that remained of the wall were chunks sold as souvenirs at the former Checkpoint Charlie Gate. I had to have my personal piece showing a portion of the graffiti that had once adorned the wall, and now I can reflect on my two visits there, before and after. (Our previous trip is recalled in my first book.)

We returned to the Berlin hotel from our tour around 5:00 P.M. and it was time for our "happy hour." Since this was a four-star hotel in a very civilized city, I thought I would have no problem getting ice for our drinks. I called room service and ordered some ice and two glasses. Promptly, there was a knock at our door. There stood a large, robust young German girl holding a tray with two of the most beautiful ice cream sundaes you ever saw. Although they looked appetizing, it was not time for ice cream. I explained that I did not order ice cream, but a bucket of ice cubes for our drinks.

"You order—you eat!" she sternly replied.

I emphatically said that I did not want the sundaes, and closed the door. I decided to go down to the bar to see if I could obtain better results. Successful with the bartender, I was just getting on the elevator with my two glasses of ice when I met the lady with the ice cream sundaes, now slightly melting around the edges. As the elevator slowly made it to our floor, no word was exchanged. I let her depart first, and watched as she went two doors down from our room (belonging to two ladies of my tour group). I quickly ducked into our room. That night at dinner, I asked the two ladies if they were able to obtain ice for their drinks. They laughed and said no, but they sure enjoyed some excellent ice cream sundaes. We later found out that "ice" in German refers to ice cream.

This trip was a disappointment because we did not get to cruise and see the sights along the Elbe River via boat, but we obtained an insight into that historical and lovely part of Eastern Germany that had been "off limits" to tourists for so many years.

*Our cruise ship never sailed but one-half day along the Elbe River.*

# South America

South America is a continent of varied scenic beauty and cultures. Yet it is not, as a rule, the favored destination of American travelers, who seem to usually select Europe or Asia. Keith and I have been in every country in South America with the exception of the tiny nations of Guyana and Suriname. Each country we visited was interesting, filled with friendly natives and outstanding landscapes.

## The Amazon

The first Amazon cruise was aboard the *Pacific Princess* in 1990. Our group flew to San Juan, Puerto Rico, and sailed to St. Thomas, Martinique, Barbados, and Devil's Island before entering the Amazon River.

We had been to St. Thomas and Martinique many times on previous cruises. In Barbados, while walking around the quiet streets, we were intrigued at the dock area where several people were cleaning fish. They were working on thousands of "flying fish," about eight inches in length with long fins resembling wings. The fishermen told us the flying fish were a delicacy, and it was their number-one export. After they had removed the fins and bones, I couldn't see much that remained to eat. Continuing our cruise, we were delighted to see some of the "flying fish" skipping their way alongside the ship.

This was our first time at Devil's Island, since it is not on the regular tourist path in the Caribbean. This evil-sounding place was just that at one time. It housed France's most notorious prison settlement, where for many years murderers, thieves, and traitors were banished. The prison was in operation from 1854 to 1948. A total of some 80,000 were imprisoned here during that time. The extremely rocky shoreline of the island and the shark-infested waters surrounding it deterred escape attempts.

Devil's Island lies ten miles off the coast of French Guyana and is included in that country's possessions. It is known for two famous prisoners. Dreyfus, falsely condemned for treason, suffered here four years before being released and given a new trial. Henri Charrie, better known as "Papillon," claimed to be the only convict to escape the island alive. He and a fellow prisoner made rafts of coconut husks stuffed into a couple of jute sacks. One night they tied themselves to these rafts and jumped into the high waves at the northern end of the island and were swept out to sea. After two days they washed up on some mud flats near a small fishing village. The other comrade, excited to be near land, foolishly tried to walk ashore and drowned in the mud. Papillon clung to his raft until the tide lifted him into the mangroves, and he then was able to escape after eleven years of prison hell.

*The vacated prison cells on Devil's Island, now occupied by jungle growth.*

As you walk through the ruins of the prison buildings you can feel the ghosts of the condemned. The government has turned the Officers' Mess Building into a hotel, restaurant, and the ever-present gift shop. (Don't know why anyone by choice would want to overnight in this creepy place—but I guess there is something for everyone.) A walk around the small island revealed former homes of the prison staff, the hospital, chapel, children's cemetery, and a lighthouse. We saw a little rodent animal, between a rat and a weasel, reddish brown in color and about two feet long and one foot high. We saw four of these little critters, but they remained in the shadows and I wasn't able to get a clear photograph. I never found out what they were called, and no one seemed to know anything about the mysterious animals.

After a day at sea and later in the evening, we noticed that the blue Caribbean was turning brownish as we were nearing the doorway of the mighty Amazon River. The brown color is from the forest runoff. For a long distance after entering the river we could not even see across the watery expanse. (Stories of our Amazon experiences are related in *Around the World in the Middle Seat.*)

## Estancias in Paraguay and Argentina

As my husband and brother are both ranchers, they wanted to see the ranching country of South America. I had read about the *estancias* (ranches) in South America that took guests, much like our bed and breakfast inns. I contacted Molly of Geeta Tours, whom we had gone to Vietnam and Cambodia with, and had her make the arrangements for us to visit *estancias* in Argentina, Paraguay, and Uruguay in 1998.

Keith and I flew with my brother Delbert and his wife, Wanda, to Asuncion and were met by our Paraguay guide, Pedro. It was about a three-hour drive to our first *estancia*, LaLita, southeast of Asuncion City. The countryside resembled Texas ranching country during good rain times, as there were plenty of green trees and grass. When we arrived at the property boundary, we had to travel along dirt roads for several miles from the main road to reach the *hacienda*. A Spanish ranch-type house with a red tile roof was surrounded with gardens of cacti and flowers. Inside the house, massive ornate Spanish-style furniture filled the living room and dining room. José, the owner, and his sister, Marice, welcomed us to their home. José's wife was in Spain at the time visiting their daughter, who was attending a university there.

Our sleeping quarters were in a long, bunkhouse-style building behind the house. Everything was nice and clean with a private bath, but very basic.

The next morning José took us for a drive to see his cattle and lands. The Brahma-type cattle looked very small and poor compared to the United States variety. He was very proud of a natural spring and waterway that ran through his property, complete with a beautiful waterfall surrounded by ferns. He said that many commercials had been filmed at this location.

When we returned in the afternoon to the ranch house, two of the ranch hands were standing by a barbecue pit with a calf hindquarter roasting on a rotating spit. The men were straight out of the movies: floppy western hat, gaucho-type pants with knee-high boots, and a holstered gun and large knife tucked in their back belts.

When we sat down with the host and hostess that evening at the dinner table, the *gaucho* brought in a large piece of meat from the outdoor cookout. He took out his knife (about two feet long), sliced large pieces from the roast, and served everyone's plate. I've never tried to eat meat that was that tough. We chewed and chewed. But we certainly weren't going to say anything other than complimentary remarks about the meat to the server equipped with a gun and large knife!

Our host and hostess were very gracious,

*Our armed* gaucho *proudly presents his barbecued beef—and it was as tough as it looks!*

but conversation was difficult as they did not speak English and we had to converse through our guide, Pedro.

Our next two *estancias* were in Argentina near the town of Salta, called the Garden of Argentina. We flew 1,000 miles northwest of Buenos Aires to reach the area. Salta is at the meeting point for two valleys and is not far from the Bolivian border. Thus many of the people of the area are related to the Ayamara Indians of Bolivia, and the women dress in a long, colorful skirts and shawls.

*A village in the mountains north of Salta, Argentina.*

Finca San Antonio Estancia was located just a short drive from Salta in the heart of the Lerma Valley. The two-story whitewashed home dated back to 1750 and had been occupied by the Cornejo Backer family for more than a century. It has been totally modernized, and we had a very lovely and comfortable suite, one of the five accessible from the open courtyard. The hosts said they open their doors so that visitors can discover the ancestral cordiality of the people of Salta, their history, and the serenity of this location. The house sits on five hectares of manicured grounds that include a swimming pool.

The family had cattle and grew tobacco, and a large orchard produced a variety of fruits they sold at a roadside market. They also had a separate fruit jelly operation. Numerous hired hands operated the *estancia*. The son of the family was a member of the Argentine government and had to be in Buenos Aires most of the time. Here dialogue was easier, for the daughter-in-law spoke English. A house servant served each meal just for the four of us in the large dining room, not with the family as in Paraguay. We did have cocktails with the mother and daughter-in-law each evening on the terrace overlooking the large pool.

Just at dusk, a loud shrill noise arose from the surrounding trees.

"Cicada," they explained. They are similar to our locust. I always thought our crickets were loud in Texas, but I have never heard anything like this. The sound continued at a high crescendo until dark.

Our last *estancia* was Finca El Bordo de las Lanzas, located not far from Salta, and was excellent in accommodations, food, and fellowship. This property is one of the oldest ranches in the area. In 1609 the Arias Cornejo family took possession of this fertile farming and ranching property, and it has remained in the same hands throughout the years. They raise tobacco, tomatoes, alfalfa, cattle, pigs, and even alligators on more than 2,500 hectares.

The Arias Cornejo family, whose first Argentine ancestor arrived with the founder of the city of Salta, proudly displays a collection of artifacts found on their land and their library contains valuable antique books and documents. Tradition and history go hand in hand with modern farm business at the *estancia*.

It was tomato-harvesting time when we were there. It was amazing to see hundreds of boxes of tomatoes stacked up and to find out that they would get about $1 per box when shipped to Buenos Aires. I thought of how tomatoes run around $1 or more a pound here in the US, and they had to sell a whole box for that amount. They were complaining about the low prices for their farm products and were upset about the U.S. crackdown on tobacco. The family employs about 100 people who live in their own village on the ranch.

The massive, two-story house was built around a courtyard, where a colorful parrot greeted us with a shrill *"Buenos días."* Our suites just off the patio were tastefully decorated in Spanish style.

Señora Cornejo spoke perfect English and welcomed us. We later met her son, who had a degree in agriculture and was currently operating the farming aspect. His other brother, a veterinarian, had begun the alligator farming to produce the skins for sale. We went with them to feed the alligators. When we approached the pond, it was startling to see about fifty alligators coming out of the water straight at us, looking for food. Fortunately, they were more interested in the raw chicken meat than us.

That evening we joined the family for pre-dinner drinks. The proprietor, Señor Dario Arias Cornejo, was dressed in the typical elegant *gaucho* fashion, which I am sure he had tailored just for him. The jacket and pants had an embossed design and were accented by shiny black boots.

We dined with the family and other guests by candlelight on the patio. Staying there at the same time were two businessmen—one from France and the other from Germany. They spoke English, as did the hostess, her son, and his fiancée, so we had a very pleasurable evening (and their beef was delicious).

It was interesting to see tradition and history combined with a modern farm business. They have the same problems the farmers and ranchers have in the United States: low prices for their crops, and naturally weather and insects.

Our last country on this tour was Uruguay. We took the comfortable hydrofoil from Buenos Aires across the Rio de la Plata for about thirty miles to Colonia, where a local guide met us. Uruguay has a population of just over three million, and nearly half of the population resides in the capital, Montevideo. The small country is resource poor, receiving most of its income from the beaches east of Montevideo that attract wealthy Argentines.

The Portuguese founded Colonia in 1680. The impressive Puerta de Campo, the restored entrance to the old city, was built in 1745. We were fascinated by the numerous antique cars, dating back to the 1930s, along the streets of the old city, many of them in excellent condition.

Montevideo was a typical bustling city, but not as cosmopolitan as Buenos Aires. We did find some excellent leather stores there to purchase rugs and wall hangings. After one night in Uruguay, we returned to Buenos Aires on the hydrofoil.

Between each venue of this tour we had to go in and out of Buenos Aires. Each time a charming local guide, Petra, met us. We stayed at the Hotel de las Americas, ideally located in the heart of the shopping district. At the end of our tour, when we returned from Uruguay, Petra showed us the city of Buenos Aires—from the Plaza de Mayo, where Evita Peron greeted her patrons, to the colorful La Boca, with its multihued houses and home of the tango. We also visited Evita Peron's gravesite.

*(Above) Evita Peron's tomb at the Recoleta Cemetery in Buenos Aires, Argentina. (Below) Buenos Aires is known as the city of the tango, and you can see demonstrations of the dance in the colorful LaBoca area.*

We had planned our schedule to be there on Sunday to go to the antique market, where each week merchants set up booths on the square and display their wares. Everything imaginable was offered for sale. On a previous trip to Buenos Aires, we had been to this market and purchased *boleadoras,* the South American Indian weapon made of stone balls, usually encased in animal hide and attached to long, thin ropes. When twirled and thrown, the tool is designed to strike an animal so as to entwine its legs, rendering it immobile. It is used in hunting rhea, guanaco, and puma. As we do not have any of these animals in Texas, our

weapon is proudly displayed with our other South American souvenirs. On this trip to the market, Petra bought a 1920s hat, and looked darling in it. We took a break from our shopping to watch a tango presentation in the street. The final night we enjoyed a delicious meal featuring Argentina wines at a local steak house, followed by a tango dance show.

For a unique and interesting visit to South America, I recommend visiting the *estancias*. Here you get to visit with the people and learn more about their way of life. A guide to the properties is published by Tierra Buena.

## Ecuador and Galapagos Islands

The primary destination of this group tour was the Galapagos Islands in 1990, but to go there, you must fly to Quito, Ecuador, and take a flight from there. The capital of the country, Quito, is 2,850 meters above sea level, thus creating a wonderful spring-like climate year round, even though it is only fifteen miles south of the equator. In 1997 UNESCO declared Quito one of the world's cultural heritage sites. A walk down colonial Quito's old town, with its whitewashed and red-tiled houses and many historic churches, is like a step into a past era. We had a few days to see some of the nearby regions of this vibrant country.

A bus took us about six miles north of Quito on the Pan American Highway to the village of Calderon, famous for its unique Ecuadorian folk art. The best examples are the bread dough ornaments and statuettes. Everyone in my group stocked up on the exclusive Christmas ornaments. They were tempting because of their unusual designs and price—about ten cents each! I bought about 50 of these cute curios and had them on our Christmas tree for several years. Then one Christmas when I opened the storage box, there was just flour dust. Silverfish had had a delightful year feasting on the bread dough.

We were there on November 2, which is the holiday of All Saints' Day, or the Day of the Dead. We drove out to the cemetery and found a big celebration. The families had gathered at the site of their relatives' graves with picnic lunches to dine with the departed. Music was playing from portable radios and boom boxes. Fresh flowers were placed all around, and everyone seemed to be having a wonderful time.

Saturday is market day at Otavalo, a small town of about 20,000, two hours from Quito. The market dates back to pre-Inca times, when jungle products were brought from the lowlands and traded for highland goods. Today

*Families celebrate the "Day of the Dead" by taking a picnic lunch to the cemetery.*

the market is for buying and bartering local food, animals, and other essentials for the locals, and to sell crafts to tourists. A variety of products was offered: food, animals, colorful weavings, sweaters, etc. With the U.S. dollar, everything was very inexpensive, and we couldn't resist the designs of the rugs and wall hangings. But to me, the most inter-

esting aspect of the venue was the picturesque women in their multicolored dresses, shawls, and black felt hats. Several had contented babies secured to their backs.

Sunday is market day at Pujili, strictly an Indian market, and not geared to the tourist as in Otavalo. I have never seen larger cabbages and carrots. They also sold rope, old batteries, brown sugar wrapped in cane straw holders, and lots of cheap western clothes and felt hats. Also, did you know that Panama hats are made in Ecuador? Several of our group purchased fine fedoras that fold up in a handy little wooden box for traveling.

Our tour continued on to Salassaca to another market that featured a little different weaving, and then on to Baños (meaning baths in English). The town is famous for thermal springs that the locals swear are good for your health. A walk around the small town revealed many shops making sugar cane syrup and taffy. I did not care to purchase any when I saw the men outside

*This native boy in a typical knitted cap is resting with his pet lamb.*

the stores pulling and throwing the taffy in the air and then hanging it on an outside stick, where flies were having a real feast.

Our hotel was once a villa. When we checked in, the manager said there were no room assignments or keys. We could pick out any room we wanted, and so we did. The next morning we drove toward the Amazon jungle, where the terrain changed to rushing rivers, long waterfalls, deep canyons, and heavy foliage. Indiana Jones-type suspension rope bridges crossed deep gorges to small houses on the mountainside. The roads were unpaved, and the only other vehicle we encountered was an Ecuadorian bus, very brightly colored, and crammed with people and their belongings.

When we returned to the Quito hotel, it was just a regular day in the life of a group travel leader. Because we had been gone overnight, they had assigned the entire group to new rooms, and couldn't locate our luggage. This mess took about an hour to settle. The lock was broken on Ray and Bill's room and they couldn't get in, so I had to convince the front desk that they needed another room. George called to say that he left his jacket on the bus with his and his wife's passports and airline tickets in it. We called the bus company and they said that the bus was locked and that they would use the same bus to pick us up the next day to take us to the airport. After worrying all night, the next morning the bus showed up with the jacket and all its contents. We stored most of our luggage at the hotel and took eleven bags to the Galapagos. As we were ready to leave, the hotel desk clerk called me and said that two rooms owed money because they ate too much breakfast.

"How is that possible when it was a buffet breakfast?" I asked.

He replied that that was the amount on the bill, and I had to pay 420 sucres, which at that time was less than $1. I quickly paid the bill and we were on our way.

Six hundred miles off the west coast of Ecuador are the numerous isolated islands called the Galapagos, so named by the Spanish because the gigantic turtle found there had a shell that resembled a *"galapaga,"* the Spanish name for a riding saddle. The islands were discovered accidentally in 1535, when Tomas de Berlanga, the bishop of Panama, drifted off-course sailing from Panama to Peru. For over 300 years after the discovery the Galapagos provided firewood, water, and fresh food for pirates, buccaneers, sealers, and whalers. The seamen, always looking for fresh meat, would capture the huge

*The Galapagos Islands are known for their large turtles, shown here at the Charles Darwin Research Center.*

tortoises and keep them on board the ship. The tortoises would survive up to one year, thus providing food for the crew.

The Galapagos were officially claimed in 1832 by Ecuador, and thereafter the islands were inhabited by a few settlers and also used as a penal colony. In 1959 the Galapagos Islands were declared a national park. These islands have been referred to as a "zany zoo" because of the unusual animals, such as the blue-footed booby, the bright red and orange Sally Lightfoot Crabs, the bearded titmouse, and oversized turtles, weighing up to 500 pounds. The area obtained fame when Charles Darwin in 1835 called it "a living laboratory of evolution." Today, despite it being a wildlife sanctuary, many forms of flora and fauna face the chance of extinction.

Our ship was the *M.V. Galapagos Explorer.* From it we took numerous land excursions by small Zodiac craft to see the various wildlife. One of the highlights was snorkeling with the sea lions. They would zoom in headed right for us, and then just before they reached our bodies, they would veer off and never touch us. They seemed to think it was some kind of game.

There were colonies of sea lions everywhere. Sometimes we would see a group of "bachelors" who were lying out sunning and healing their wounds. Many had bloody gashes on their bodies from fights with other males over the possession of females.

As we unloaded on the beach of one island, there, swimming around and barking loudly in a watery nook, was a large bull sea lion talking at full volume to his harem of six females. I had been snorkeling, and for protection from the extreme heat so near the equator I had black tights on my legs. My bathing suit was also black. I rushed ahead of everyone and sat on a rock right in front of the sea lions to get a close-up picture. As I was focusing my camera, the bull lion suddenly reared out of the water straight for me. Keith came up behind me, and, recognizing the danger, grabbed me and literally pulled me across the rocks to safety. I don't know if the sea lion thought I was a male intruder due to my black garb, a new female seal, or somehow he just did

not like me. The results of this encounter were a very close photo of the sea lion's face, plus a sore rear end and the bottom ripped out of my bathing suit. The tights under my suit saved me from an embarrassing exposed condition.

Unique wildlife abounds, but most prevalent are the birds. There are fifty-eight resident bird species on the islands, and twenty-eight of them are found nowhere else in the world, unless in captivity. Thirteen species of the famous Darwin's finches are found here, usually small birds and some with

*This picture is the result of a bull sea lion thinking I was going to harm his harem on the Galapagos Islands.*

a delightful song. Also, penguins can thrive here due to the cool Humboldt Current flowing from the South Polar regions up the South American coast.

Large albatrosses circled high in the sky above the waters and then would suddenly dive in to lunch on unsuspecting fish. At this time of the year the large bird had chicks that were about six months old and stood about two feet high. They were just shedding their down feathers. Albatrosses live to be up to sixty years old and mate for life. From December to April they go out to sea to feed and then return to the same beach with the same mate to lay eggs and hatch chicks in June. The male goes out for food while the female stays with the chicks.

It was most fun to watch the blue-footed booby, as they are fast fliers and exceptional plunge divers. These cute critters with bright blue feet are entertaining when they perform their courtship display. The mating ritual features bowing, wing spreading, and sky pointing, with the neck, head, and bill stretched upward. There is also a red-footed booby, but it is not seen as often as the blue-foots. The third booby of the Galapagos is the masked booby—pure white with a black facemask. There are also many pelicans, petrels, and gulls.

My favorite had to be the Sally Lightfoot Crab. This colorful cutie is about three or four inches across, with bright red on its back and blue underneath. The crabs scurry all around the rocks in the surf and are even capable of running across the surface of the water in tide pools when frightened.

Another endemic specie of this area is the marine iguana, the only seagoing lizard in the world. These prehistoric-looking creatures are red and brown. However, when they get ready to mate, the male turns green and red to attract females.

We visited the Charles Darwin Research Center that began operation in 1962. At the research center you can see giant tortoise hatchlings and walk in an adult tortoise enclosure to meet the big boys up close and personal. One turtle was said to be at least 150 years old.

The Galapagos Islands are special because of the rare and unusual wildlife found there. Try to visit before the wonderful species become extinct.

# Argentina and Chile

Collette Vacations was putting together a circle tour of South America in 1993. The president and CEO, Dan Sullivan, Jr., called me and wanted to know if I thought I could get a group together to try out the new tour. I said, "Why not?" I was able to enlist twenty-six of my faithful followers to be the first passengers for the trip. Dan was on the trip, plus four Collette guides who were training for the tour. So we were very well taken care of.

We flew to Buenos Aires, the "Paris of South America," where we had a city tour, dinner with a tango show, plus a visit out on the Pampas to see *gauchos* perform their horsemanship and partake of a typical Argentine *asado* (lunch) barbecued over an open fire.

We flew south to Patagonia, the enormous Argentine area that reaches just south of Buenos Aires all the way to the bottom of the country at the Straits of Magellan. Our destination was the Reserva Provincal Punta Tombo, home to one- half million Magellanic penguins, the largest penguin nesting ground in continental South America. These little birds set up housekeeping here from September to April. when they lay their eggs and hatch their young. The remainder of the year they are out to sea along the Brazil coast. We walked along trails that took us right up to the birds, but the penguins seemed to pay us no attention. We spent the night at Trelew, a nearby Welch village with bountiful fruits and flowers.

The next day we were amazed at the wildlife on the Peninsula Valdez. From a boat ride we viewed monstrous elephant seals lounging on the beach. They are so named because the males have on their nose an excrescence that they can blow up at will until it measures some twenty inches. The rocks all around the shores were covered with sea lions and sea birds.

We flew to Ushuaia, Argentina, "the world's southern-most city," and held our breath as our plane swooped down between the mountains and sea to land on a very short runway. We had dinner with a local family (called Feugians), who told us about life at the bottom of the Americas, where it is winter about six months of the year, and not very warm the other six. Being so close to Antarctica, it is cold here most of the time and they experience extremely high winds. But the locals consider themselves to be adventurers, and seemed to be content with their surroundings. Give me hot Texas any day!

A drive through the Tierra del Fuego National Park displayed forests, streams, and snow-capped mountains. We boarded a vessel for a cruise of the Beagle Channel where, even though the waters were rather rough and the winds blowing cold, we enjoyed seeing albatrosses and sea lions.

We flew north to Rio Gallegos and boarded a motor coach to Calafate, a small village located on Lake Argentine in the spectacular Patagonia Region. The following day we stopped to see the awesome Moreno Glacier, one of the planet's few advanc-

*The Moreno Glacier in Argentina is one of the world's few advancing glaciers.*

ing glaciers. The thirty-foot-high glacier, formed from ice in the Andes, is gradually flowing eastward. This wall of ice breaks off in mammoth iceberg chunks that slowly float down to Lake Argentina.

A short bus ride brought us to Puerto Natales, Chile, a serene village perched on the eastern shore of Last Hope Sound near the bottom of the country. At our hotel here we were served the best fresh salmon I have ever tasted. This long nation of Chile has 2,625 miles of coastline in length and only 312 miles across at the widest part. I was amazed at this land of contrasts from fertile valleys (much of our fruits and vegetables in the winter come from Chile), mountain rivers, and green fields in the north to a wild southern waste-land of glaciers, fjords, and tall mountains. The people were happy and congenial.

Our excursion in the south was to the Torres del Paine National Park. Here a sapphire-colored lake mirrors the massive rock towers, some covered with snow. We were so lucky that day to have crystal clear weather, for often the mountains are

*The magnificent vistas of the Torres del Pain National Park in southern Chile.*

*The guanacos, a cross between a llama and a deer, are found only in South America.*

shrouded in fog and clouds. Further into the park we took pictures of rainbows forming on raging waterfalls. The guanacos were all about. This South American animal that looks like a cross between a llama and a deer intrigued us.

After a very colorful and exciting day in the park, we began our return bus trip along a dirt road through barren and uninhabited land. All at once our bus came to a stop. As if this occurred frequently (and I am sure it did), our driver reached in the bins overhead, took out his coveralls, put them on, and proceeded to the back of the bus where the engine was located. After some time, he concluded that it was the fuel pump. We were about eighty miles from the nearest town or station. I assumed we would just have to spend the night in the bus, as there was no means of communication from the bus (this was before the wonderful invention of cell phones). After a while, another tour bus came by and stopped, asked what the problem was, and immediately handed us a new fuel pump. Apparently they carry extra parts with them in these remote areas, but our driver had not been so prepared. Anyway, in no time he had the new part in place and we were on our way. I am always astonished how things work out!

A flight north took us to Santiago and then back south to Puerto Montt. The next two days we experienced what is possibly the most scenic lake crossing in the world through the Argentine-Chilean Lake District. We traveled by bus-boat, bus-boat, etc., for seven exchanges that revealed the grandeur of the massive snow-capped peaks of the Andes and the deep blue lakes with waterfalls flowing in from all directions. Frequently we would spot high in the sky the huge condor floating along on the mountain updrafts.

We spent the night in a delightful lake lodge with hiking trails abounding in clear streams, waterfalls, and tropical foliage. The culmination of this fantastic journey was Bariloche, Argentina, which resembles European alpine resorts, complete with the wonderful aroma of chocolate candy, one of their specialties. Skiing is very popular here, and many Olympic skiers practice here during the United States summer. Wonderful sweaters are found in the shops, and naturally, I had to have one.

From there we went to Iguassu Falls and Rio de Janeiro in Brazil (which I covered in my first book).

I am so glad that we were included on this first Collette Vacations Discover South America Tour. The original one was twenty-five days and covered all the places mentioned above. Now the tour is fifteen days, and does not include the southern part of Argentina where we saw the sea lions and penguins and Ushuaia, nor the beautiful Moreno Glacier and the Torres del Paine Park in Chile. Realizing that the tour was too long, and after experiencing difficult airline schedules in those areas, they decided to make it a more concise trip including the highlights of South America, with Santiago, the Argentine-Chilean Lake District, Buenos Aires, Iguassu Falls, and Rio de Janeiro. It is still a wonderful trip.

# Bolivia

We had been to Peru but never to Bolivia, and when Collette Vacations presented the Legends of Peru and Bolivia Tour in 1998, I rounded up a group of my faithful followers.

Bolivia is landlocked in the southwestern part of South America, bordering Brazil on the

*Market Day in Bolivia is a colorful event.*

north and east, Peru on the northwest, Paraguay on the southeast, Argentina on the south, and both Peru and Chile on the west. It experiences heat in its equatorial low lands and extreme cold in its mountains. Approximately 75 percent of the inhabitants are descendants of the Aymara and Quechua pre-Columbian cultures. The colorful costumes of the Indians are still worn throughout the countryside.

*(Above) This Bolivian woman is spinning thread from llama wool. (Below) Bolivian markets offer a wide variety of colorful merchandise.*

When we arrived at the capital of La Paz, we quickly noticed the oxygen-thin air at 11,900 feet elevation. Bruce, our Collette guide, advised us to go to the hotel to rest and drink the local "coco tea." He recommended we call the hotel desk if we needed oxygen to help in the acclimatizing. I had two passengers who were very sick, and that afternoon on the city tour, we had to frequently stop the bus for someone to rush off and vomit. One woman never did overcome the altitude sickness, and we had to send her home after three days.

The children, dressed in brightly hued Indian regalia, greeted us at each stop and we could not resist the photo

*(Left) This interesting lady caught my attention at a Bolivian market. (Above) Spinning thread straight from the source—the llama.*

opportunity. The ladies wear long, full-patterned skirts, long-sleeved solid-color sweaters, and woolen shawls around their shoulders. Their long black hair, usually in a plait, is often topped with a brown felt hat (similar to a man's hat).

The third day we drove to Bolivia's most important archeological and mystical zone, Tiwanacu, located not far from La Paz. These ruins, some dating back as far as 7,000 B.C., are considered to have been occupied by the oldest pre-Incan Andean cultures. The magnificent monuments represent a perfection of building and decorating technique. The most famous is the Door of the Sun, where even today about 1,000 Bolivian Aymara Indians gather for the sacred Solstice Celebrations that begin at dawn in the Sun Temple. The Aymara spiritual leader and the Kalawalla medicine man perform the ceremony.

Our destination for the day was Lake Titicaca, the highest navigable lake in the world at 12,500 feet. This gigantic expanse of water stretches some 3,500 square

*Reed boats are the primary source of transportation on Lake Titicaca, Bolivia.*

miles and is up to 700 feet deep in some places. The vistas across the lake are breathtaking, with the snow-covered Andes in the distance. The lake is known for the totora reed that grows profusely around the lake. These thick reeds are pliable but durable. They break free from the lakebeds and join with other matter to gradually form floating islands that become living spaces for many Indian tribes.

When Thor Heyerdahl sailed from South America to Polynesia aboard the *Kon Tiki*, it was a copy of an Inca balsa-log raft. Later Heyerdahl thought that the explorers could have made the journey on reed boats similar to the early ones of the Nile, Tigris, and Euphrates. So in 1969, on the sands behind the Great Pyramids of Egypt, he and his helpers constructed the *Ra I* by lashing together many small reed bundles with separate ropes. This boat proved to be unsuccessful, for the waves tore the boat apart, and the *Ra I* had to be abandoned short of Barbados. Not to be defeated, Heyerdahl decided to build *Ra II*, but this time from the reeds from Lake Titicaca in Bolivia. He enlisted four Aymara Indians to be the shipwrights. We were honored to meet one of those men at the Inca Utama Hotel on the lakeshore, and had our picture taken with him. I was duly impressed because I had read *Kon-Tiki*, which led me to want to go to Easter Island, and had seen the *Ra II* in the Kon-Tiki Museum in Oslo, Norway. To actually meet the man who helped in the construction was overwhelming! A full-size replica of the ship is in the Andean Roots Cultural Complex at the Inca Utama Hotel.

*The gentleman in the center assisted Thor Heyerdahl in constructing Ra II from the reeds of Lake Titicaca.*

During our three days at Lake Titicaca, we took various boat rides. On one excursion we stopped at the Island of the Sun, which according to legend is the birthplace of the Inca Empire. The island boasts white sandy beaches, Inca stone ruins and terraces, and splendid views. We trudged up the stone staircase that leads up from the beach to the flowing Inca springs that produce fresh water and are considered to be sacred. As we stopped to get our breath along the way up, we visited darling youngsters with their llamas, and of course, we had to take a picture and give them some money for the privilege.

Another stop was at Copacabana to visit the cathedral, the home to the Virgin de Candelaria, Bolivia's patron saint. She is known as the Saint of the lake, embodying symbolism of the Aymara faith. Her dress is triangular to resemble the local mountain, and she is depicted above a crescent moon, below a shining sun, with stars between.

It was time to leave the beautiful Lake Titicaca and reluctantly return to La Paz to get our flight to Peru for more outstanding scenery and colorful people. (I recounted our visit to Machu Picchu in *Around the World in the Middle Seat.*)

South America has so many varied sights and interesting cultures, and you can travel from the United States with hardly any jetlag, so take advantage of the many exciting activities and unequaled scenery it has to offer.

*This scene is from a typical village in northern Bolivia.*

# North America

Needless to say, the first continent I stepped on was North America, my birthplace. As this was the only continent I saw until I was forty-two years old, it is very difficult for me to pick out favorite places. There is so much beauty and diversity in North America: the splendor of the mountains and rugged coastlines of Canada, the totally different culture and heritage of Mexico, the lovely and exotic islands of the Caribbean, the Mayan civilizations and tropical jungles of Central America, and the many interesting cities, spectacular national parks, and grandeur of the United States. I have selected a few places from this bountiful area that were special to me.

## Canada

### Chateau Lake Louise

As I look back to all the places I have spent away from home, and that includes hundreds, Chateau Lake Louise at Lake Louise in Canada has to be my favorite. This place has everything: outstanding scenery (I think the most beautiful setting of any hotel I have ever seen), old world atmosphere in décor, gracious service, and excellent food.

Chateau Lake Louise is located thirty-five miles west of Banff, Canada. As you drive up the mountain road, you are spellbound when you come to this storybook castle perched high in the Rockies surrounded by snow-capped mountains, and in the center a round emerald green lake. From the hotel terrace, during the summer you can see the snow-tipped peaks of Fairview Mountain to the south and the Beehive Mountains to the north. Straight across the lake is Victoria glacier. It resembles a waterfall frozen in place flowing down to the lakeshore. As you walk along the water's edge, you immediately notice that the serenity is undisturbed by motorcraft of any type, and canoes glide silently across the calm waters.

The hotel was established in this striking setting in the 1890s when the Canadian Pacific Railroad was built and mountaineering and tourist adventures in the remote

Canadian wilderness started to become popular.

Any time of the year is great to visit, but I personally prefer the winter. The rates are lower, and the snow and ice create a fairyland. The lake is totally frozen. Hotel employees design gigantic ice sculptures such as ice castles and snowmen right out on the lake surface. Glittering lights surround the lake ice rink that is lit for night skating, adding to the mystical effect. Twinkling lights adorn the surrounding trees to fashion the ultimate Christmas card.

*Winter is a great time to visit the Chateau Lake Louise in Canada. Here I am standing inside an ice sculpture on the frozen lake.*

Keith and I were there in February 1983, on an inspection trip, and they generously gave us a turret room (a bedroom with a sitting room in one of the towers). From our window each evening we watched the cross-country skiers snake their way single-file across the frozen lake to the hotel. In the distance, we could see two men attempting to climb a frozen waterfall—no simple task.

Winter activities available, other than the obvious downhill and cross-country skiing and snowmobiling, were dog sled rides and horse-drawn sleigh rides. We had been on a sleigh ride before, so opted to take the dog sled ride. The driver carefully seated Keith in the sled and placed me in front of him. Just as the driver was tucking the fur blanket around our legs, the nearby horse team with the sleigh took off. Apparently, the dogs thought that the movement was their cue to go, and go they did. The dogs took off running so fast that the driver could not take hold of the reins and came running behind, shouting, "Stop!" The driverless canine group was not about to stop. In the meantime, Keith and I were bouncing along with our rear ends on what seemed just like a board, hitting the high spots on the trail. (We needed that fur wrap under us, not on top!) At the end of the walkway around the lake (about one-third of a mile), our dog power stopped. The driver came running up, to apologizing for the wild ride, and offered us another try. We politely refused, untangled ourselves from the contraption, and gladly walked back to the hotel.

It is very difficult to get an individual reservation during the summer months, so if you want to go during that time, it is best to book very early or with a tour group. I suggest you go in the wintertime, even if you are not active in winter sports, for you won't find a more picturesque place in the world.

## The French Island of Saint Pierre et Miquelon

Did you know that you could go to France just twelve miles off the eastern Canadian coast? On our Collette Vacations Tour of Newfoundland and Labrador in 1995, our group boarded a ferry at Fortune, located at the far southwest point of

*St. Pierre et Miquelon is the only possession of France in the Western Hemisphere and is located just off the coast of northeastern Canada.*

Newfoundland's outer banks. On the short trip out we saw the tips of whale's tails as they frolicked in the cold Atlantic waters. We also spotted numerous puffins, those cute little sea birds that are black and have a bright orange beak. When puffins fly they resemble those cutout whirlybirds you sometimes see in yards as their wings go round and round in a circular motion.

Here, just off the coast of Canada, we had to show our passports as we entered Saint Pierre et Miquelon, a possession of France, and their only holding in the Western Hemisphere. The tiny island, about 1.5 times the size of Washington, D.C., has approximately 6,000 citizens and is known for its shops containing French goods. There are several small islands in the area of the French holdings, but Saint Pierre is the largest with the most population. All the natives migrated from the northern part of France, and today the island is not accepting any immigration. When we were there in 1995 there was a moratorium on cod fishing, once the main industry. The fish processing plants were canning fish they received from Russia.

Colorful houses and gardens greet visitors who are interested in the French boutiques and restaurants. Many private yachts are anchored in the harbor.

The island's most profitable time was during the American prohibition era. Bootleggers needed a place to receive booze from Canada, France, and Cuba, and this was the closest legal place. Warehouses were built, and up to 350,000 cases a week were smuggled out of Saint Pierre into the U.S. The smugglers discovered that the wooden cases which held the liquor were noisy when handled to ship out, so they transferred the bottles to burlap bags. Thus Saint Pierre ended up with thousands of wooden crates. They were used for heating homes, but still standing today is a Cutty Sark house made from the Scotch crates.

Al Capone, the main rumrunner, headquartered at the Hotel Robert where we stayed. Our room number, 29, was located in Capone's suite of rooms. His hat remains today in the hotel lobby.

Historians believe the islands were also used as a gun-smuggling outpost during the United States' battle with the British for independence in 1776. Many Acadians sought refuge here when deported in 1755 on their way south to Louisiana.

Other items of interest were numerous '50s-style jukeboxes at the hotel. The manager explained that during the 1950s some latter-day pirates on the island would extinguish the island's lighthouse lamp. They would then go out in boats in the ocean and hold up a light, imitating the lighthouse. When cargo ships hit the sand reef, the men would board the boat and tell the captain they would pull them off the sand bar in exchange for merchandise.

We also learned that all Charolais cattle from France were brought to Saint Pierre for quarantine before entering the United States. The Hotel Robert wasn't anything special, but the history of the place intrigued me for I really did not know that a piece of France was so near. (You can stock up on French perfumes and wines there for less than sold in the United States.)

# Prince Edward Island

Another delightful island in Canadian waters, and owned by Canada, is Prince Edward Island (referred to as PEI), located in the Gulf of St. Lawrence on the country's east coast. Only 140 miles long and 40 miles wide at its broadest part, no area is more than 20 miles from the sea, making it a haven for beach lovers. Approximately 56 percent of its 140,000 population live in rural areas, because farming is the number-one industry. And potatoes are the number-one crop. When you are chowing down on McDonald's French fries, they probably came from PEI, as McDonald's is their largest contractor. The high iron-oxide content of the red soil is perfect for growing potatoes.

My first trip to this wonderful island was with a Collette Vacations group tour in the summer of 1993. At this time we flew to Halifax, Nova Scotia, toured captivating Peggy's Cove (the most photographed site in North America), and then to Evangeline country in Acadia, where we later took a ferry ride (of a little more than an hour) over to PEI. Today they have opened the Confederation Bridge, a thirteen-kilometer link from the mainland. I liked the place so much that I wanted to return. My brother and his wife, and Keith and I, included the island on our fall foliage tour of the Northeast in 1999. We zipped across the bridge in about ten minutes and marveled at its efficient construction. It curves to ensure that drivers remain attentive.

On this personal trip we stayed at the Island Way Farm Bed and Breakfast, nestled among trees and flowers in the middle of a working potato farm. It was harvest time, and the farmer/host was very upset because it had rained so much, he couldn't get into the fields to gather the potatoes. He was afraid they would rot in the soil.

Other than pastoral scenery of fields and cattle, PEI is known as the home of Lucy Maud Montgomery, author of *Anne of Green Gables.* You can visit the Green Gable House, and of course, purchase lots of cute "Anne" souvenirs. They also present an enchanting musical play about Anne during the summer months.

Lobster fishing is the second largest industry on the island, and on both trips there we indulged in a scrumptious lobster dinner with all the trimmings. The lobster season runs from the first of May to the end of

*Wanda and Delbert enjoy a bountiful lobster dinner on Prince Edward Island.*

June and from mid-August to mid-October. Try to go during these times for mouth-watering feasts.

For beauty, peace and tranquility, visit Prince Edward Island. Just remember, when you return over the Confederation Bridge, you have to pay a toll to leave. It is such a neat place, you might just want to stay and avoid paying the exit toll.

# Manitoba

After our successful farm visits in South America and PEI, we decided to try a similar vacation in Saskatchewan and Manitoba, Canada. We had enjoyable stays at six different properties, but one hostess certainly outperformed all the rest.

Willow Point Farms B&B was listed on the Internet as located near Fisher Branch in the northern Interlake region of Manitoba, where we planned to travel through on our return to Winnipeg to catch our plane home. The farm had been in the family for generations, and they enjoyed exchanging travel tales. Sounded right down our alley.

We were welcomed by Pauline Gulay, a widow who had started the B&B to fill her

lonely time. The ancestors of Pauline and her husband had migrated to this area of Canada from the Ukraine of Russia. They were farmers, raising wheat, canola, and alfalfa, and her family continues the management of the farm, plus they are involved in many other activities. Two sons, Jim and Glen, were pilots and crop sprayers, although Jim had started a new business called "Pooper Scoopers."

*Pauline Gulay and her dog welcome us to her bed and breakfast in Manitoba, Canada.*

With large machinery, he went to a farmer's cattle lots, scooped up the poop, and spread it on farmland as fertilizer.

When I called Pauline to reconfirm our reservation, she said she hoped we planned to stay a long time for she had many tours planned. And she certainly did!

She served us a hearty early dinner of soup, pork roast, and various vegetable dishes from her garden, topped off with lemon meringue pie. Afterward we visited Greenridge Farms, where they raised the best herd of polled Herefords we have ever seen (and even us Texans admitted that). The people were so gracious, and the wife insisted we have some of the rhubarb meringue squares she had prepared especially for us. We were already so very full from Pauline's meal, but did not want to hurt her feelings. So we added a few more pounds with the extra delicious dessert.

It was just getting dark when we stopped by to see Pauline's son, Glen, the crop duster, who was taking off and spraying crops in the twilight.

When we returned home, I asked Pauline if she had any ice for our drinks.

"Ice?" she repeated. "I don't have any ... we never use it." Yet she had two refrigerators and one large freezer. I guess when you live where it is cold most of the time, you have no need for ice. For us Texans, it is a necessity.

"No problem," I said, "just give me a shallow metal pan and I will quickly freeze some water." And in no time, we were able to have our cold drink.

After a gigantic breakfast the next morning, Pauline had a full day scheduled. All along our travels in this area we were puzzled by little round buildings, resembling doghouses, out in the fields. We found out their purpose when we went to a nearby industry—Interlake Forage Seeds. These people put out 1,200 honeybee colonies in these little huts on the area farmers' alfalfa fields for a percentage of the seeds, which they then process, warehouse, and market. They also are researching and developing new native species of seed. They sell the honey from the bees, and we sampled some of their delicious product.

Pauline wanted us to meet her friends in the Hutterian community. This religious sect was new to us, but we learned that there are 36,000 Hutterites in 434 colonies in North America, mostly in Canada.

The Hutterian Brethren is a religious group that originated in Switzerland and Austria, migrating to Canada in the early 1900s. They speak a Tyrolean dialect, from southern Austria, but English is taught in the commune schools. All Hutterites live in settlements of about 100 inhabitants. There were 111 members at the one we visited. The minister is the chief executive, and he and an advisory board make all the colony's decisions. All goods are owned communally, and all monies earned from different industries go into the central fund. If a member needs anything, it must be requested. If necessary, it will be bought for them. This colony had the most up-to-date farm equipment, kitchen appliances, etc. available.

When we arrived, the current spiritual leader, Jonathan, was cleaning some hogs that would be cooked for an upcoming event. His wife, along with their three-year-old grandson, was gathering herbs. Jonathan quickly washed his hands and was eager to show us around. His greenhouse produces tomatoes year round, and he proudly demonstrated how he manages to pollinate them in the enclosure by spraying the vines each day with warm water.

The Hutterites take their meals together in a large hall, and we toured the perfectly organized kitchen. The women are assigned in groups to cook for one week, and the duty rotates every six weeks. The spiritual leader's wife plans all the menus and orders the supplies.

A modern laundry facility was on the premises, and on the wall was a chart indicating the day each family was assigned to wash. The only way a family could veer from this schedule was if they had a baby and required extra washing.

Typically, the Hutterite men wear black trousers with suspenders, and any kind of buttoned shirt, and traditionally have a beard. The women wear below-the-knee-length dresses in a dark pattern print; younger girls tend to wear brighter colored frocks. All females wear a small white caps.

The adult males are assigned to a certain duty—raising hogs, building metal trailers, tending the cattle or chickens, or farming the fields. The schoolmaster is in charge of the garden, where schoolchildren work in the summer months.

It was nearing noon during our tour, and Jon invited us to come inside their home. The housing was two family units connected in a long barracks duplex-style. Inside were all the usual modern furnishings, with the exception of a television or phone,which are not permitted. There is one phone in the colony, at the manager's office.

"You must have some of my sassafras wine," the minister's wife stated, as we sat down in the living room. She served the wine in small glasses. "Now I will go get the lunch," she announced sternly.

"We did not intend to impose on you for lunch. We need to go on," I said.

"You don't argue with her," Jonathan stated, and I agreed with him.

She went over to the main kitchen and returned with steaming pots, inviting us to sit at the kitchen table. She served us some kind of noodle soup, some greasy, thin-sliced fried potatoes, and an apricot square for dessert.

"They had some chicken, but I don't like chicken, so I did not bring any," she stated.

Personally, I wish she had brought some chicken. I didn't care for the rest of the food.

"Eat the apricot square with the fried potatoes—they are good together," she instructed.

That was a matter of opinion.

We thanked the Hutterites for their gracious hospitality and lunch, and departed with appreciation, respect, and knowledge of a culture we did not even know existed before our trip to Manitoba.

Pauline then took us to a place that manufactures machines which cut a carpet just the size you want without having to roll it out on the floor. A local man invented this, and they are now sold all over the world.

We kept telling Pauline we had to get on the road to Winnipeg, but she said that we must go to see Patrick's machine shop, owned by another son. Then we walked around the town and she introduced us to everyone we met as her "Texicans." Just before we left, we stopped by to see her last child, a daughter who served us a glass of tea. (She had ice.)

We will always fondly remember Pauline and her efforts to show her "Texicans" a good time. We plan to return to see her in the future.

## Vancouver Island

Several times, prior to departing on Alaska cruises with our groups, we visited the lovely Butchart Gardens in Victoria on Vancouver Island, just a ferry ride from the city of Vancouver. These gardens were created when Robert Butchart, who had made a fortune out of cement at the turn of the century, was stuck with an exhausted limestone quarry. His wife suggested turning the whole thing into a garden. Thus today visitors can enjoy a beautiful

*The Butchart Gardens are a spectacle not to be missed on Vancouver Island, Canada.*

array of fountains, lakes, trees, and flowers. We had always wanted to see the rest of Vancouver Island, so we planned a trip for the two of us in 2001.

After flying to Vancouver, we rented a car, took the ferry over to the island at Nanaimo, and began our exploration. The island is about 285 miles long and 50 miles wide, and we covered most of it. The terrain is mountainous and is covered by large territories of lumber, a boon to the province's economy and also a magnet for nature-lovers. The waters around the island lure salmon fishermen and kayak enthusiasts.

We stayed at interesting and picturesque bed and breakfast inns throughout our journey. First, we drove from Nanaimo across the island to Port Alberni, claiming as many other places, to be the salmon capital of the world. From there we took the Lady Rose Ferry, passengers only, down inlet waters for about two hours to Bamfield, located on the western side of the island, and the beginning of the Pacific Rim National Park. Bamfield has been called the "Venice of North America," as most travel around it by boat. This is the place to go on sea otter and whale watching charters, kayak adventures, and guided fishing trips. We stayed at the Bamfield Lodge, a comfortable inn catering to fishermen. It was so pleasant to sit out on the large porch and watch the wildlife and human life activities in the harbor below.

A boardwalk starts at the lodge and runs along Bamfield Inlet. As you stroll along you can see bald eagles, blue herons, kingfishers, cormorants, crows, ravens, gulls, loons, plus many ducks and a variety of other birds. From Bamfield hikers start on the forty-eight-mile West Coast Trail of the Pacific Rim Park that leads through the coastal rainforest. Reservations must be made to hike the trail to protect overuse of this delicate environment. To return to our car at Port Alberni

*We toured a small portion of the Wild Pacific Trail on Vancouver Island.*

we took the land route via the Western Bus Lines, a drive along logging dirt roads most of the way.

Our next stop was at Ucluelet, right on the windswept Pacific rugged coast. I selected the Ocean's Edge B&B here because the host, Bill McIntyre, offered a half-day personalized walking tour of a portion of the Pacific Rim Park whose trail was accessed just down from his house. We saw thousand-year-old cedars, spruces and hemlocks, many leaning from the fierce winds that come in from the Pacific. Bill focused on the natural environment of the area and its resources, pointing out individual trees and mosses, which made the scenery much more meaningful. Bill said that his most popular tours were by storm-seekers. Desolate winters have become high season for storm watching. When a storm is raging, Bill leads groups to safely witness the majesty and power of the Pacific Ocean performing with peak force, hurling itself against the shoreline in a never-ending series of breakers up to fifty feet high. In these storms, tons of giant kelp are swept shoreward, along with large tree logs tossed in the surf like straws. I am not inclined to want to be part of a storm, so I was glad it was a cool but beautiful day when we made our trek.

At mealtimes, Keith enjoyed the hand-sized, farm-raised oysters that are grown in the area. I was content to eat the delectable fish dishes the local restaurants prepared.

We continued our tour of the island, crossing over to Campbell River on the eastern shore, where we took a ferry to Quadra Island, the largest and most populous of the Discovery Islands that lie between Vancouver Island and the mainland coast of British Columbia. It is home to 3,500 year-round residents and is a popular destination for tourists in the summertime. The area is attractive for its natural beauty, unlimited recreation, and friendly people. Sport fishing is the prime activity. The intricate shoreline, dotted with beaches, sheltered coves, protected channels, and islets, is ideal for exploration.

We chose to go there because it is the home to the First Nations Indians, and we are very interested in Native American cultures. Long before European explorers made their way to the Pacific Northwest, Cape Mudge on Quadra Island was called "Tas-Kwa-Luten," meaning a gathering place in the Kwak'wala language. Today the Laichwiltach people have built a modern beachfront lodge where their ancestors once lived, hunted, and fished for salmon in the rich Discovery Passage. The lodge features authentic Pacific Coast native architecture, art, and culture based on traditional Kwagiulth historical values. Exuding the warmth of West Coast wood construction is the design of a historical "Big House" as the main foyer and lounge area. From our comfortable sea-view room, we enjoyed watching a family of eagles nesting in a nearby tree. The food and service were excellent, and we were renewed from our long trip on the road with our two-day stay here.

Reluctantly, we had to get back on schedule. A ferry ride took us back to Port Campbell, and we motored north to Port Hardy to overnight before catching the ferry to Bella Colla on the British Columbia mainland. This eight-hour journey did not meet our expectations of a wonderful boat ride. It was raining and cloudy, with rather rough seas at times. When we landed in Bella Coola it was pitch dark, and we had difficulty finding our reserved motel.

The next morning we started the 185-mile drive over unpaved mountainous roads to our next stop, Chilko Lake Resort. I now know why the resort brochure states that they will fly their guests in a private plane directly to the resort. It took over five hours to make the journey over dusty and rough roads, but Chilko Lake Resort was worth the trip. Situated at the north end of Chilko Lake, the resort has eleven deluxe waterfront bungalows. It would have been wonderful to sit on our front porch overlooking the lake, but unfortunately, it was cold and rainy (and this was in July). Lodge personnel said the time to come is from mid-August to mid-October, when hundreds of thousands of red sockeye salmon return to their spawning grounds in the lake. They said the entrance to the lake would be red during this time. During the rest of the year, Dolly Varden and rainbow trout are popular prizes for the fishermen.

Their very moderate-priced American Plan includes the accommodation, all meals, afternoon coffee hour with homebaked goodies and "happy hour snacks." It was all wonderful.

Our neighbor to the north, Canada, has so much to offer in scenery, activities, and gracious people. I fully recommend that you plan a visit there soon.

# United States

When it comes to the United States, there are so many fantastic places, I don't know what to include! Each part of the country offers a special attraction. My group tours to the fall foliage in New England, and the national parks of the West were always popular. New York City cannot be equaled with its sights, Broadway plays, and shopping, or Washington, D.C. with its many monuments and museums.

And there is no other place in the world like one of my favorites, Las Vegas. This Disney World for adults has now become a mecca for family entertainment. You don't have to go around the world to see the Pyramids (Luxor), pirate ships in the Caribbean (Treasure Island), the Eiffel Tower (Paris), the canals of Venice (Venetian), the lake region of Italy (Bellagio), a jungle forest (Mirage), a castle with King Arthur and the Roundtable (Excalibur), continuous circus acts (Circus Circus), lions in the jungle (MGM Grand), Caesar's magical empire (Caesar's), the Hard Rock Café, and much, much more. You don't even need to like to

*Fun for all ages and a place like no other on earth—Las Vegas, Nevada.*

gamble to have a great time in Vegas. You can spend your time going from one exciting hotel to the next.

It was difficult to narrow them down, but here are just a few of my much-loved places in the United States.

## San Francisco and the Wine Country

San Francisco, California, is my favorite city in the United States. I guess one reason is that this city was the first stop Keith and I made on our honeymoon. It was my first time in this alluring city, and as the song goes, "I left my heart" there. I love the city's rolling hills, coming right down to the sea at Fisherman's Wharf, where you can sample all kinds of appetizing seafood, usually while watching a street performer at the same time. It is eerie to look out into the bay and see the vacated buildings of Alcatraz, the infamous federal prison. Now you can tour this landmark. I don't like to see places like that, so we just viewed it from afar.

This first trip to San Francisco was in July 1974, and coming from Texas, I had no idea that July was their coldest month. We were going to continue on to Hawaii, so I had only summer clothes with me. It was very chilly, and I had to purchase a sweater to go over my lightweight fabrics.

The first thing I wanted to do was ride the trolley cars. We came out of our hotel

*Fisherman's Wharf, where good food and entertainment are plentiful.*

our first morning there and climbed aboard. The car was very crowded, and we just squeezed in at the front.

"Get in the back," the driver bellowed, as he released the brake and thrust the trolley car uphill.

In my haste to obey, plus the sudden movement of the car, I tripped over a man's foot and fell down on my knees, knocking a hole in my new white linen pantsuit, plus one in my knee. We managed to jump off at the next stop and return to the hotel to doctor my bloody injuries and change clothes—not the way you want to start a honeymoon. Patched up and in warmer clothes, we proceeded to Fisherman's Wharf. We stopped at a shop that sold redwood burl tables. Before I realized what was happening, Keith had bought a large redwood coffee table and was having it shipped home. Now, every time I look at the table, I have fond memories of our honeymoon and San Francisco, and it will always remain my favorite city in the United States.

My next visit to San Francisco was when I was working at the public television station in Austin as auction manager and fundraiser. I read where California had wine-tasting parties to raise money for the stations. I wanted to see if I could persuade the vintners to come to Texas. I contacted the Wine Institute in San Francisco, and they invited me to come out in 1976 and discuss the possibility. After meeting with the group and convincing them that Texans liked wine as much as beer, they agreed to give our state a try. I am happy to say that now, many years later, the Wine Tastings have produced many dollars for public television in Texas.

While we were there, the Wine Institute people suggested we visit some wine producers, and they set up appointments for us at Cakebread, Mondavi, and Domaine Chandon wineries. Keith and I rented a car and started out early for our trip to the Napa Valley. On the Golden Gate Bridge they had set up reversible lanes in 1963. The bridge's six lanes were thereby adjusted to meet the demands of the traffic. On that morning, most of the traffic was coming into the city, so there were four lanes inbound and two, where we were, outbound. Just as we entered the bridge's 4,200-foot span, the bottom (it seemed) fell out of our car. A rod broke and was dragging on the pavement, creating a terrible noise and making sparks fly everywhere. People were honking and pointing at us, as if we did not know we had a problem! Keith kept on gunning it, and miraculously we reached the other side where there was pull-off and a phone. We contacted the rental company, and shortly they arrived with a bigger and better vehicle.

A few Golden Gate Bridge facts: The bridge was completed in May 1937, taking four years to build. (I escorted a group to the 50th Anniversary Celebration in 1987, reviewed in my first book.) A group of ironworkers and painters battle wind, sea air, and fog to maintain the bridge year-round. The bridge has always been painted orange and is named Golden Gate because it spans the Golden Gate Strait, entrance to the San Francisco Bay from the Pacific Ocean. When the bridge was completed in 1937, it was the longest span bridge in the world. Since that time the Golden Gate Bridge has been demoted to number seven in size in the world. A Japanese bridge holds first place at 6,532 feet.

With a different automobile that seemed to perform well, we continued on our planned tour to have breakfast on the outdoor dining deck of the Alta Mira Hotel and Restaurant in Sausalito, known more for its famous madam in the early 1900s than the food. But the view of the bay and the city of San Francisco is unmatchable.

*The famous Golden Gate Bridge leading you into San Francisco or out to the Napa Wine Country.*

On the way to the wine country, we had to make a stop at the breathtaking Muir Woods National Monument. Pamphlets at the park entrance state that until the 1800s, many northern California coastal valleys were covered with redwood trees similar to those now found only in Muir Woods Park. Noting that the area of Redwood Creek

contained the last uncut stands of old-growth redwood trees, Congressman William Kent bought 295 acres for $45,000 in 1905. In 1908 he donated it to the federal government to become a national park. It was named for John Muir, a conservationist at the time. You can get a crick in your neck trying to look up to the tops of the giant trees that are hundreds of years old. We are so fortunate that the Kents protected this jewel for us to appreciate many years later.

*Muir Woods—home to the few remaining giant redwood trees just outside San Francisco.*

On to the Napa Valley wine country. Our first stop was at

Cakebread Cellars at Rutherford. At this time, Jack Cakebread was just starting his winery, and we were privileged to taste his wine straight from the casks. Today Cakebread Cellars has grown into a thriving internationally distributed wine company. Jack became a personal friend during the public television tastings, and he hosted many visits for my tour groups to Napa Valley.

On this visit to the wine country we had lunch at Domaine Chandon, a champagne vintner where wine and cuisine are as luscious as the setting of their grounds. Domaine Chandon was the first California sparkling wine producer to be established by a Frenchman using only the traditional method, and the first to introduce smaller containers to preserve the delicate grapes during harvest. They also introduced four-star dining to Napa Valley. When I brought my groups to Napa, we always took pleasure in a gourmet lunch at Domaine Chandon, accompanied by their mouth-watering champagnes.

Our last stop this time was at the Robert Mondavi Winery, recognized for their superior wines all over the world and known for supporting diverse cultural programs to educate the public about the many enjoyable aspects of wine. On a later group tour, we had a private wine seminar at Mondavi.

After a thoroughly delightful day of sampling the wines of Napa Valley, I was positive I could promote a successful wine tasting in Texas, and later, this was one of the first places I brought my groups for some very lovely and tasty experiences.

## Pacific Northwest and the San Juan Islands

Collette Vacations announced a new tour in 1997 that I thought my faithful followers would like: "Pacific Northwest and the San Juan Islands." After checking the

map to see where the San Juan Islands were located, in Puget Sound north of Seattle, I decided this would be an excellent trip to take in July to escape the Texas heat. Our group of almost fifty flew to Seattle and spent the night before boarding the *Island Spirit*. The captain, owner and operator, Jeff Behrens, and his sailing mate, a magnificent Dalmatian named Bosun, welcomed us aboard. The ship was to be our transportation and restaurant during the day, and each evening we would be at a hotel on one of the islands.

There are more than 175 islands in the San Juan region. Captain Jeff has over fifteen years of experience and knows just where to go to get the best sightings of wildlife and natural beauty of the area. Ports of call for us were LaConner, with antique shops and Indian artifacts; Roche Harbor, known as John Wayne's favorite

*Captain Jeff and First Mate Bosun by their sailing cruise ship,* Island Spirit, *which tours the San Juan Islands in the Puget Sound north of Seattle.*

docking place; and Friday Harbor, where we visited the Whale Museum and enjoyed the quaint shops. One afternoon Jeff received word that a pod of whales were nearby, so off we rushed in search of the spouts on the water surface. Soon we spotted them! We were able to get great pictures of the whales as they cavorted in the waters around our ship. We also saw porpoise, eagles, and harbor seals, plus numerous waterfowl.

A highlight of the cruise, other than the great fun of having the entire ship to our-selves and complete attention of the captain and crew, was the delicious food and com-plimentary open bar cocktail hour. One night we were treated to a hearty Crab Feed as we watched the sun set over the Gulf Islands. It was like being on our own private yacht.

Now Captain Jeff has converted the *Island Spirit* to a comfortable overnight cruise ship accommodating thirty-two passengers in sixteen outside cabins, complete with private bath and individual cabin thermostat. A special feature that appeals to me (as I have trouble sleeping with noise) is that after 8:00 P.M., the generators are shut down and the entire ship operates on battery. How wonderful to have a peaceful night's sleep.

All too soon we had to depart the ship at Port Townsend, located in northern Washington, but we had more treasures awaiting us. We switched to a motor coach and traveled through the Olympia National Forest to Lake Quinault Lodge, which boasts that President Franklin Roosevelt was one of their guests.

We continued to the Alpine village of Leavenworth, where it seemed like we were are really in the charming Bavaria region of Germany, not the state of Washington. German architecture, food, and entertainment dominate the town.

The next night we were staying at the Sun Mountain Lodge located on its own Cascade Mountain peak outside the old western mining town of Winthrop, Washington. This year-round resort is listed as one of the 100 World's Best Resorts and Great Hotels. Entertainment for the evening was a wagon ride to a camping area. Here they had a BBQ dinner, where some of the local cowboys provided country/western music. They were not the greatest, and finally one of group, Joy,

*Wagon transportation to an evening BBQ dinner, Sun Mountain Lodge.*

took the guitar and showed them how it's done—"Texas style." She had been on several trips with us, and I did not even know she could sing, much less play a guitar.

After the scrumptious meal and good music, we climbed back on the wagons to return to the hotel. Two horses pulled the wagons. Bench seats had been installed in the back of the open wagon for the passengers. Our wagon and horses were plodding along, last in line of the parade, when all of a sudden, a large tree limb was struck by the wagon in front of us. With a crash, it fell right down on the front of our wagon, where, thankfully, no one was sitting. The driver expertly managed to contain the frightened horse team after several jumps and runs. There were six of us in the wagon, plus the driver. We were thrown down on the floor, but other than a few bruises, were OK. When the driver was able to stop the horses, the guys extracted the large tree part and we went on our way. Who would have ever thought you could have an accident on a non-traffic road out on a ranch in a wagon?

## Skiing in Colorado

At the age of forty-one, I took my first snow skiing lesson. Keith, the kids (then ages eight and eleven), and I went to Aspen, Colorado. Keith was the only one of the group who could ski, so the children were enrolled in their age group classes and I signed up for the adult lessons.

The first morning there I donned all that ski stuff—thermal underwear, ski pants and jacket, and those terri-

ble heavy boots—and reported to class. I had great apprehensions about doing this thing, but was determined to give it a try. As I looked around the class, I was pleased to see that there were a few older than I was, and a few appeared to be in worse physical shape. The instructor told us to form a circle around him and start moving our skis back and forth— *shush-shush-shush.* As I was *shushing* I suddenly became very warm, then sick at my stomach.

*The Brooks family out on the slopes at Aspen, Colorado (many years ago).*

*What if I throw up right here on the snow in front of everyone?* ran through my mind. Then, I guess my subconscious took over, and I passed out right on the snow! When revived, all I saw was a big red cross on the medic's jacket. I thought I must have died and gone to heaven. Then I realized what a spectacle I had made of myself. The medics assured me, when they discovered that I was from Texas, that I needed to adjust to the altitude and told me to go to the warming house and rest for a couple of days to get acclimated.

I trudged off to the warming house, feeling devastated that I had failed at skiing because my husband could already ski and I knew the kids were probably doing Olympic runs on the slopes. I took off my coat (which had an attached belt in the back) and draped it over the back of the chair. I was soothing my spirits by sipping a hot buttered rum when some clod in ski boots walked behind my chair, caught his boot in the coat belt, and pulled me and the chair over backwards, bruising my shoulder. I feel sure that I am probably the only skier who has ever been injured sitting in the warming house!

After the children learned how to ski, we started a traditional ski trip each Christmas to a western ski resort. My mother, my brother, and his wife and son accompanied us and this was how we celebrated Christmas each year for eleven years. We gave no presents; the trip was our gift. All members of our family look back to these times as some of the best family activities in our lives.

Through practice on the "bunny slopes," I gradually learned to stay upright and, after a fashion, get back up when I fell. On one trip to Colorado, I had the kind of ski poles that have straps, and I had my hands through the straps while skiing. On my way down the mountain, somehow I lost control and sailed right off the edge of the run into a deep snowdrift. I fell with my thumb caught in the ski pole strap, and *crack*—it was broken. At first I thought it was just sprained, but by the time I returned home, I realized I had more than a sprain, and had to have an operation to set it correctly. This resulted in a cast for six weeks, but conveniently, it was on the left hand, so I could still manage fairly well. After that, I added breakaway ski poles to my skiing equipment.

To continue my skiing saga, we were in Vail for the family Christmas trip. This was ten years after my first attempt to ski, and by this time, I had become moderately adept at the sport. (At least on the blue and green runs.) I was feeling good about my ability and was cruising down a long run ahead of the rest of the family group. A kid, about five years old, came zooming very close past me. I swerved to dodge him and hit an ice patch. My skis went right out from under me, and I landed on my head with such force I was knocked out. When I came to, the medics were already at my side. I looked down the slope, and here came Keith side-stepping back up the hill. He had skied right past me, not realizing the one down on the snow was his wife. The medics checked me and wanted to take me back down on the stretcher, but I said that I could make it slowly. Other than a large bump on the head (caused even through a fur hat) and an ice scrape on my cheek, I was OK, but I could have broken my neck.

Thus, that little episode ended the skiing career of Joyce Brooks. I never was any good anyway. We transferred our Christmas trips from the snow to the tropics, and went to Belize to snorkel and fish instead.

## Snowmobiling in Jackson Hole, Wyoming

Snowmobiling is no big deal in areas where you have lots of snow, but to this Texan, it is. It looked like such a great sport, but I had never had the opportunity to try it. In 1999, Collette Vacations announced they had a tour in Jackson Hole, Wyoming, that included a day of snowmobiling. I immediately jumped at the chance, and found many patrons who wanted to try it also. This was my last trip as a group travel leader.

I was hesitant, for when we were in Bermuda some years prior, Keith and I had rented motorbikes to see the island. I had never been on any type of motorized bike, and found out quickly that I was no candidate for "Hell's Angels." We were instructed that to stop, you turn the handles forward, and to go forward, you turn the handles back. That seemed totally opposite of logic to me, and consequently, as we pulled out in the teeming traffic in Hamilton, the first thing I did was run a stop sign, having turned the handle the wrong way. Immediately, Keith motioned me to follow him back to the rent place, where we promptly returned the bikes and caught a bus to tour the island.

After this experience, I was afraid I would have the same problem with the snow-mobile. When the outfitter picked up this bunch of old warm weather troops (the youngest one was in her fifties), everyone was ready to tackle the snow trails. First we signed all kinds of forms stating that we would not sue them if we were injured (which didn't help your confidence). Then we were issued insulated coveralls, gloves and boots, visored helmets, and traveled by bus to the beginning of the trails outside Jackson Hole.

We were blessed with a totally gorgeous day. The sun was shining brightly with the

*Great fun! Snowmobiling for the first time at Jackson Hole, Wyoming.*

temperature around 30 degrees. When we arrived at the starting point our guide gave us about five minutes of instructions. I was so relieved to find out that the vehicle would stop by just releasing the power switch on the right handlebar. That was all there was to it. There were hand warmers on the handlebars to keep our hands nice and comfy, and our feet were next to the engine that would radiate heat to keep them feeling snug.

You should have seen us aged Texans hot-dogging it along the snowy trails. Along the way we encountered a group of bighorn sheep so accustomed to seeing the vehicles that they didn't even move as we roared up to them. The snowy covered mountains against the clear blue Wyoming sky were breathtaking.

We rode all morning and stopped for an appetizing lunch at a resort about eighteen miles into the wilderness and then returned to the starting place around 5:00 P.M. As the day came to an end, we were getting braver and speeding along the trails like professionals. I rate snowmobiling as one of my all-time travel highs.

Just on the outskirts of Jackson Hole is an elk refuge. Here reportedly 10,000 elk come every winter to be fed. A large horse-drawn wagon sleigh took us up close and

personal for some un-
believable photos of
the elk. Large bulls,
still carrying magnifi-
cent antlers, were
sometimes "facing off
with each other" while
the cows and calves
just sat or stood
around and ignored
them and us. The
National Elk Refuge
was set up in 1912 to
protect the elk winter
range and provide a
supplemental feeding
program during the

*Huge herds of elk come to the National Elk Refuge at Jackson Hole each winter.*

snow-covered months. Our guide explained that when the elk shed their horns in the
spring, the local Boy Scouts collect them to be shipped to the Orient, where they are
sold to make an aphrodisiac drug. Collecting the elk horns has been a very profitable
project for the Scouts.

As an option, several of my group took an excursion to Yellowstone National
Park. We took a bus to the south entrance of the park. There we crowded into a snow
coach, a funny-looking contraption that looks likes a minibus half-track. Talk about
an uncomfortable ride! If you were in the back, you were burning up from the heat of

*A snow coach took us to Yellowstone National Park.*

*It was a real blast to see Old Faithful do its thing, with the snow as a backdrop.*

the rear engine. Up front, you froze, as the driver had to have his window open for ventilation, plus there was an open hole in the top where snow and wind entered. This machine went max twenty miles an hour. The rough ride rewarded us with the dazzling snow-covered Yellowstone Park. All the park roads are closed in the winter. The only admittance is by snow coach or snowmobile. And there were plenty of snowmobiles—they were whizzing noisily around us all day.

The big thrill was to see Old Faithful shooting its steam from the boiling geyser high into the clear winter sky with a snowy backdrop. As the foliage is gone from the trees, it's easy to spot wildlife on the snow. We saw bison, elk, deer, and a wolf.

If you have an opportunity to take a trip to Yellowstone Park in the winter, plan to spend the night at the beautiful new lodge near Old Faithful. We made the trip in one day, and that was too tiring a ride on the snow coach. You can snowmobile in, but I have heard they are considering limiting their access because of the snowmobiles' effect on wildlife.

Everyone on the trip was elated with the fantastic winter experiences at Jackson Hole and eager to go again someday.

## Salmon Fishing in Alaska

Keith and I love to fish and always wanted to go salmon fishing in Alaska. One day I noticed Shelter Lodge in Juneau, Alaska, was offering a FAM trip at a reduced rate, so we quickly signed up. We went the last week of August 1998, just before they closed down the lodge after Labor Day.

The lodge is located on the lush, heavily forested Shelter Island, five miles by boat from Juneau. Nestled among giant spruce trees, the main lodge contains the kitchen and lounge/dining area, plus living quarters for the owners, Richard and Jackie. A deck with benches for telling fishing stories connects sleeping rooms that will accommodate a total of twelve guests. Two of the rooms at that time had private bath facilities.

On the week program, you fish five days, allowing two days for arrival and departure. Before departing for the island, you stop by a grocery store and stock up on beverages and snacks of your preference.

The fisherpeople are divided into parties of four to a boat. The three twenty-six-foot Olympic cabin cruisers are captained by Richard, his son, Kenji, and Frank, all experienced in locating and catching fish. Everyone is issued all-weather gear of overalls, coat, and boots. Even if it is not raining, these are necessary to keep your regular clothes clean. Each morning, after a bountiful breakfast, you pack your individual lunch from a sandwich buffet, put it in a paper sack labeled with your name, and deposit it in the cooler for your assigned boat for the day. The cook always sneaks in some special goodies such as brownies, fruit, cookies, etc.

By 8:00 A.M. you are in your boat headed for the "fishing for the day," be it salmon, halibut, river trout, or rockfish. For everything except salmon, each person is given a rod and bait or lure appropriate for the type of fish being caught. When seeking salmon, four lines are set by the captain in each corner of the back boat deck. You are assigned a number, and as the fish strike the line, you take your turn reeling it in.

Now, this is my kind of fishing. The captain baits the line and puts it out. When there is a fish on it, you have the fun of reeling it in, and then he takes it off the hook. When you get back to the lodge around 5:30 P.M., the crew cleans the fish and packages it in plastic bags with your number and puts it in the freezer. The morning of departure, your catch is packed in insulated boxes, correctly labeled for the plane travel. The only thing you have to worry about is that your plane is not delayed, or the fish may thaw out. But we were successful in bringing over 200 pounds of still-frozen salmon and halibut all the way back to 100-degree temperature in Texas.

It's hard to explain the special thrill of bringing in a twenty-pound salmon as it leaps high in the air or takes your line way out and you have to bring it back in, or the excitement in cranking the reel to bring up a forty-four-pound

*It doesn't get much better than this—catching salmon in the Pacific Ocean near Juneau, Alaska.*

halibut from depths of over 300 feet. Another shock is to bring up a rockfish from around 300 feet. When it surfaces, its eyes bug out about two inches from the pressure. We caught our limit each fishing day, and the time passed so quickly.

Fishing with Keith and me were a young couple on their honeymoon. When she brought her first salmon in, she remarked: "I have never experienced anything this exciting!" Made me wonder about her groom.

Even if fishing is not your thing, you should go to Shelter Lodge just for the food.

*A weekly treat was a king crab dinner freshly caught in the Shelter Lodge's private traps.*

Each morning and night you have a choice of two or three entrées. The fresh seafood is usually a feature of the evening meal, but they also offer other meats. Once a week we would run the crab pots and that night have a crab boil feast. Every meal was a hearty, home-cooked delight.

Richard and Jackie work diligently to offer first-class fishing with a friendly, home-style atmosphere. With only twelve guests, you soon become one big happy family, and in the evening, each angler has to try to outdo the other with their fish stories. At the end of a very quick week, we regretted leaving the island paradise and our new friends.

We were so fond of Shelter Lodge that we have been back once, and plan to go again. I can assure you that your Alaska experience at the Shelter Lodge will be a delight.

## Grand Hotel—Mackinac Island

The Grand Hotel on Mackinac Island, Michigan, offers the ultimate in American style and grace. This destination was part of an Around Michigan Tauck Tour for my group in 1988. Located offshore of the northern tip of Michigan, the only way to arrive at the hotel is by plane or ferry across the lake and then transfer to horse-drawn carriage. No cars, except emergency vehicles, are allowed on the island. There are more than 500 horses on the island to serve as transportation, adding more work to the street cleaning crews known as "pooper scoopers."

The Grand Hotel's front porch is the world's longest at 660 feet long, furnished with comfortable rocking chairs for relaxation and a view out to the lake. The hotel opened as a summer retreat for vacationers who arrived by lake steamer in 1887. Through the years remodeling and additions have taken place, but the charm and elegant atmosphere remain. At only four floors high, the Grand Hotel has a total of 343 rooms. The movie *Somewhere In Time*, starring Jane Seymour and Christopher Reeve, was filmed here.

Our tour guide somehow managed to obtain one of the top-floor corner suites, with a small balcony overlooking the lake, for Keith and me. Each room at the hotel is decorated differently with period antiques, and ours was a symphony of blue and green.

The gardens are worth the trip. Each year the hotel's gardeners install more than 100,000 bedding plants to create the profusion of color and fragrance around the grounds.

When you are not rocking on the front porch, you can have afternoon tea, browse the unique shops of the village, and sample the world-famous fudge (the mouth-watering aroma fills the air), or take a carriage ride around the island to the old Fort Mackinac.

*Tulip time in Michigan is a special time. Here we are among the tulips in the beautiful gardens of the Grand Hotel.*

Dinner is a special occasion, and one of the few resort places today that require men to wear a jacket and tie and the ladies a dress. You might grumble as you have to get dressed up, but once in the dining room, you feel part of a by-gone era, when people took time to dine formally and leisurely. It took us nearly three hours for dinner, but what an extraordinary experience.

All too soon you have to take the ferry back to the mainland and reality. The Grand Hotel is open May through October, and again, it is probably best to book with a tour company to insure a reservation during the peak summer months.

## Natchez, Mississippi

When I became a group travel leader at the bank, one of my first motor coach trips out of Texas was to Natchez, Mississippi. The bank president's wife was from Mississippi, and she thought we should have a trip to the Spring Pilgrimage in 1982. The morning the forty-four passengers arrived to depart, I noticed one woman, Bessie, in her eighties, was wearing a bonnet, the old-fashioned kind that my grandmother had worn in the fields, with a big shade and tied under her chin. This was her first trip with me. She was traveling with her daughter, who had been on many of my previous trips. I was glad her mother had joined us.

Every spring Natchez celebrates the season with a Spring Pilgrimage in which they open about thirty of their pre-Civil War mansions to the public. The event is held in March, when the city is decorated with a profusion of azaleas, dogwood, and wisteria. Natchez has more antebellum houses than any other place in the United States, including over 500 buildings dating back before the Civil War.

Our local guide had a pleasant Southern accent and told us: "You may call the conflict the 'Civil Warwa,' but we refer to it as the 'Warwa Between the States,' for there was nothing civil about that warwa."

Lovely hostesses dressed in long hoop skirts greeted us at each home. The opening of these heirlooms to the public for a fee has enabled the owners to maintain the buildings in mint condition and preserve the historical monuments. The entire Pilgrimage was like stepping back into life during the *Gone With the Wind* era. Our group had a private tea at one of the homes arranged by our bank president's wife.

The weather was warm and humid, and after a tiring morning of house touring, we were all ready for lunch. I had arranged for the group to eat at the Carriage House Restaurant, and had ordered a mint julep for each place setting. The liquid is amber in color and resembles ice tea. Unknown to me at the time, my little "bonnet lady" rushed in, and, being very thirsty, drank the whole thing down immediately. Some of my group told me that when she was told she had just drunk a mint julep made with bourbon, she had said that was the first alcoholic drink she had ever tasted.

The next morning I approached her. "Bessie, I want to apologize to you. You have lived all these years so pure, and I had to be the first one to corrupt you with an alcoholic beverage."

"Honey," she smiled, "I never slept better in my life!"

To personally relive the plantation owner's life in the deep South during the pre-Civil War days, and to experience authentic Southern hospitality, visit Natchez, Mississippi.

## Hell's Canyon—Snake River, Idaho

My group was on a Tauck Tour of the state of Idaho in 1987, which, incidentally, should be known for its fabulous scenery instead of its potatoes. We flew to Spokane, Washington, where we met our guide and bus. The first stop in Idaho was the pretty resort town of Coeur d'Alene located right on a scenic lake. This appealing resort city offers great shopping, and the lake presents all shades in the color range of blue.

We continued through silver mining country, an Indian reservation, and fertile farming land to Lewiston, named for the Lewis of Lewis and Clark explorers. Here we boarded a jet boat for an eighty-mile journey along the Snake River through Hell's Canyon, the same area traveled by Lewis and Clark. The canyon was carved over millions of years by the Snake River, and the walls are as high as 7,900 feet in some places. Hell's Canyon is the deepest and narrowest river gorge in North America. The river flows north through the canyon and forms the border of Idaho and Oregon. This site played an important role in American history, sheltering Indians and pioneer settlers. The mile-deep canyon is bordered by Seven Devils Mountain on one side and a steep wall of basaltic rock on the other.

All forty of us were on one large jet boat that raced at top speed along the waterway, dodging rock up-croppings and fallen trees. Halfway at noon, we stopped at a camp for lunch. Afterward, we continued down the picturesque waterway, and all was wonderful until the loud roar of the engine died and there we were, stranded in the canyon, many miles from the area where our bus was to pick us up. This was before the day of cell phones, but I doubt they would have worked in that remote area anyway. We floated over to the side and unloaded. There we remained for several hours, literally cooling our heels in the Snake River, while the drivers tinkered with the motor to no avail. Finally, when we had not arrived at the pick-up site at the proper time, the company had sent out another boat to our rescue. We finally arrived at our hotel after dark, thinking we had really been to hell.

In 2002, Keith and I were on an auto and book signing tour through Wyoming, Montana, Oregon, and Idaho and made many stops in the Hell's Canyon area to view from the top overlooks where we had traveled in the jet boat.

On our route I found one of the neatest little towns I have ever seen—Joseph, Oregon. Located in the northeastern part of the state, not far from Lewiston and Hell's Canyon, Joseph sits in the beautiful Wallowa Valley with snow-covered Mount Joseph watching over the area. Years before white man invaded this paradise, the Nez Perce Indians lived and hunted abundant game here. The most famous chief of the tribe was Chief Joseph, who was friendly to the whites and in 1855 signed the initial treaty between Nez Perce bands and the U.S. government. In 1863 the U.S. government amended the treaty to state that the Nez Perce would surrender Wallowa Valley and 90 percent of the 1855 land grant. Old Chief Joseph refused to sign. In 1872 the first permanent white settlers of Wallowa County arrived and established a community. In 1877 Chief Joseph's band was forced out of Wallowa Valley, beginning the Nez Perce War and making Chief Joseph one of the most famous American Indians in U.S. history.

The little town progressed slowly until 1982, when a sculptor moved there and the first bronze sculptures were poured at Valley Bronze foundry, the initial step to growth of the county's arts industry. Artists soon were lured to the area. The second foundry, Parks Bronze, opened in 1988, and the third foundry, Joseph Bronze, opened between Joseph and Enterprise in 1996. In 1999 the residents of Joseph, about 1,000 strong, obtained a grant and began street improvement projects. Today the main street of Joseph boasts numerous outstanding sculptures by famous artists. The monumental works are placed in planter boxes laden with colorful flowers and greenery at each intersection on the main street through town, aptly called "Art Walk." Citizens maintain the landscape in the boxes, and have added hanging baskets of flowering plants all along the sidewalk, decorating galleries and boutiques.

We stayed at the Bronze Antler Bed and Breakfast at the end of the street. The house was built for one of Joseph's sawmill supervisors in 1925, and our room on the second floor had a lovely view of Joseph Mountain. As we entered the establishment, the wonderful aroma of chocolate chip cookies baking invaded us. The host came out from the kitchen to greet us. We found that cookies and excellent western hospitality reigned there.

If you are ever in the area, make an effort to visit the unique and artsy town of Joseph, Oregon.

## Monument Valley and American Indian Country

Regardless where you live, once in your lifetime you should experience the amazing diversity and natural beauty of the Western United States. One publication speculated that the ultimate road tour would be from Las Vegas to Bryce and Zion Canyons, Grand Canyon, Lake Powell and Monument Valley Navajo Tribal Park. All these places are downright awesome, but I want to tell you about Monument Valley and the Indian reservations, often overlooked in tour itineraries.

If you are an old movie buff, and especially like westerns, you have seen the spectacular scenic region of Monument Valley as a backdrop to the cowboy action. The

*The Navajo weaver poses with the rug we bought from her at her hogan in Monument Valley.*

park covers about 2,000 square miles in northeastern Arizona and southeastern Utah. The landscape is characterized by tall, red sandstone buttes, mesas, and arches created by erosion, some rising up to 1,000 feet from a sandy plain. You can fantasize all kinds of objects from the unusual shapes. We were there once on a Tauck Tour when we took a small plane and landed right in the park next to a Navajo hogan, a round hut constructed of mud and straw. Inside was an elderly Indian woman weaving Navajo rugs. At this time, Keith and I were interested in the Navajo weavings, but had not started our collection.

In the early 1990s, when we moved out to our ranch at Evant, we decided we wanted to decorate the living room in a Southwest motif, and decided to start collecting small (about 18x24") Navajo rugs to place over the windows on both sides of the room. We always regretted not buying the rug from the little old lady in the hogan in Monument Valley, so we flew to Las Vegas, rented a car, and made our way back to this captivating land. We stayed at Goulding's Lodge, located amidst the astounding red rock formations. From there we took a tour of the monuments at sunset—an incredible sight. And to add to the atmosphere, at one ridge, an Indian on a horse appeared—the perfect Kodak moment. The next day we returned to the same hogan and found the same Indian rug maker, and this time we bought one of her rugs that now proudly hangs on our wall, along with many other fine Navajo weavings. The park is inside the Navajo reservation. The Navajos are the largest American Indian tribe in the United States.

On another car trip in our quest for Indian art, Keith and I toured the Hopi Mesas in Arizona. The Hopi Indians call themselves "The Peaceable People." The small Hopi reservation is totally surrounded by the large Navajo reservation. Today there are twelve Hopi villages located on the top of, or at the foot of, three flat top mesas which rise a mile high. The Hopi Clans are deeply united by their religion, which has survived the challenges of outsiders and newcomers to their land for the past seven thousand years.

The First Mesa is fifteen miles west of Keams Canyon. We visited Walpi, the most spectacular of the Hopi villages. A drive on top of the mesa brought us to a settlement of cliff-edge houses and scenic views, mostly unchanged for centuries. Here the local women showed how they used cow dung to fire their pottery.

The guide told us that the Hopi ancestors, the Anasazi, probably arrived in the re-

gion around 10,000 years ago. Pueblos of stone and mud were constructe[d]
the mesas for protection from their enemies. Kivas, underground round [...]
the pueblo homes, were used for religious ceremonies.

We were looking for a Hopi Kachina Doll. All true Kachina Dolls are [...]
from the roots of the water-seeking cottonwood tree and clothed in masks and costumes to look like the men who dressed up as Kachina spirits, or gods. These creatures were known to come down to earth and actually help the Indians tend their
fields, and give them wisdom about agriculture, law, and government.

The Third Mesa village was started in 1050 and is the oldest continuously lived-in
settlement in North America. On this mesa we were at a trading post looking at the
Kachina Dolls, and were a bit astonished at the prices. Despondent that we did not
think we should spend that much for the art at this time, I noticed an Indian woman
come in with an attractive Kachina sculpture that had not one but three Kachina figures, all carved from one piece of wood. She spoke to the shop manager, and I heard
the manager say that she was not buying any new items at this time. I followed the
Indian maiden outside and asked if she would sell us the art.

"You have to talk to my husband, the artist," she said. "Just follow me."

She zoomed off in a pickup, and we followed her cloud of dust to a small pueblo
dwelling. She led us to a small wooden shop nearby. Inside, the first thing I noticed
were several wire cages with small chickens chirping loudly. Sawdust and wood shav-
ings covered the floor. There at a small counter sat the carver, Coolidge Roy, Jr. We
introduced ourselves and stated that we were interested in purchasing his Kachina.

He explained that he grew up on the Third Mesa learning about his Hopi heritage
and culture. He is of the Coyote clan. He has two brothers who also are Kachina
carvers. Coolidge taught himself the craft of woodcarving by observing other works
and slowly perfected his finished product to the true-to-life figures he produces today.
He has had Kachinas on exhibit at the Heard Museum in Phoenix and gives carving
demonstrations at the Arizona State Fair.

When we had settled on what we considered a fair price for his outstanding work,
he commented to his wife, "Now we can go see the sons."

I asked where their sons lived, and he laughed. "I was referring to the Phoenix
Suns, the basketball team."

I guess everyone was very pleased with the outcome of our encounter.

## Central Texas Hill Country

To me, the Central Texas Hill Country in the springtime is one of the most beautiful places in the world. Of course, I am a little prejudiced since I live here.

During the first two weeks in April, the roadsides of Texas turn to an artist's
palette of blues, orange, and pale pink, with some yellow and purple thrown in. Texas
is blessed with about 5,000 kinds of native flowering plants, and to assist the bounty,
many years ago the highway department planted bluebonnet seeds (the state flower)
all along the major roadways. The bluebonnet is of the lupine family, but smaller in
stature than the varieties we have seen in other countries. Interspersed among the
bluebonnets frequently the picture is enhanced with the presence of orange-pink
paintbrushes and an occasional pale pink primrose. In some areas you can see a whole

*Spring transforms Texas into a colorful wonderland of bluebonnets and other wildflowers.*

sea of bluebonnets, a true masterpiece. Bright green grass surrounds the flowers, and the trees are just showing off their new foliage—brilliant and shiny green leaves. The only bad thing is that they last only about two to three weeks. Other wildflowers then take their place, but they are not as spectacular or showy.

So come to Central Texas in the spring. You will experience a feast for the eyes, plus the weather is delightful this time of the year.

Many people from other countries have the conception of the United States as revealed to them through movies or television. I invite them to come and see for themselves the real America—a country of untold natural wonders, exciting cities, rural communities, hundreds of ethnic cultures, and sociable people.

I am sure you have your favorite destinations in North America; I hope you have enjoyed visiting mine.

*Bluebonnets as far as you can see at the Wild Flower Farms near Fredericksburg, Texas.*

196

# Epilogue

Travel is the love of adventure and learning. Travel is experiencing new places and sights. Travel is an unknown where you learn to deal with what comes along. My rewards are the extraordinary memories that can never be recaptured: viewing the lovely and peaceful Dal Lake from the top of a houseboat in Kashmir, India (now the scene of strife between India and Pakistan); walking on top of the ancient wall around the enchanting town of Dubrovnik, Yugoslavia (now damaged due to civil war); seeing the Berlin Wall, and then again happily viewing where it was torn down; and most sadly, to never again have dinner and look out at the magnificent vistas of New York City and the harbor from atop the World Trade Center's Windows on the World Restaurant.

Another benefit of travel is acquiring a new awareness of the entire universe and the inequalities that exist therein. We become involved in our own lives and do not realize that conditions are different around the world. I now appreciate the common everyday items here in the United States that we take so very much for granted, like comfortable housing, running water, indoor plumbing, excellent health care, plenty of food in bountiful supermarkets, and freedom in general.

Keith and I realize how lucky we were to go all around the world during a time when travel was more relaxed. We also recognize that through my job and travel contacts, we were able to go to places that would have been financially impossible for us otherwise.

I feel blessed to have had the opportunity to see so much of this wonderful world of ours, and to understand the many cultures and ways of everyday existence, and to learn to respect all peoples of the planet as they go about their daily lives. I hope you enjoyed your exploration of the seven continents with me. You can view pictures of these destinations on my website: www.joycebrookstravel.com.

I would love to hear from you by e-mail (jbrooks@centex.net) or snail mail (Box 280, Evant, TX 76525). If you would like me to speak to your club, school, or organization about my many travel experiences, call 254-471-3134.

See the seven continents, and try to do it before you are seventy!

# Joyce Brooks Was Here

## AFRICA

Cape Verde Islands    Mauritius
Canary Islands        Morocco
Comoros Islands       Reunion Island
Egypt                 Seychelles
Kenya                 South Africa
Madagascar            Tanzania
Madeira               Zimbabwe

## ANTARCTICA

## ASIA

Brunei            Hong Kong
Cambodia          Japan
China             Macau
India             Malaysia
Indonesia         Nepal
  Kalimantan      Philippines
  Sumatra         Sabah
  Java            Sarawak
  Sulawesi        Singapore
  Irian Jaya      Thailand
  Bali            Vietnam

## AUSTRALIA AND PACIFIC AREA

Australia         New Zealand
Easter Island     Papua New Guinea
Fiji              Tahiti
Guam

# EUROPE

| | | |
|---|---|---|
| Andorra | Hungary | Russia |
| Austria | Iceland | Scotland |
| Belgium | Ireland | Sicily |
| Bulgaria | Italy | Slovakia |
| Czech Republic | Liechtenstein | Spain |
| Denmark | Luxembourg | Sweden |
| Finland | Monaco | Switzerland |
| France | Netherlands | Turkey |
| England | Norway | Ukraine |
| Germany | Poland | Vatican City |
| Greece | Portugal | Wales |
| | Romania | Yugoslavia |

# NORTH AMERICA AND CARIBBEAN

| | | |
|---|---|---|
| Antigua | | Haiti |
| Aruba | | Honduras |
| Bahamas | | Jamaica |
| Barbados | | Martinique |
| Belize | | Mexico |
| Bermuda | | Nicaragua |
| British Virgin Islands | | Panama |
| Bonaire | | Puerto Rico |
| Canada | | St. Barts |
| (all 10 provinces) | | St. Maarten |
| Cayman Islands | | St. Pierre et Miquelon |
| Costa Rica | Greenland | (French) |
| Curaco | Grenada | Trinidad |
| Dominican Republic | The Grenadines | United States |
| El Salvador | Guatemala | (all 50 states) |
| | | U.S. Virgin Islands |

# SOUTH AMERICA

| | |
|---|---|
| Argentina | Ecuador |
| Bolivia | Galapagos Islands |
| Brazil | Paraguay |
| Chile | Peru |
| Columbia | Uruguay |
| Devil's Island (Guyana) | Venezuela |

# Joyce Brooks

At age nine, Joyce Brooks made a vow as she picked cotton on her Texas farm birthplace that she would see the world and write a book about it. She was unable to realize this dream until she became a group travel leader at the age of forty-eight. As a Pied Piper she has led groups of forty or more people on over two hundred tours to more than one hundred countries in eighteen years.

Her first book, *Around the World in the Middle Seat: How I Saw the World (and Survived!) as a Group Travel Leader,* was published in 2001. On January 14, 2003, at the age of sixty-nine, she stepped on Antarctica, her seventh continent, thus providing the title for *Seven Before Seventy: One Woman's Quest for the Seven Continents.* Her inspiring stories, reminding us to never lose sight of our goals, are told with her own personal flair and delightful humor.

Joyce currently lives on a ranch in Central Texas with her husband, Keith, and devotes her time to promoting her books and guest lecturer appearances. For further information, visit her website: www.joycebrookstravel.com.